My Life in the Service

THE WORLD WAR II DIARY
(OCTOBER 7, 1944–OCTOBER 14, 1945)
OF
STAFF SERGEANT JACK E. BATES

2ND SQUADRON
22ND BOMBARDMENT GROUP
FIFTH AIR FORCE

COMPILED BY *Wayne N. Horton*

HERITAGE BOOKS
2012

HERITAGE BOOKS
AN IMPRINT OF HERITAGE BOOKS, INC.

Books, CDs, and more—Worldwide

For our listing of thousands of titles see our website
at
www.HeritageBooks.com

Published 2012 by
HERITAGE BOOKS, INC.
Publishing Division
100 Railroad Ave. #104
Westminster, Maryland 21157

Copyright © 2007 Wayne N. Horton

Library of Congress – Txul – 356 – 343
Front graphic design of the 22nd Bomb Squadron's logo
courtesy of Cyril Klimesh: www.redraiders22bg.com

All rights reserved. No part of this book may be reproduced or transmitted in any form or by any means, electronic or mechanical, including photocopying, recording or by any information storage and retrieval system without written permission from the author, except for the inclusion of brief quotations in a review.

International Standard Book Numbers
Paperbound: 978-0-7884-5389-2
Clothbound: 978-0-7884-9484-0

DEDICATION

To my father Roland E. Horton and all those who have served our country.

TABLE OF CONTENTS

Dedication	Page iii
Acknowledgements	Page vii
Introduction	Page ix
The Diary	Page 1 - 3
The Author	Page 5 - 20
The Crew	Page 21 - 23
The Plane	Page 25 - 30
The Mission Chart	Page 31 - 35
Pacific Theater Map	Page 36
Philippines Map	Page 37
Formosa/Taiwan Map	Page 38
The Opposition and Losses	Page 39
Enemy Fighters	Page 41 - 44
"My Life in the Service"	Page 45 - 175
The List	Page 176 - 182
Odds & Ends	Page 184 - 192
Poems	Page 194 - 199
The 22nd B. G. - 2nd B. S.	Page 200 - 203
Memorabilia	Page 204 - 212

TABLE OF CONTENTS

B-24 Nose Art	Page 214 - 215
Memorial	Page 216 - 217
In Tribute	Page 218 - 219
Lest We Forget	Page 220
Bibliography	Page 222
Research Resources	Page 224 - 226
Photo Credits	Page 227 - 228
Index	Page 229 - 238

ACKNOWLEDGEMENTS

I feel very privileged and especially honored to be given the opportunity to record the WW II diary of S/SGT Jack Bates for posterity. The result is the culmination of many hours of hard work and research more enjoyable than you can imagine.

I would like to thank each and everyone who contributed information (see research resources). Especially noteworthy are Col. Don Evans, USAF (deceased) and the 22nd Bombardment Association veterans who graciously allowed me to quote extensively from "The Supplement" and Charles Mason, past Secretary/Editor of the 22nd Bombardment, 2nd Bomb Squadron's monthly newsletter. I would be remiss if I didn't mention the following who allowed me use of their incredible web sites: Cy Klimesh who allowed me to access and use his web site on the 'Red Raiders'. Also, Justin Tylan who allowed me to quote extensively from his informative web site 'Pacific Wrecks' rightly advertised as "Since 1997, the internets most comprehensive reference on the topic" and Dave Hanson whose web site on American aircraft of WWII is one of the best on the subject. Dan Stockton of 'B-24 Best Web' - the most complete web site on B-24's statistics and nose art. As well as Ted Williams a member of the 'B-24 Best Web' research team. Also Paul Yarnell and the 'Navsource' team.

Special thanks, to my nephew, Jeffrey Tham for his graphic editing and advice. As well as my son Eric Horton and Steve Smith for their technical assistance.

A very special thanks to Jamy Brice-Hyde whose assistance editing this work and encouragement was invaluable.

The diary is currently in the possession of Mr. Bates' son Ken and I am thankful that he has allowed me access to the diary and to take the time to record his father's life in the service. I am also very thankful Mr. Bates took the time to record "My Life in the Service".

INTRODUCTION

I can't remember the exact day or even the conversation I had with Ken Bates concerning our mutual interest in military history, but I can remember my excitement as he told me that his father had flown as a gunner on B-24's during World War II and had left a diary. Needless to say, I was even more excited when he told me he would allow me to read it. Words can't describe how much I enjoyed each and every minute of my time reading the diary. As I read the diary I couldn't help but think how sad it was that I would be one of a chosen few who would have access to all the information in the diary. That is when I asked Ken if I could record his father's diary. This is the result of that effort.

I have added some things I thought would be interesting to the reader. For historical context and reference I have included a brief description of the B-24 Liberator bomber on which Mr. Bates flew. Several diagrams are included as well. I have also added several maps, one of the Philippines, one of Formosa/Taiwan and the other of the South Pacific area of operations, in which Mr. Bates and his comrades flew their missions against Japan. I have also attempted to "flesh out" the diary by including as much information concerning the people, places and things Mr. Bates refers to including pictures of planes and ships. I hope this material will add an interesting sidelight.

It has been almost sixty five years and three generations since the aptly named "Greatest Generation" laid down their weapons of war. Over 16.1 million Americans participated in WW II. Of that number approximately 2,583,000 survive. With each passing day an estimated 900 pass away and take with them the precious memories of their participation in that conflict.

I fear that the years since have dimmed our memories and dulled our senses to the tragedy, horror and meaning of that conflict. This diary is one of the few precious legacies' left to us from those who fought so bravely and gave up so much. It reaches out from the past to our generation and those to come, a reminder of the sacrifices made by those who fought for their homes, families and country. My greatest desire is that in reading *My Life in the Service* the reader will gain a greater appreciation for and remember all those who with their "blood, sweat and tears", secured for themselves and their posterity, the freedoms and liberty we so richly enjoy.

THE DIARY

Weather beaten, war torn, aged for nearly fifty-six years like the finest of scotch; it is the darkest of blue like the skies it flew in and the seas it flew over. Fragile yet strong like the freedom its' owner defended. Small enough to fit a pocket at six by four and a half inches, yet big enough to hold an epic, heroic story. On its' cover a red shield emblazoned with the words, "My Life in the Service"

THE DIARY

The publishers (Consolidated Book Publishers, Inc., Chicago, Ill.) included the following instructions to the serviceman turned diarist (some of the printing is illegible due to tears in the pages).

"Your experiences in the armed forces of our country are your part of living history. By all means KEEP A DIARY! Times without number, historians and writers have found more information of real human interest in the diaries of enlisted men than in the studied accounts of generals and admirals. This book conscientiously kept, may prove to be the living record of your destiny five hundred years from now!

'By keeping a diary, you provide a record that can be referred to in later years for verification should any question arise. Although, Army, Navy and Marines keep official records of all the men in the armed forces, (cont.) - 'there are many ways in which their records can be lost or destroyed in time of war. Your personal record may supply vital information that is available to no other source. It is particularly essential to record any disability or hospital treatment received, whether on duty or on leave. This should be a detailed account - giving dates, names of Medical Officers and Examining Physicians - with complete facts concerning hospitalization.

'Because the events recorded in these pages are likely to be the most significant of your life, and the ones most worthy of remembrance. DON'T TRUST THEM TO MEMORY.

'Keep a written record. You will be glad you did so - countless times - when you have need to recall incidents, places, dates, and close companions. In many cases diaries have been turned to profit for their authors: newspapers and magazines have published them - with permission from the War or Navy Department - to give their readers a true, firsthand picture of service life.

'Especially planned for convenience, this book has designated pages for every pertinent entry - names, addresses, dates, places, people, autographs, and photographs. By all (means take) PHOTOGRAPHS!! One picture is said to be worth a (thousand) words.....get as many pictures as you can, (of people) and places, for an illustrated diary is the best.

'(Illegible) if for any reason it becomes inadvisable for you to keep your diary with you, if your duties are such that the book should not be in your possession, DON'T STOP MAKING ENTRIES! Send your diary home or to a friend for safekeeping. Then while you are away, send your entries home in letters - regularly. Keep your diary up to date by proxy.

'Remember, the value of this record lies in the future; the time to create that value is now. Resolve to make an (illegible) however short, EVERY SINGLE (illegible) this book a treasure trove (illegible) memories."

Purchased for the grand total of one whole American dollar ($1.00) on September 30, 1944 the diary met its owner. Their meeting place, ironically the very place that brought Staff Sergeant Jack Bates into the war, Pearl Harbor, Hawaii.

Mr. Bates noted that he left the United States on September 29, 1944. The first "dated" entry is October 2, 1944 written while he was aboard B24L, serial number 44-1536, while it was being ferried to Townsville, Australia.

(cont.) - Subsequent entries are a meticulous record of his service with the 2nd Bomb Squadron, 22nd Bomber Group, known as the "Red Raiders", until his return to the United States on October 14, 1945.

Along with the daily diary entries are a chart, which is recreated further on, of each of his forty-one bombing missions. Included are a record of his transfers and changes in rank, citations, awards and decorations. The diary also contains articles concerning the war as well as poems.

The diary reveals every place on the itinerary of this American serviceman including a timeline of events. Another fascinating entry is a list of handwritten signatures. These were signed by those people with whom he had contact during his duties as Post Master. Although time has made some of the names illegible every effort to recreate them accurately has been made.

Mr. Bates had excellent handwriting skills but some of the entries, due to a lack of space, are rather small and not easily legible. Only minor changes have been made to the entries - some spelling and others for clarification. Entries made noting missions are bolded for emphasis.

Otherwise, the diary and each entry are exactly as Mr. Bates wrote them. Along with the diary Mr. Bates kept an extensive array of memorabilia. One of the more interesting articles is a piece of foil dropped by the bomber crews to confuse enemy radar. I have taken photos and scanned as many of these items as I could and included them in this work.

THE AUTHOR

Jack E. Bates was born on May 11, 1923, the son of Wellington and Esther (Austin) Bates of 303 Mill St., Horseheads, NY. He graduated from Horseheads Central High School (where he excelled in baseball and basketball), in Horseheads, New York, in 1942. He was the second oldest of seven children: Wellington Jr., Robert (June 18, 1925 - December 8, 2008), Gene, Gloria, Clark and Helen.[1]

He was employed by the Eclipse in Elmira Heights, NY at the time of his enlistment. (known as Purolator) He notes that he was 120 lb., 5 ft. 4 in. tall with brown hair.

Mr. Bates recorded in the section of the diary known as "Things I Did While in the States" on Feb. 20, 1943 he went to Binghamton, N.Y. and passed the physical for the Army. He left home on Feb. 27, 1943, for Fort Niagara, Niagara, NY. In March 4, 1943, he started for Camp Swift. He was then assigned to Co. L, 386th Infantry, 97th Division on March 7, 1943. He started basic training in a weapons platoon on March 16, 1943, where he notes - he was the only one in his company to rate "expert" with the M-1, machine gun and carbine.

Pvt. Jack Bates

1 - Bates, Louise in personal interview with author, 2005.

Sometime after March 1943 Mr. Bates decided to volunteer[1] for the Army Air Corp. His wife Louise relates: "You know Jack loved sports especially baseball. He heard that men in the Air Corp had a lot of extra time to participate in baseball, etc. I heard that is why he transferred to the Air Corp."[2] He passed the Cadet exam (with a 200) and physical in late August 1943 and was assigned to the Cadets on September 11, 1943 and sent to Sheppard Field, Texas on Oct. 18, 1943. The diary states he was "eliminated" from the Cadets but doesn't elaborate on the reason. It is common knowledge that there was a lack of crews to man the bombers and enlisted personnel were extensively recruited for this duty.

Nevertheless, he graduated from gunnery school on May 27, 1944 with the designation of armor gunner. An armor gunner's duties included: the ability to take care of all the guns on the ship, and could handle any gun position waist, turret, tail, and belly or nose guns. After more training at various airfields he left for the Pacific theatre on September 29, 1944. He flew forty-one combat missions and was awarded the air medal with three Oak Clusters and eight battle stars.

After the war Mr. Bates returned to his hometown and his job at the Eclipse. He met his wife Louise Bednarchik there. Louise graduated from Elmira Free Academy, Elmira, New York in 1943 and went to work at the Eclipse immediately thereafter. According to Louise "I was working at the Eclipse when Jack returned to work after the war. I was laid off shortly thereafter. When work picked up I was called back. I was told, when I got laid off, Jack asked some of his co-workers what had happened to me." They got married December 27, 1950. They have two children John E. and Ken.[3] Mr. Bates died on September 27, 1990. Louise passed away on December 15, 2006 and is buried with Jack in plot # K O 219 at the Woodlawn National Cemetery in Elmira, NY.

---

1 - "They were all volunteers. The U.S. Army Air Corps - after 1942 the Army Air Forces - did not force anyone to fly. They made the choice.", Stephen Ambrose, The Wild Blue, The Men And Boys Who Flew The B-24's Over Germany (Simon and Schuster, New York, 2001), 27.

2 & 3 - Bates, Louise in personal interview with author, 2005.

Prepare in Duplicate

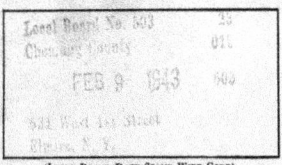

Feb 9, 1943
(Date of mailing)

(LOCAL BOARD DATE STAMP WITH CODE)

ORDER TO REPORT FOR INDUCTION

The President of the United States,

To   Jack   E   Bates
   (First name)   (Middle name)   (Last name)

Order No. 12,220

GREETING:

Having submitted yourself to a local board composed of your neighbors for the purpose of determining your availability for training and service in the armed forces of the United States, you are hereby notified that you have now been selected for training and service in the   Land or Naval Forces
(Army, Navy, Marine Corps)

You will, therefore, report to the local board named above at   Greyhound Union Bus Terminal
E Church St & State Sts. Elmira N Y
(Place of reporting)

at   7:15 A.m., on the   20th   day of   February , 1943
(Hour of reporting)

This local board will furnish transportation to an induction station of the service for which you have been selected. You will there be examined, and, if accepted for training and service, you will then be inducted into the stated branch of the service.

Persons reporting to the induction station in some instances may be rejected for physical or other reasons. It is well to keep this in mind in arranging your affairs, to prevent any undue hardship if you are rejected at the induction station. If you are employed, you should advise your employer of this notice and of the possibility that you may not be accepted at the induction station. Your employer can then be prepared to replace you if you are accepted, or to continue your employment if you are rejected.

Willful failure to report promptly to this local board at the hour and on the day named in this notice is a violation of the Selective Training and Service Act of 1940, as amended, and subjects the violator to fine and imprisonment.

If you are so far removed from your own local board that reporting in compliance with this order will be a serious hardship and you desire to report to a local board in the area of which you are now located, go immediately to that local board and make written request for transfer of your delivery for induction, taking this order with you.

ALLYN P. HOFFMAN CH.
Member or clerk of the local board.

D. S. S. Form 150
(Revised 7-13-42)

Mr. Bates "Orders to Report for Induction"

Things I Did While in the States:

Feb. 20, 1943 - went to Binghamton and passed physical for Army.

Feb. 23, 1943 - went to work for last time at Eclipse. Got paid and bonds. Hated to leave.

Feb. 24, 1943 - had farewell party at Melody Gardens by Eclipse gang and had swell time.

Mr. Bates farewell party at Melody Gardens
Jack is fourth from the right seated at the table

Feb. 25, 1943 - played last basketball game as civilian, took Mary Peterson and had good time.

Feb. 27, 1943 - went to Ft. Niagara at reception center.[1]

March 4, 1943 - started for Camp Swift[2] and went into Canada from Niagara Falls.

1 - 'New' Fort Niagara, Niagara County, Youngstown, NY. "1940 to 1943 it was a Reception Center for Army draftees…From 1943 to 1945 it was a Reception Center, then Separation Camp, and also served as a POW camp. In 1945 the base was closed.....", *New York Military Museum and Veterans Research Center - NYS Division of Military and Naval History*, 2005, www.dmna.state.ny.us/forts/fortsMP/niagarafort.htm.

2 - "Camp Swift, established in 1942 as a major combat infantry training area for WWII.... near the small town of Bastrop, (Texas)….was officially activated….on May 4, 1942….The US Government acquired 52,191 acres (52,092 fee acres and 99 lease acres), on 23 March 1942. The site was used by the Army as an infantry replacement training camp....This army training facility housed, at its peak, over 90,000 US servicemen. It also served as a German prisoner-of-war camp with 4,000 prisoners captured in North Africa from Rommel's Afrika Corps and at Normandy during the invasion of Europe.", John Pike, Military, *GlobalSecurity.org*, 2005, www.globalsecurity.org/military/facility.

March 7, 1943 - came to Camp Swift in early morning. Assigned Company L, 386 Infantry, 97th Division.

March 16, 1943 - started basic infantry training in weapons platoon.

Received in basic training in the infantry.

Aug. 4 - 15, 1943 - was home on furlough all this time and had good time.

Aug. 24, 1943 - took cadet exams and passed with 200.

Aug. 27, 1943 - passed cadet physical at Bergstrom Field, Austin, Texas.[1]

1 – "Originally activated in Sept. 19, 1942 as Del Valle Army Air Base it was renamed March 3, 1943 Bergstrom Field in honor of Captain John Bergstrom first Austinite killed in the war. It was used throughout WW II as a USAAF training facility.", City of Austin, *Austin-Bergstrom International Airport*. Jim Halbrook, Public Information Manager, Aviation Department, 2005, www.ci.austin.tx.us/austinairport/bergstromhistory.htm.

DISTRICT HEADQUARTERS
SAN ANTONIO RECRUITING DISTRICT
AVIATION CADET EXAMINING BOARD
THIRD FLOOR CALCASIEU BLDG.,
SAN ANTONIO, 5, TEXAS

SPECIAL ORDERS: 11 September 1943

NO.   224:

2. Pursuant to provisions contained in Instructions for Aviation Cadet Examining Boards, War Department, dated January 7, 1942, and Aviation Cadet Manual, AGO, War Department, dated September 10, 1942, Chapter Ten, Par. 310.01 (Transfer of enlisted applicants), and Par. 310.02 (Unit Commander to be notified), the following named enlisted men are transferred to the Air Forces Unasgd in grade, effective this date, 11 September 1943, and will remain attached to their present organization for duty, pending announcement of appointment as Aviation Cadet from this Headquarters. In event a soldier is now on detached service, or has been transferred, this office will be notified at once.

Pfc. Bates, Jack E., 32838983, Co.L, 386th Inf., APO#445, Camp Swift, Texas
Cpl. Bechtel, Oscar F.,   Co.H, 386th Inf., APO#445, Camp Swift, Texas
Pfc. Cring, Robert E.,   Clr.Co., 322nd Med.Bn., Camp Swift, Texas
Pvt. Filler, William S.,   Co.D, 387th Inf., APO#445, Camp Swift, Texas
T/5gr. Forgey, Howard L.,   97th Signal Co., Camp Swift, Texas
Pfc. Fosnot, Charles F.,   97th Rcn.Trp, APO#445, Camp Swift, Texas
Pvt. Gutlian, Harold J.,   Co.M, 387th Inf., Camp Swift, Texas
Pfc. Hueneke, Robert A.,   Hq. & Hq.Co., 387th Inf., Camp Swift, Texas
Pfc. Martin, Hobart B.,   Cannon Co., 387th Inf., Camp Swift, Texas
S/Sgt. Mennie, James R.,   Co.C, 322nd Engr.Bn., Camp Swift, Texas

Cpl. Ferranti, Philip J.,   389th N.T.S., AAFNS, SMAAF, San Marcos, Texas
Pfc. Foley, Francis J.,   389th N.T.S., AAFNS, SMAAF, San Marcos, Texas
Cpl. Gassie, Robert E.,   456th B.Hq. & A.B.Sq.AAFNS,SMAAF,San Marcos,Texas
Sgt. Hudson, Val J.,   390th N.T.S., AAFNS, SMAAF, San Marcos, Texas
S/Sgt. Lain, Lee T.,   89th N.T.S., AAFNS, SMAAF, San Marcos, Texas
Cpl. Lovell, Richard R.,   89th Hq. & Hq.Sqdn.AAFNS, SMAAF,San Marcos,Texas
Pvt. Henricksen, Walter P.,   1096th Guard Sqdn., AAFNS,SMAAF,San Marcos

Pfc. Bell, Connie M.,   26th T.C.Sq. 89th T.C.Gp.Bergstrom AAF, Texas
Pfc. Haulter, Howard E.,   25th T.C.Sq.89th T.C.Gp.Bergstrom AAF, Texas
T/4gr. Massie, Harold W.,   Med.Det., Bergstrom AAF, Austin, Texas
T/Sgt. Valencic, Anthony,   31st T.C.Sq.89 T.C.Gp.Bergstrom AAF, Texas

Pvt. McDonald, William C.,   944th Guard Sqdn., Goodfellow Field, Texas
Sgt. Mercer, Jessy W.,   56th Air Base Sqdn., Goodfellow Field, Texas

Sgt. McElroy, Sylvester L.,   85th B.Hq. & A.B.Sqdn., Moore Field, Texas
S/Sgt. Strickland, Warren G.,   504th S.E.F.T.Sqdn., Moore Field, Texas

Pfc. Chung, Matthew,   6th Training Sqdn., HAAF, Harlingen, Texas

Pfc. Joacobowsky, Vincent G.,   11th B.Hq. & A.B.Sqdn., Kelly Field, Texas

                                   By Order of the District Recruiting Officer:

OFFICIAL

CHARLEY A. LEINWEBER, 1st Lt., AGD,   VINCENT D. PHILIPS, Major, Air-Inf
Recorder.   Aviation Cadet Examining Board,
                                       President.
DISTRIBUTION:
6-Each Orgn. listed.
6-CG, 8th S.C.
4-CO, USA, Ft.Sam Houston.

Transfer records from infantry unassigned pending announcement of appointment as Aviation Cadet

3486

DISTRICT HEADQUARTERS
SAN ANTONIO RECRUITING DISTRICT
AVIATION CADET EXAMINING BOARD
THIRD FLOOR CALCASIEU BLDG.,
SAN ANTONIO, 5, TEXAS

SPECIAL ORDERS: 29 September 1943

NO.   241:

3. Pursuant to provisions contained in Instructions for Aviation Cadet Examining Boards, War Department, dated 7 January 1942, and Letter, Headquarters, Eighth Service Command (ASF), Dallas, Texas, dated 26 September 1943, and AR 30-920, the following enlisted men having been found qualified for Aviation Cadet appointment, are ordered in present grade to the Army Air Force Basic Training Center, Sheppard Field, Wichita Falls, Texas, for pre-aviation cadet (Air-Crew) basic training, reporting upon arrival thereat to the Commanding Officer, for disposition. Their departure will be so timed as to insure their arrival at destination on 18 October 1943. Unit Commanders will forward the service records to the Commanding Officer, Army Air Force Basic Training Center, Sheppard Field, Wichita Falls, Texas, within 48 hours.

Cpl. Ackley, Bruce B.,   Btry.A, 389th F.A.Bn.APO#445, Camp Swift, Texas
Cpl. Amick, Hugh M.,   Co.D, 307th Inf., Camp Swift, Texas
Pvt. Babcock, Robert L.,   Co.E, 303rd Inf., APO#445, Camp Swift, Texas
Pvt. Barker, Zanas V.,   Co.B, 387th Inf., Camp Swift, Texas
Pfc. Bates, Jack E., 32833903,   Co.L, 386th Inf., APO#445, Camp Swift, Texas
Cpl. Bechtel, Oscar F.,   Co.H, 386th Inf., APO#445, Camp Swift, Texas
Pvt. Connors, Robert P.,   97th Rec.Troop, APO#445, Camp Swift, Texas
Pfc. Cring, Robert E.,   Clr.Co., 322nd Med.Bn., Camp Swift, Texas
Pvt. Cunningham, Malcolm K.,   322nd Engr.Co.C.Camp Swift, Texas
Pvt. Filler, William S.,   Co.D, 387th Inf., APO#445, Camp Swift, Texas
Pfc. Fisher, Louis A.,   Hq.Co., 97th Inf.Div.APO#445, Camp Swift, Texas
T/5gr. Flisnick, Walter E.,   97th Signal Co., 97th Inf.Div.Camp Swift,
T/5gr. Forgey, Howard L.,   97th Signal Company, Camp Swift, Texas
Pfc. Fosnot, Charles F.,   97th Rcn.Trp., APO#445, Camp Swift, Texas
Pvt. Gutlian, Harold J.,   Co.H, 387th Inf., Camp Swift, Texas
Sgt. Hartzog, Eugene E.,   Co.C, 387th Inf., Camp Swift, Texas
Pfc. Hueneke, Robert A.,   Hq. & Hq.Co., 387th Inf., APO#445,Camp Swift
Pvt. Jones, James K.,   241st Med.Bn., Co.A, Camp Swift, Texas
Cpl. Kruse, George W.,   Hq. & Hq.Btry.922nd F.A.Bn.Camp Swift, Texas
Pvt. Lee, Roger R.,   Co.B, 322nd Med.Bn., APO#495, Camp Swift, Texas
Cpl. Luchetti, Lucas R.,   Co.E, 387th Inf., Camp Swift, Texas
Pfc. McCleary, Francis J.,   Hq. & Hq.Btry.922nd F.A.Bn., Camp Swift,Texas
Pfc. McKinley, Lyle L.,   H. & S.Co., 554th Engr.(HP) Co.Camp Swift,Texas
Pfc. Martin, Hobart B.,   Cannon Co., 387th Inf.Camp Swift, Texas
Pfc. Matthews, Clarence,   314th M.P.(ZC) MI, Camp Swift, Texas
Pfc. Maust, Lee B.,   Co.F, 386th Inf., APO#445, Camp Swift, Texas
S/Sgt. Mennie, James R.,   Co.C, 322nd Engr.Bn., Camp Swift, Texas
Cpl. Merico, William D.,   Co.D, 387th Inf., APO#445, Camp Swift, Texas
Pvt. Moyer, Raymond L.,   Hq. & Hq.Co., 387th Inf., Camp Swift, Texas
Pfc. Muir, Dean R.,   529th Engr.(LP) Co., Camp Swift, Texas
Pfc. Noland, Carroll V.,   A.T.Co., 387th Inf.APO#445, Camp Swift,Texas
Pvt. Powell, Dalton,   Co.H, 386th Inf.APO#445, Camp Swift, Texas
Pvt. Snyder, James L.,   97th Rcn.Trp., APO#445, Camp Swift, Texas
T/5gr. Urban, John P.,   A T Co., 387th Inf., Camp Swift, Texas
Pvt. Valenti, Jr., Philip C.,   Hq.Co.2nd Bn.386th Inf.Camp Swift,Texas
Pfc. Van Duzer, Robert E.,   97th Signal Co.APO#445, Camp Swift, Texas
T/5gr. Zahuta, Michael,   Service Co.303rd Inf., Camp Swift, Texas

Sgt. Kurtz, Harrison D.,   390th N.T.S., AAFNS, SAAAF,San Marcos, Texas
Pvt. Payne, Robert L.,   1096th Guard Sqdn. AFNS,SAAAF,San Marcos, Texas
Sgt. Reichwein, Gordon C.,   389th N.T.S.AAFNS, SAAAF,San Marcos, Texas

Oct. 18, 1943 - came in cadets at Sheppard Field,[1] Texas for one month.

Introduction booklet for Sheppard Field,

1 - "During World War II, Sheppard conducted basic training.....In addition to the basic flying training, the base also provided advanced pilot training for ground officers....The field reached its peak strength of 46,340 people while serving as a separation center for troops being discharged following World War II from September through November 1945. Sheppard Field was deactivated August 31, 1946 and declared surplus to the War Department's needs...", John Pike, Military, *GlobalSecurity.org*, 2005, www.globalsecurity.org/military/facility.

Dec. 23, 1943 - arrived at Buckley Field, Denver, Col.[1] to armament school.

Front cover of training manual used by Mr. Bates at Buckley Field

1 - "Originally known as Lowry Army Air Field. The field was enlarged and renamed Buckley Field in honor of 1st Lt. John Harold Buckley, a World War I flier from Longmont, CO. Buckley lost his life in France on Sept. 17, 1918. Donated to the Department of the Army by the city and county of Denver in early 1941. The Army Air Corps Technical School, offering B-17 and B-24 bombardier and armor training, was opened July 1, 1941.", *A Brief History of Lowry Air Force Base*, *Wings Over the Rockies Air & Space Museum*. 2005, www.wingsmuseum.org/lowryafb.php.

March 18, 1944 - graduated from armament school.

Jack (on the right) and two of his buddies from armament school

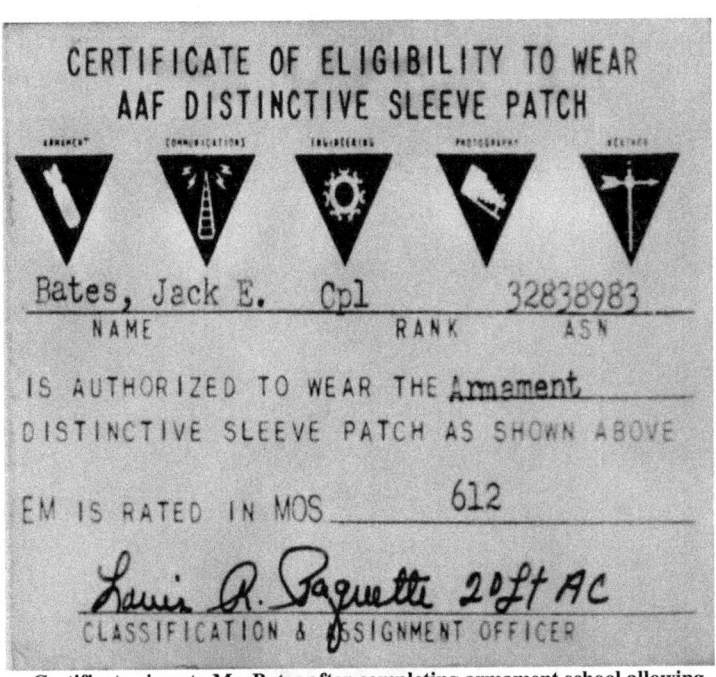

Certificate given to Mr. Bates after completing armament school allowing him to wear the patch below

Armament Patch

March 25, 1944 - started for Harlingen, Texas[1] from Denver and had good trip.

Booklet for Harlingen Gunnery School

1 - "Harlingen Army Airfield opened in July 1941 and was used by the United States Air Forces as a training base during World War II....as a flexible gunnery school. Training was conducted in both air-to-air & air-to-surface gunnery. The air-to-air training used a variety of aircraft, including....B-24's", *Air Force Historical Research Agency*, 2005, www.afhra.af.mil.

May 14, 1944 - first time I ever flew and in AT-6 at gunnery.

North American AT- 6   DH

"A two-seat advanced trainer powered by a Pratt & Whitney 550 hp R-1340-AN-1 Wasp Engine. No armament. Range: 750 miles, Cruise Speed: 170 mph, Max Speed: 205 mph, Ceiling: 21,500 feet.", Dave Hanson, *American Aircraft of World War II*, September 2004, www.daveswarbirds.com/usplanes.

Certificate of Proficiency from Gunnery School

May 21, 1944 - flew my first time in B-24 at gunnery.

May 27, 1944 - graduated at gunnery and got Corporal rating.

Diploma from Gunnery School

June 3, 1944 - came to Lemoore Field, Calif. [1]

June 14 - July 1, 1944 - had furlough to home from Lemoore and then to Tonopah. [2]

```
                        SHIPPING TICKET
      Prepared by       Shipping Officer's Voucher No.       Page 1
      Date 7/3/44       Shipping Order: Class     No.
      Squadron "T"                       as listed
Consignor  XXXX XXXXXXXXXXXXXXX, TAAF, TONOPAH, NEVADA

Consignee  Bates, Jack E, Cpl.  32838983

Accountability                               Date Shipped
                             Ship by
Auth. or Reg. No. AAF REG:  65-23 WD Cir 170  Via Consignee    Packed By
                             T. O. 00-30-41
```

ITEM	ISSUED	UNIT	STOCK-LIST NO.	NOMENCLATURE	COST
				Class 13	
1.		Ea.	8300-022100	BAG ASSY - Flyers Clothing, Type B-4	
2.		Ea	8300-022200	BAG - Flyers Kit, Type A-3	
3.		Pr	8300-290400	GLASSES - Flying Sun Comfort Cable 6¼	
4.		Pr	8300-336000	GOGGLE ASSY - Flying Type B-7	
5.	1	Pr	8300-	GLOVES - Winter Flying, Type A-10, Size 10	
6.		Ea	8300-	HELMET - Summer Flying, Type A-9, Size	
7.		Ea	8300-	JACKET - Winter Flying, Type B-3, Size	
8.		Ea	8300-	PARACHUTE - Complete Type	
9.		Pr	8300-	SHOES - Winter Flying Type A-6, Size	
10.	1	Pr	8300-	SUIT - Summer Flying Type A-4, Size 38	
11.		Ea	8300-	TROUSERS - Winter Flying Type A-3, Size	
12.		Ea	8300-971200	VEST - Life Preserver, Type B-4 Complete	
13.		Ea	8300-145000	CUP - Headset, retaining cup helmet	
14.		Ea	8300-	JACKET - Summer Flying Type A-2 Size	
15.		Ea	8300-	VEST - FlyingWinter, Type C-2, Size	
	1	Ea		Harness	
				Class 05-A	
16.		Ea	6200-305000	KIT - Navigation Pilot, Complete	
				-LAST ITEM-	

Shipping ticket – list of equipment assigned to Mr. Bates at Tonopah, Nevada

1 - "Located nine miles southwest of town (it) was a dirt air field usable only in dry weather…This base was built during WW II as an Army Air Corp training center.", Daniel M. Sebby, Command Sergeant Major, The California State Military Museum, California State Military Department, *Historic California Posts Lemoore Army Air Field*, March 23, 2005, www.militarymuseum.org/LemooreAAF.html.

2 - "This World War II era facility located 8 miles east of Tonopah, Nevada was used for training B-24 and B-25 bomber crews. Improvements made at the site included runways, barracks, mess halls, a hospital, and maintenance and hanger buildings. The airfield was deactivated and sold in 1946 and presently serves as Tonopah's municipal airport.", State of Nevada, Division of Environmental Protection, *Formerly Used Defense Sites*, 2005, http://ndep..gov/bca/dod_fuds.htm.

Sept. 15, 1944 - left Tonopah to go to Hamilton Field (Calif.).[1]

Left States Sept. 29, 1944 for overseas. Fairfield-Suisun Airfield[2] was Embarkation Point and flew over Frisco (San Francisco, California) on the way over.

1 - "Construction of Hamilton Airfield commenced on July 1, 1932....Built as a bombardment base and the headquarters for the 1st Wing of the Army Air Corps....played a significant role during World War II in training and national defense by serving as an overseas staging area, acting as one of three major bases of the West Coast wing of the Air Transport Command's Pacific Division and for its role in the Operational Training Unit Program.", Justin Taylan, *Pacific Wrecks*, 2005, www.pacificwrecks.com.

2 - "Known today as Travis Air Force base...Activated on May 11, 1943, the field was named Fairfield-Suisun Army Air Base, after the two closet towns. Planned shortly after Pearl Harbor, the base served as home for medium bombers and fighters assigned to the West Coast. The first runway and temporary buildings were constructed in the summer of 1942. Shortly after construction was begun the base's potential as a major aerial port and supply transfer point for the pacific theater led the Army Air Corps to assign it to the newly-designated Air Transport Command. The base officially opened June 1, 1943, with a primary mission of servicing and ferrying tactical aircraft from California across the Pacific to the war zone.", Daniel M. Sebby, Command Sergeant Major, California Center for Military History, California State Military Department *Historic California Posts Travis Air Force Base (Fairfield-Suisun Army Air Base)*, 2005, http://www.militarymuseum.org/TravisAFB.html.

THE CREW

As noted Mr. Bates was sent to Tonopah, Nevada in July of 1944. The Tonopah facility was used for the training of B-24 and B-25 flight crews. It is most probable that it was here Mr. Bates and those who were to become his 'crew members' were brought together and trained.

The above photo is a picture of Mr. Bates and his fellow crew members. The photo was taken in September 1944 at Tonopah, Nevada probably just prior to the crews assignment to Hamilton Field were they were assigned to overseas duty. The crew was identified using information from the diary and provided by Richard Faletti: Bottom row (left to right) Arthur Deter - engineer; Joseph N. Tosto - radio operator; Jack Bates - gunner; William F. Bridge - nose gunner and assistant radio operator; Richard E. Schoen - waist gunner and assistant engineer; James J. Perry - tail gunner. Top row (left to right) Richard J. Faletti - pilot; Wilford W. Crockett - co-pilot; Camillus A. Raymond - navigator; William D. Coleman - bombardier.

A misconception concerning B-24 flight crews was the fact that once flight crews were "put together", in basic training, they continued flying missions together and in the same airplane on each mission; throughout the war. Pilot Richard Falletti wrote: "Generally we flew together as a crew, but on some occasions crew members were assigned to other pilots when, for one reason or another, there may have been a shortage of one (cont.) or two crew members on account of sickness, leave, etc. I was assigned for a three-month period early in 1945 as an instructor pilot in Nadzab, New Guinea. During this time the crew members flew with other pilots." It is clearly evident from reading Mr. Bates diary "his crew", the crew that obviously trained together and flew B-24L #44-41536 from the states to Townsville, Australia, with the exception of radioman Joseph Tosto. - who flew twenty-five missions with Mr. Bates[1] - very rarely flew together. Mr. Bates wrote in his Oct. 26, 44 entry: "They have split our crew up for the first few missions to fly with experienced crews." Then, Mr. Bates notes in his diary entry of Nov. 28, 1944, that this was "Perry and Tosto's first mission"; by this time Jack had already flown three missions. Mr. Bates notes in his Dec. 13, 1944 entry "Crockett went on first mission". Also, as late as Jan. 27, 1945, Mr. Bates notes "Schoen has been evacuated to Australia...he has yellow jaundice. Hasn't had a mission yet". Finally, in his Apr. 23, 1945 entry he writes, "Our whole crew flew together for the first time since Wewak" (their first mission). In fact, of the numerous references Mr. Bates makes concerning the composition of the flight crew; I find only two references to the whole crew flying together. Also, from reading the diary and noting information sent by Richard Faletti (see Missions Chart), they very rarely, if ever flew in the same plane from mission to mission. It is noted on the 22nd web site "crews flew whatever aircraft assigned to them by operations at briefing." [2]

Information concerning the crew as of 2006:

William F. Bridge - Latrobe, PA[3]
Wilford W. Crockett - Born: Mar. 19, 1923; Died: Aug. 22, 2000; Buried: Pima Cemetery, Pima, AZ ; enlisted April 15, 1944
Richard Faletti - Born: 1922: Died: Dec. 25, 2006, Phoenix, Arizona
Arthur Deter - Cumberland, MD[4] (known as "Pappy" as he was the oldest of the crew [3])
James Perry - Klamath, California
Camillus A. Raymond - Born: June 16, 1917; Died: May 25, 1971; enlisted June 30, 1942

---

1 - Tosto, Joseph Sr. in correspondence with author, June 2005.

2 - Cy Klimesh, *22nd Bomb Group*, 2001, www.redraiders.com.

3 - Bates, Louise in personal interview with author, 2005.

4 - 2nd Squadron Newsletter, December 2001.

WILFORD CROCKETT   WILLIAM COLEMAN

RICHARD FALETTI   C.A. RAYMOND

PHOTOS TAKEN 1945 AT CLARK FIELD, PHILIPPINES

THE PLANE

The B-24 Liberator was a heavy bomber designed by Consolidated Aircraft for the US Army Air Corp. The first prototype flew on December 29, 1939. Although, overshadowed by the more famous B-17, it was built in greater numbers than the B-17 and was the most extensively produced aircraft in WW II. The B-24 was one of the most versatile aircraft of the Second World War. It was not only used as a long-range bomber but also used for maritime and photographic reconnaissance, anti-submarine, passenger freight transportation, and flying tanker purposes. During the war Liberators dropped 635,000 tons of bombs on Europe, Africa and the Pacific and shot down 4,189 enemy aircraft.[1]

Mass-produced by five different manufacturers it could be produced easily and in sufficient numbers. At the Consolidated factory in San Diego, California B-24's moved along the production line at a rate of 8 1/2 inches per minute. This facility alone produced 6,500 Liberators. Altogether, over 18,000 Liberator bombers were built from June 1941 through May of 1945. A greater number than any other heavy bomber built during World War II.[2]

It carried a crew of 10, which consisted of: Pilot, Co-Pilot, Navigator, Bombardier, Engineer, Radioman and four gunners. Its armament consisted of 10 - .50 cal. Browning M-2 machine-guns. These were located in the waist, tail, nose, top and ball turrets. Mr. Bates was a gunner on the B-24 and served the guns[3] in every position including: waist, tail, nose and ball turret.

---

1 - *Fiddlers Green,* September 2004
www.fiddlersgreen.net/models/aircraft/Consolidated-B-24.html

2 - Ibid.

3 - "Each gun had about 150 working parts and the men had been required to strip and assemble it blindfolded wearing gloves. The guns weighed sixty-four pounds and fired 800 rounds of ammunition per minute to a range of 600 yards." Stephen Ambrose, The Wild Blue, The Men and Boys Who Flew the B-24's Over Germany, (New York: Simon and Schuster, 2001), 158 & 159.

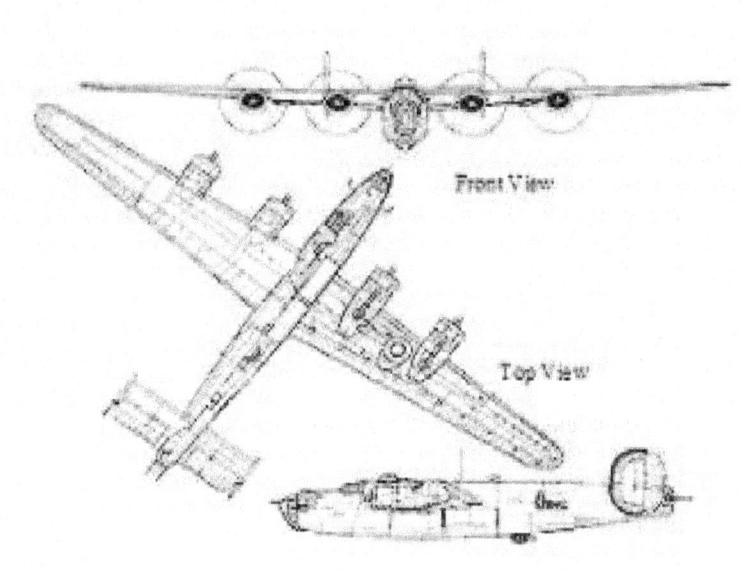

The B-24's specifications varied with each model but the general characteristics are as follows:

Length - 67' 2", Height - 18', Wingspan - 110'

Powered by four Pratt & Whitney engines it could carry: Empty weight - 36,500, Maximum weight - 65,000

It had a range of 2,300 miles and could reach a cruise speed of 215 mph and maximum speed of 303 mph with a ceiling of 30,000 feet.[1]

1 - *Fiddlers Green,* September 2004
www.fiddlersgreen.net/models/aircraft/Consolidated-B-24.html

From its inception the B-24 went through many modifications and improvements noted through a series of models:

B-24A - It had an armament of six 50. caliber and two .30 caliber machine guns.

XB-24B - The first B-24 to be fitted with turbo-supercharged engines, self-sealing tanks, armor and other modern refinements.

B-24C - Armament augmented to include two power-driven turrets, one dorsal and one tail, each fitted with two .50 caliber guns. Also, there was one .50 caliber nose gun and two similar guns in waist positions.

B-24D - Armament further increased by the addition of two further nose guns and one tunnel gun, making a total of ten - .50 caliber guns. Fuel capacity increased by the addition of auxiliary self-sealing fuel cells in the outer wings and there was provision for long-range tanks in the bomb bay.

B-24E - Similar to B-24D except for minor equipment details.

B-24F - An experimental version of the B-24E fitted with exhaust-heated surface anti-icing equipment.

B-24G, H and J - Similar except for details of equipment and minor differences. Armament further improved to include four two-gun turrets, in nose and tail and above and below the fuselage.

B-24L - Similar to the B-24J but fitted with a new tail turret with two manually operated .50 cal. guns.

B-24M - Same as B-24L except fitted with two-gun power operated tail gun.

B-24N - The first production single-tail Liberator. Fitted with new nose and tail gun mountings.[1]

---

1 - Stephen Sherman, *AcePilots.com World War Two & Aviation History*, 2010
http://acepilots.com

According to www.warbirdregistry.org of the over 18,000 B-24 Liberators produced there are only a handful surviving B-24's; of which most are static museum displays. The Collins Foundation restored B-24J is the only one of its kind airworthy. Some years ago that B-24J, known at the time as "The Dragon and His Tail", made a visit to the Elmira/Corning Regional Airport, Elmira, NY. The author was privileged to be able to tour the aircraft. Follows are pictures taken of "The Dragon and His Tail" which will give the reader a better perspective of the features of the B-24. The gun positions are particularly interesting as Mr. Bates occupied each of these positions during his forty-one missions. The color scheme of "The Dragon and His Tail" has since been changed to "Witchcraft". For further information see www.collinsfoundation.org.

"The Dragon and His Tail"
Note the cockpit and top turret are covered with tarp.

Rear View

Nose Guns

Tail Gun (with protective coverings)

Interior view of the left side waist gun

Ball Turret – located in the 'belly' or underneath the plane

THE MISSIONS CHART

Mr. Bates kept a very detailed chart of each of his forty-one missions. The chart is replicated on the following three pages and is included as a reference guide.

The chart includes the following information:

DATE - Date of mission

MISSION - Mission objective

OPPOSITION - The opposition encountered which includes a sub listing which notes if the bomber took a hit on the mission and on occasion the number of hits taken

BOMB LOAD - Type of bombs used, number and weight of the bombs carried on each mission

DEPARTURE FIELD - Field from which the bombers took off

POSITION - The position Mr. Bates occupied on the plane

TARGET - The type of target

As an added feature I have tried to obtain information concerning the bomber Mr. Bates flew on during each mission such as number, name and history of the plane, as well as, the pilot who flew the plane. Although, not as successful as I would have liked to be I think what little information was found is interesting.

Following the mission chart is a map of the Pacific Theater, the Philippines and Formosa. It will give you a perspective on the large area the bombers flew and I'm sure you'll note the names of many of the places Mr. Bates mentions in his diary.

For convenience and clarity I have bolded the dates, in the diary, which correspond with Mr. Bates missions.

THE MISSIONS

DATE	MISSION	OPPOSITION	# OF BOMBS/ BOMB WEIGHT	DEPARTURE FIELD	POSITION	TARGET
Oct. 22, 1944 (P)	New Guinea Wewak[TO]	None	8 - 1000 lb.	Nadzab	Scarf Guns*	Gun Positions
Nov. 14, 1944 (P)	Davao Mindanao	Flak	5 - 1000 lb.	Owi	Tail Turret	Airstrip
Nov. 21, 1944	Davao Mindanao	Close Flak (H)	9 - 500 lb.	Owi	Waist Guns	Flak Positions
Nov. 28, 1944	Davao Mindanao[TO]	None	16 - 250 lb. Fragment	Owi	Nose Turret	Planes
Dec. 6, 1944	Cebu Anguar	None	9 - 500 lb.	Palau	Waist Guns	Airdrome
Dec. 8, 1944	Cebu[TO]	None	18 - 250 lb.	Anguar	Nose Turret	Bad Weather
Dec. 13, 1944	Cebu	None	9 - 500 lb.	Anguar	Waist Guns	Planes
Dec. 20, 1944 (P) B-24J (#333)** [1]	Fabrica[TO] Negros	None	9 - 500 lb.	Anguar	Scarf Guns	Supply Buildings
Dec. 24, 1944	Clark/ Luzon[TO]	Flak (12H) Fighters	240 - 20 lb. Fragment	Anguar	Waist Guns	Planes
Dec. 26, 1944	Clark/ [TO] Luzon	Flak (7H) Fighters	240 - 20 lb.	Anguar	Waist Guns	Planes
Jan. 3, 1945 (P) B-24J (#971)** [2]	Clark/ Luzon [TO]	Flak (3H)	40 - 100 lb.	Anguar	Waist Guns	Revetments

* "The 'scarf' mount Jack refers to is a replacement for the ball turret, which was removed on long missions to save weight and fuel. It is similar to the gun mounts in WWI. The gun rotates on a circular gear permitting 360 degree firing range." Cucurullo, Cookie in e-mail to author.

** B-24 model and bomber number - Faletti, Richard in correspondence with author, January 2001.

TO - Indicates mission that Joseph Tosto flew on with Mr. Bates, Tosto, Joseph in correspondence with author, June 2005.

1 - Known as "TRIPLE THREAT" noted in diary, see 1/22/45 entry.

2 - "One of the original 2nd Squadron Liberators..... "It (#42-109971) flew its last mission on February 17, 1945 when it was damaged by flak over Heito, Formosa, with 1Lt. Horice Cunningham piloting.", Lawrence Hickey, The 22nd Bombardment Group in World War II, Volume III, Photo Supplement, ed. Don Evans (Bonsall, California: Alliance Business Services, 2001), 183.

P = Pilot (noted in diary): 10/21/44 - Canepa; 11/14/44 - Canepa; 12/20/44 - Faletti; 01/03/45 - Faletti

H indicates the plane was hit by flak and if accompanied by a number indicates how many hits

THE MISSIONS

DATE	MISSION	OPPOSITION	# OF BOMBS/ BOMB WEIGHT	DEPARTURE FIELD	POSITION	TARGET
Jan. 9, 1945 (P) B-24J (#978)** [1]	Clark^{TO}	Flak (2H)	8 - 500 lb.	Anguar	Scarf Guns	Revetments
Jan. 15, 1945	Clark^{TO} Samar	Flak (1H)	8 - 500 lb.	Anguar	Waist Guns	Barracks
Jan. 17, 1945	Legaspy/ Luzon^{TO}	None	6 - 1000 lb.	Samar	Nose Turret	Rail Yards
Jan. 20, 1945	Negros^{TO}	None	5 - 1000 lb.	Samar	Tail Turret	Supplies
Jan. 28, 1945	Subic Bay^{TO} Grande Is.	None	9 - 500 lb.	Samar	Waist Guns	2 - 14" Naval Guns
Feb. 4, 1945	Caballo Is.^{TO} Manila Bay	None	6 - 1000 lb.	Samar	Waist Guns	Naval Guns
Feb. 7, 1945	Bogo/Cebu^{TO}	None	21 - 250 lb.	Samar	Tail Turret	Japanese Personnel
Mar. 5, 1945	SW Manila^{TO}	None	8 - 1000 lb.	Samar	Nose Turret	Japanese Personnel
Mar. 10, 1945	East Manila^{TO}	None	6 - 1000 lb.	Samar	Waist Guns	Japanese Personnel
Apr. 17, 1945 (#157)** [2]	Shinchiku^{TO} Formosa	Flak	Fragment	Clark	Waist Guns	Airdrome
Apr. 18, 1945	Tainan^{TO} Formosa	Intense Flak (H)	Fragment	Clark	Waist Guns	City
Apr. 20-21, 1945	Taihoku^{TO} Formosa	Search Lights	500 lb. Incendiary	Clark	Waist Guns	City

** B-24 model and bomber number – Faletti, Richard in correspondence with author, January 2001.

TO - Indicates mission that Joseph Tosto flew on with Mr. Bates. Tosto, Joseph in correspondence with author, June 2005.

1 - "#42-109978, was called BAYBEE......carried 63 mission symbols on her scoreboard when she was salvaged after the nose wheel collapsed during take off for a mission on February 22, 1945." Lawrence Hickey, The 22nd Bombardment Group in World War II, Volume III, Photo Supplement, ed. Don Evans (Bonsall, California: Alliance Business Services, 2001), 149.

2 - "# 42-100157 known as "PLEASURE BENT", Ibid., 159.

P = Pilot (noted in diary): Faletti; 01/09/45

H indicates the plane was hit by flak and if accompanied by a number indicates how many hits

THE MISSIONS

DATE	MISSION	OPPOSITION	# OF BOMBS/ BOMB WEIGHT	DEPARTURE FIELD	POSITION	TARGET
Apr. 23, 1945 (P) B-24J (#182)** [1]	Matsuyama Formosa	Intense Flak (H)	12 - 500 lb. Fragment	Clark	Waist Guns	Taihoku Airdrome
May 1, 1945 (P)) B-24J (#318)** [2]	Tainan^{TO} Formosa	Light Flak	12 - 500 lb. Incendiary	Clark	Waist Guns	Clouded Over
May 14, 1945 (B-24J #365)**	Toshien^{TO} Formosa	Inaccurate Flak	12 - 500 lb. Incendiary	Clark	Waist Guns	City
May 18, 1945 (P)	Tainan^{TO} Formosa	Flak (H)	12 - 500 lb. Fragment	Clark	Waist Guns	Airdrome
May 29, 1945	Kiirun^{TO} Formosa	Flak (H)	8 - 1000 lb.	Clark	Tail Turret	Installations
May 30, 1945 (P) (#043) [3]	Takao^{TO} Formosa	Flak	32 - 250 lb. Fragment	Clark	Waist Guns	Anti-aircraft positions
May 31, 1945	Taihoku	Flak (H)	8 - 1000 lb.	Clark	Waist Guns	Center of City
June 1, 1945	Amoy China	Weather Recon	None	Clark	Tail Turret	China, Amoy, etc.
June 2, 1945 B-24M (#240)** [4]	Kiirun^{TO} Formosa	Light Flak	8 - 1000 lb.	Clark	Waist Guns	Buildings Harbor & Docks

** B-24 model and bomber number - Faletti, Richard in correspondence with author, January 2001.

TO - Indicates mission that Joseph Tosto flew on with Mr. Bates. Tosto, Joseph in correspondence with author, June 2005.

1 - "#44-4182 - lost on Clark Field, Philippines on 05/08/45" (see diary entry of the same date), Lawrence Hickey, The 22nd Bombardment Group in World War II, Volume III, Photo Supplement, ed. Don Evans (Bonsall, California: Alliance Business Services, 2001), 197.

2 - "#42-100318 -'Titian Temptress' - Assigned and serviceable on April 1, 1944. She flew the 22nd Bomb Groups final bombing attack; a strike on Kiangwan Air Drome at Shanghai, China - Pilot Lt. R.G. Arand", Cy Klimesh, 22nd Bomb Group, 2001, www.redraiders.com.

3 - # 44-4043 - Ibid.

4 - # 44-42240 - Ibid.

P = Pilot (noted in diary): 04/23/45 - Faletti; 05/01/45 - Faletti; 05/18/45 - Cunningham; 05/30/45 - Cunningham

H indicates the plane was hit by flak and if accompanied by a number indicates how many hits

THE MISSIONS

DATE	MISSION	OPPOSITION	# OF BOMBS/ BOMB WEIGHT	DEPARTURE FIELD	POSITION	TARGET
June 13, 1945 *B-24M (#845)*** [1]	Formosa	None	8 - 390 lb. Incendiary	Clark	Waist Guns	Town
June 15, 45 *B-24M (#240)*** [2]	Taichu Formosa	Flak (H)	32 - 260 lb. fragment	Clark	Waist Guns	Flak Positions
June 18, 1945	Kiirun	Intense Flak (H)	8 - 1000 lb.	Clark	Nose Turret	Buildings
June 19, 1945	Kiirun	Flak (H)	8 - 1000 lb.	Clark	Nose Turret	Residential
June 20, 1945 *B-24J (#427)*** [3]	Shinchiku	None	8 - 1000 lb.	Clark	Tail Turret	H2X Planes
June 22, 1945	Toshien	Flak (H)	32 - 260 lb.	Clark	Nose Turret	Flak Positions
June 26, 1945	Celebes	Fighters	6 - 1000 lb.	Morotai	Nose Turret	Air Strip
June 28, 1945	Borneo	None	5 - 1000 lb.	Morotai	Nose Turret	Air Strip
July 2, 1945	Toyohara Formosa	Flak (H)	40 - 100 lb.	Clark	No Entry	Planes

** B-24 model and bomber number - Faletti, Richard in correspondence with author, January 2001.

TO - Indicates mission that Joseph Tosto flew on with Mr. Bates. - Tosto, Joseph in correspondence with author, June 2005.

1 - # 44-41845 - 'Daisy Mae , With a Little Persuasion' - Cy Klimesh, *22nd Bomb Group*, 2001, www.redraiders.com.

2 - # 44-42240 - Ibid.

3 - "With the end of the war several of the high-mission aircraft had their scoreboards updated and were then photographed for posterity......B-24J-160, #44-40427.....carried an unusual version of the Red Raiders insignia, along with the group motto, "WE LEAD". It's scoreboard showed 88 missions highest in the squadron"., Lawrence Hickey, The 22nd Bombardment Group in World War II, Volume III, Photo Supplement, ed. Don Evans (Bonsall, California: Alliance Business Services, 2001), 208.

P = Pilot (noted in diary): 06/13/45 - Faletti; 06/15/45 - Berry; 06/18/45 - Berry; 06/19/45 - Peterson; 06/20/45 - Faletti; 06/20/45 - Co-pilot - Paul Davies (Davies in personal correspondence with author)

H indicates the plane was hit by flak and if accompanied by a number indicates how many hits

THE PACIFIC THEATER

22nd Bomb Group Area of Operations
1942-1945

THE PHILIPPINES

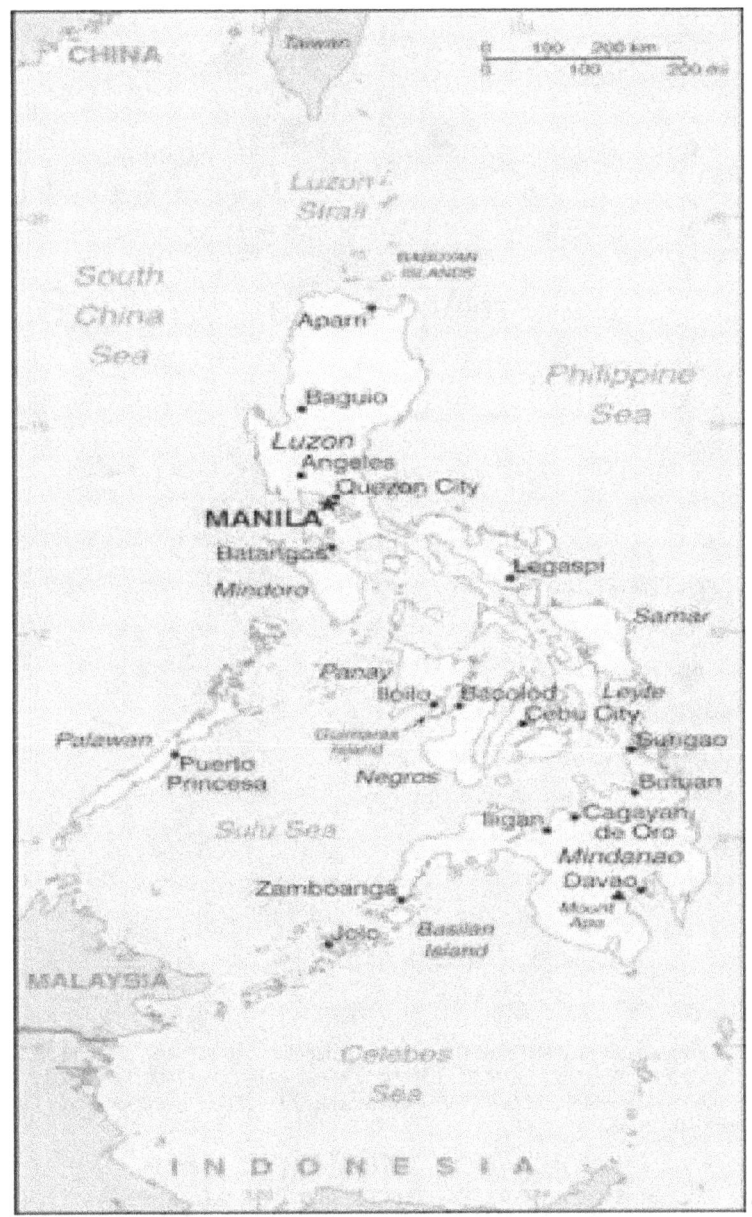

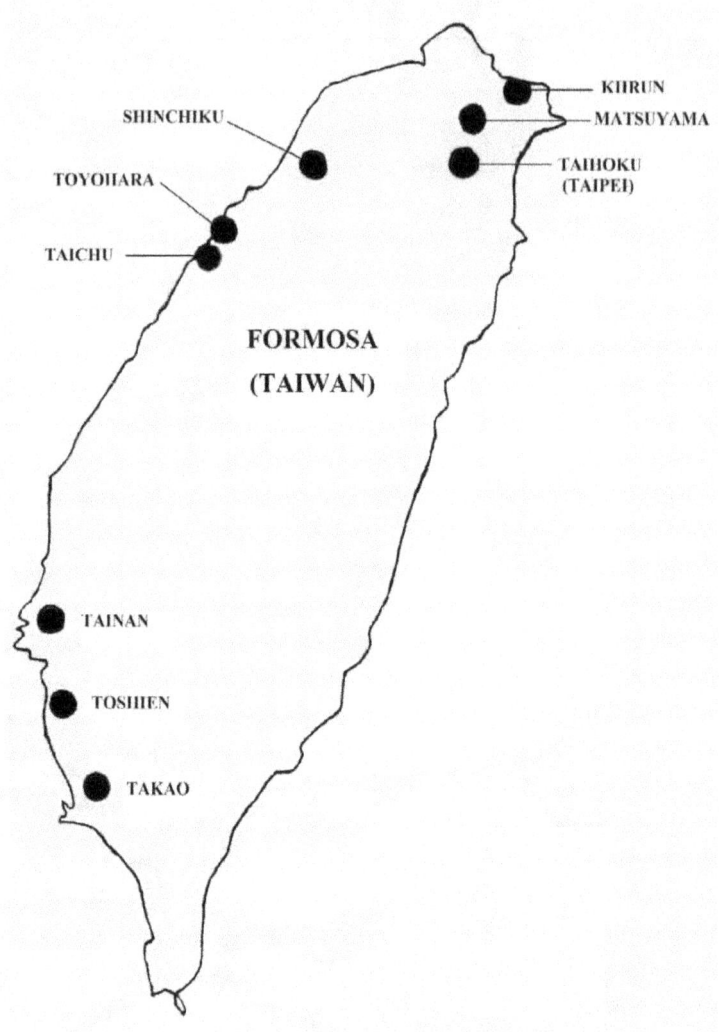

Mission Dates: Tainan - 04/18, 05/01, 05/18/45; Shinchiku - 04/17, 06/20/45; Toshien - 05/14, 06/22/45; Taihoku - 04/20-21, 05/31/45; Matsuyama - 04/23/45; Kiirun - 05/29, 06/02, 06/18, 06/19/45; Takao - 05/30/45; Taichu - 06/15/45; Formosa - 06/13/45; Toyohara - 07/02/45

**MAP OF FORMOSA WITH CITIES BOMBED DURING
MR. BATES MISSIONS AGAINST THE ISLAND**

THE OPPOSITION/LOSSES

The causes for the losses incurred by the B-24 bomber included numerous things: the weather, mechanical failure, human error and the enemy.

The missions chart listed on pages thirty-two, thirty-three, thirty-four and thirty-five notes the type of opposition encountered by the B-24's, Mr. Bates, and his fellow crew members during his forty-one bombing missions - primarily anti-aircraft fire or flak, enemy fighters or a combination of the two. Eighteen missions were flown against no opposition. This includes one mission listed as "searchlights" and another listed as "weather recon". On twenty missions the bombers encountered flak. Two missions the bombers encountered flak and fighters. One mission encountered fighters only. The percentages are:

No Opposition: 44 % Flak: 49 % Flak/Fighters: 5% Fighters: 2%

Flak or anti-aircraft fire typically came from artillery placed in and about valuable Japanese assets - airfields, harbors, factories and ground forces. This artillery consisted of 75 mm and 120 mm guns. Flak was very dangerous and much feared by the B-24 crews - as noted in Mr. Bates diary. Flak was encountered a total of twenty-two times. Of those the bomber took hits on 16 different missions.

Japanese 75 mm anti-aircraft artillery

ENEMY FIGHTERS

Enemy fighters consisted of the much feared and vaunted Mitsubishi A6M 'Zero', Nakajima Ki-43 'Oscar', Nakajima Ki-84 'Frank' and Mitsubishi J2 'Raiden' fighters. Although, very dangerous they were encountered only three times during Mr. Bates forty-one missions.

One reason for the lack of fighter opposition is what most crews would call the "luck of the draw". Some missions due to the very nature of the target - its military importance - encountered more fighter opposition than others. Looking back I imagine Mr. Bates must have felt fortunate in some of the missions he was assigned to.

As the war progressed so too did the American aircraft. The early technical advantages Japanese planes had over American models diminished. Development of planes such as the F4U Corsair, P-51 Mustang, P-38 Lightning and the P-47 Thunderbolt (noted several times in the diary as escorting the B-24 bombers on long range missions) with their technical superiority, maneuverability, range and fire power gave the advantage, even to the least inexperienced, American pilots in air combat.

Another interesting factor was America's seemingly limitless supply of manpower. America was able to replace combat loses more readily than Japan. Veteran American pilots were more likely to be "rotated" back home where they trained the new recruits. Veteran Japanese pilots remained in combat and when they were lost, were replaced by ill-trained recruits. Over time Japan, with its limited manpower, could not afford to lose or replace these valuable assets.

Finally, as the war progressed, the capture of territory nearer and nearer to the Japanese homeland made it possible for American bombing raids to target Japanese manufacturing thereby severely limiting the Japanese ability to replace the lost airplanes.

The combination of the these factors led to the eventual dominance of American Air Forces and the lost effectiveness of Japanese air assets. In fact, towards the end of the war the "Zero" and other types of enemy fighters were typically limited in use as kamikaze - suicide attacks - on American shipping.

Mitsubishi A6M "Zero"

At the start of hostilities between America and Japan the Mitsubishi A6M "Zero" fighter was undoubtedly the best fighter airplane on either side. It was a small, lightly built (due to it's lack of armor plating, typically used on American fighters to protect the pilot and gas tank), highly maneuverable aircraft. It was commonly armed with two 20-mm cannon in its outer wings and two 7.7-mm machine guns in the fuselage. Powered by a 925 hp Nakajima NK1c Sakae 12, 14-cylinder radial engine,. It had a maximum speed of 316 miles per hour with ceiling of 33,790 ft. and range (w/drop tank) of 1,940 miles. Bill Gunston, The Illustrated Directory of Fighting Aircraft of World War II, (Salamander Books Ltd., London, 2002), 284

Mitsubishi J2 "Raiden"

Powered by a Mitsubishi 1,820 hp MK4R-A Kasei 23A engine it had a maximum speed of approximately 380 mph, range of 655 miles. Its armament typically consisted of two 7.7 mm machine guns in the fuselage and two - 20 mm cannon - one in each wing. Bill Gunston, The Illustrated Directory of Fighting Aircraft of World War II, (Salamander Books Ltd., London, 2002), 290.

Kawanishi N1K1 "George"

Powered by a 1,990 hp, Nakajima Homare 21, 18 cylinder engine it had a maximum speed of 369 mph, range of 1,069 miles and ceiling of 35,400 ft. Its armament typically consisted of 4 - 20 mm cannon and 2 - 7.7 mm machine guns. Bill Gunston, The Illustrated Directory of Fighting Aircraft of World War II, (Salamander Books Ltd., London, 2002), 272

Nakajima Ki43 "Oscar"

Powered by 1,250 hp Ha-112 Kasei engine it had a maximum speed of 363 mph, range of 1,060 miles and a ceiling of 36,800 ft. Its armament typically consisted of 2 - 12.7 mm machine guns. Bill Gunston, The Illustrated Directory of Fighting Aircraft of World War II, (Salamander Books Ltd., London, 2002), 306.

Nakajima Ki84 "Frank"

Powered by a 1,900 hp, Nakajima Homare Ha-45 engine it had a top speed of 388 mph, range of 1,025 miles and a ceiling of 34,450 ft. Its armament typically consisted of 2 - 12.7 caliber machine guns and 2 - 20 mm cannons. Bill Gunston, The Illustrated Directory of Fighting Aircraft of World War II, (Salamander Books Ltd., London, 2002), 310.

"MY LIFE IN THE SERVICE"

The first entry in the diary is undated: Came back from delay enroute July 1 and stayed at Tonopah until Sept. 15. There were over 30 persons killed while at Tonopah, all but 3 were plane wrecks. The three being officers burned when barracks caught fire. Nineteen men in one day.[1] Dropped 12 practice bombs while there and had quite an easy life. Was assigned to my crew there also and had 87 hours of flying when I left. I left Tonopah Sept. 15 and arrived in Hamilton Field Calif. on the 16th. This was our staging area and was issued new equipment including flying suit, parachute harness, headset, oxygen mask, etc. also suntans.

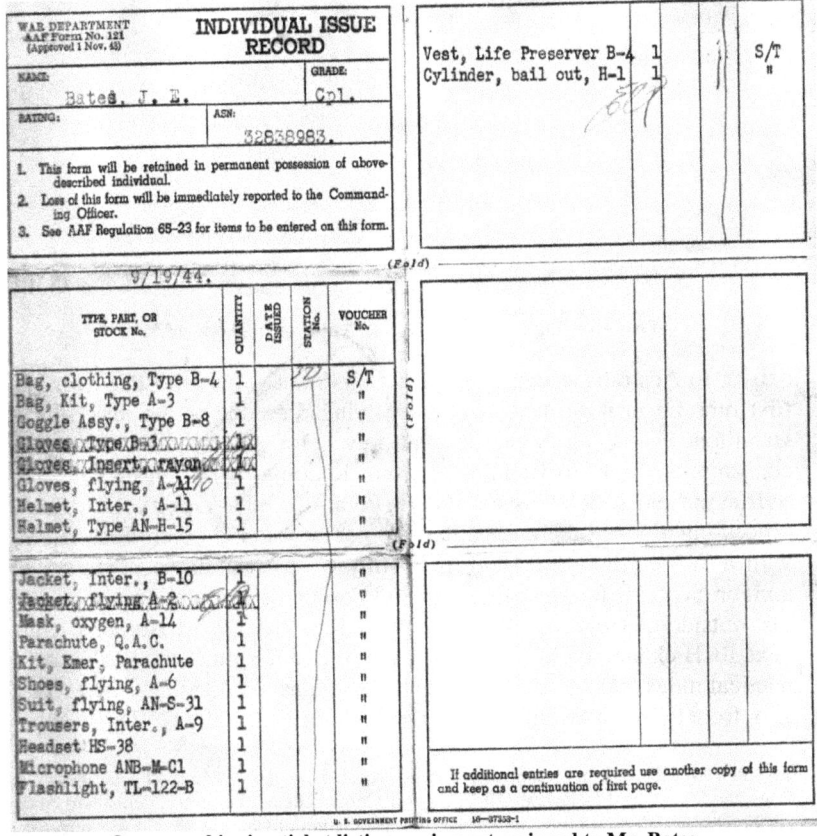

Overseas shipping ticket listing equipment assigned to Mr. Bates

---

1 - "35,946 airmen died in accidents during the war. In 1943 alone, 850 airmen died in 298 B-24 training accidents." - Stephen Ambrose, The Wild Blue, The Men and Boys Who Flew the B-24's Over Germany, (New York: Simon and Schuster, 2001), 100.

It (Hamilton Field) was at the edge of the bay and I went to San Francisco once and saw Treasure Island, Alcatraz, Golden Gate and other interesting spots. We was delayed for three days due to a gas leak in the main cell of our airplane. We received a new B-24-L (#44-41536) to

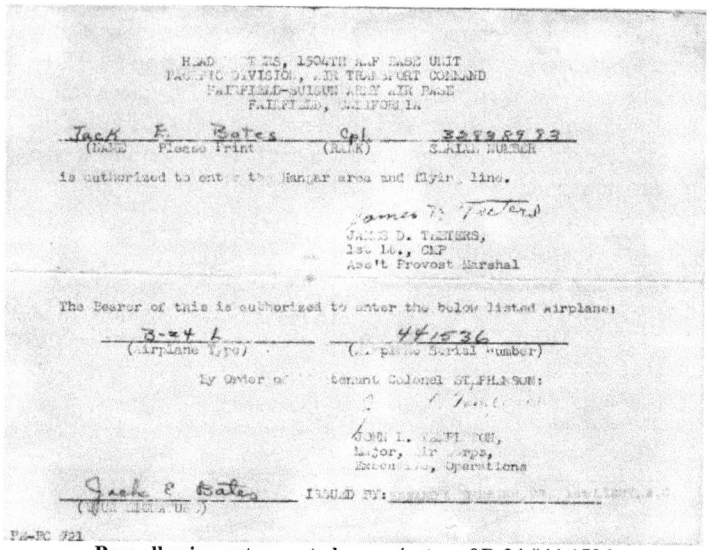
Pass allowing entrance to hanger/entry of B-24 #44-1536

deliver to Australia which I'm writing this in now over the Pacific. The first time up in it we had 4 minutes flying time due to the leak. I left Hamilton Field on Sept. 25 and flew for five hours on a fuel consumption flight to Redding, Fresno, Redding[1] and then to Fairfield-Suisun airfield which was my P.O.E (Point of Embarkation). Did some processing and was there for three days. The last night there I had a date with a WAC (short for Women's Army Corp) and shoved off at 6:15 a.m. on Sept. 29 for John Rodgers Field on the island of Oahu in Hawaii just outside of Honolulu and three miles from Pearl Harbor. Right next to Hickham Field. It took 13 hrs. and 23 min. to fly the 2100 nautical miles and we had 500+ gallons of gas on landing there. Had two front bomb bay tanks and carried 3300 gallons of gas. The weather

1 - "In 1942, the site of Redding AAF was acquired for the Air Corps by the Corps of Engineers ....On 9 December 1942, the Air Corps became the semi-independent Army Air Forces. Initially, Redding AAF was a sub-installation of Chico AAF and was under the operational control of that field's 433rd Army Air Forces Base Unit....As with all of the operational and training airfields in the southwestern United States, the overall operational control of Redding AAF rested with the Fourth Air Force of the Army Air Forces." Daniel Sebby, Command Sergeant Major, *The California State Military Museum*, California State Military Department, 2005, http://www.militarymuseum.org/ReddingAAF.html.

was fine with quite a few clouds. It took from 7 to 12 days for boats to come that far. Stayed there one day and two nights. Had a pass the day I was there and went to Honolulu and Waikiki. The island was beautiful from the air and also on the ground. I left there this morning, the 1st of October and am starting this diary now. I got this book in Honolulu for $1.00. It is 1600 nautical miles to Canton,[1] an island in the Phoenix Islands; where we're headed for and we took off about 6:30 am and had very bad weather on take off. It just stopped raining as we took off and the cumulus clouds toss the plane around at times up here. Have seen three ships so far. Passed the equator at about one p.m. Our ETA (Estimated Time of Arrival) is 15:05 for Canton. Was issued our ammunition for our 45 cal. pistol before we took off this a.m. It took exactly 11 hours to come to Canton. The island is horseshoe shaped and no more than 300 yards wide at any place with water in the middle. There was one tree on Canton. No vegetation and our barracks were called hotel Astor but were very poor. No women on the island. Our plane was in good shape and we took off at 7:30 a.m. the next morning for Nandi[2] in the Figi Islands, an eight-hour trip.

Oct. 2-3, 44 - We landed at 14:27 and its quite pretty on this island. We passed the International Date Line coming here so lost one day. Just before hitting Nandi we passed over one large island and many small islands, some only specks. Flew over the city of Nandi and all the houses are red roofed. There are real natives here and most of the houses are the grass huts just like you've seen in pictures. The natives are quite fascinating with large head of hair. There is vegetation all over the island even on the mountains. We had some very bad weather coming here and the plane really tossed around in the clouds. There are natives working on this post and (they) live in the barracks next to mine. We're making this trip under A.T.C. (Air Transport Command - DE) and have to pay for meals, barracks, etc. but get $7 a day to pay for it. We clear about $4 a day, which isn't bad. We take a box lunch to eat while flying with coffee also. It was terribly hot when I got here and there are mosquito nets over our beds to prevent malaria. Am all mixed up on the time now.

1 - "Canton Island is the largest and most northern of the Phoenix Group...(it's)...an atoll, made up of a low, narrow rim of land surrounding a large shallow lagoon. It is 4-12 miles wide on the west, from which it narrows to the southeast point, which is nine miles distant from the northeast point. Americans and British occupied the island in two separate camps....Remembered for having only one tree and one landing strip (Canton Airfield). A refueling point for American flights between Hawaii and......or to Australia." - Justin Taylan, *Pacific Wrecks*, 2005, www.pacificwrecks.com.

2 - "Located on the western coast of Viti Levu, largest island of Figi, part of the Mamanuca Island group. It had a 5,000 foot airfield used on the aircraft ferry route from Hawaii to Australia.", Ibid.

Oct. 2-3, 44 (cont.) - Have changed every day and lost a day so this is really the 3rd of October. The ocean is seen from one side of the barracks and a row of mountains on the other. It rained just before I went to bed and is cloudy most of the time. I talked with a fellow in the New Zealand Army whose home was in Australia and had quite a hard time understanding him. He'd been in the battle of France. It was 1100 nautical miles to this island.

Oct. 4, 44 - I got up at 7 a.m. ate and went down to the plane. It was given a 50 hour inspection yesterday and only has about 60 hours of flying time on it. Got a Figi dollar bill and coins. We have some athletic equipment, football, two softballs, harmonica, checkers etc. which was put on for our recreation. We played football and softball all morning. The E.M. (enlisted men) against the officers in tackle (football). Got ready and went to Nandi at 3 p.m. They had pure silver bracelets and necklaces but was short on cash. <u>Very</u> cheap too.

Figi Coin

Pass to Nandi

Oct. 4, 44 (cont.) - We haven't been paid yet for last month. The natives are fascinating and treat us swell. The missionaries converted all of these to half way civilization and though everyone goes bare footed they have shabby clothing around them now. Until just lately they wore nothing. They speak broken English which I could hardly understand and are quite dirty. The vehicles drive on the left side of the road here and I thought that funny. The New Zealander couldn't figure out how we made a left hand turn in the states. We were scheduled to take off this morning but Faletti went on sick call and was grounded so we stayed today. There is about fifteen ships in our flight and are separated through about one weeks time. We're one of the last ones now and there are four planes with us, one plane coming in today. Everyone knows each other so we try and keep in contact. Half went a different route to Canton, going to Tarawa and Guadalcanal but we all end up in Townsville, Australia. Beer is plenty scarce and we had some tonight with steak for supper. I gave mine to Deter as I don't like it. One bottle per person once a week. Nandi is only four miles from here. It's <u>very</u> hot out today. Went to the show an outdoor one and saw "Sensations of 1945". It was a new picture and free too. Wrote one letter afterward and went to bed.

Some of the children mentioned in the diary entry above

Oct. 5, 44 - Got up bright and early 4:45 a.m. and was to the plane before 6:00. We shoved off from Nandi at 6:30 heading for Australia which is due west. It's 7 a.m. now. We passed some islands on the way, there was Mare Island which is in the Loyalty Is. (East of New Caledonia) and

Oct. 5, 44 (cont.) - then New Caledonia.[1] Which was a very big island and had a very crooked coastline with small island just off the coast. There were jungle country there too just heard the news on radio compass in our plane about the air raid in Honolulu last Sat. the 30th and I was there at the time. It was at night. (most probably one of the many false alarms during this time) Landed at Townsville[2] airport at 7:45 which made the trip 12 1/2 hours long. It's very pretty and we passed a lot of coral reef just before hitting Australia. We thought we were running out of gas but really had 700 gallons. To show the inefficiency of the Army, they took our parachute and harness which was fitted perfect to us and Mae West (life jackets) which all was stenciled with our name. They also took our plane. The barracks are poor and the chow was lousy tonight. It was two hours difference in time and it gets dark at 6:30 here. Quite cool too. There is every kind of plane there is about here. Some people live in tents here too. It was about 1800 nautical miles here. Raymond said he'd give me the true reports of the trip.

Mr. Bates wearing some of the gear he notes in the diary entry above

1 - "archipelago, to the east of Australia.....the area became a major Allied staging base for the Americans, and a ferry point for aircraft to Australia. During its height, 40,000 American servicemen were based in New Caledonia, and also as a rest and hospital area for combat troops. As the war progressed, fewer came thru the island, as other more forward bases were established.", Justin Taylan, *Pacific Wrecks*, 2005, www.pacificwrecks.com.

2 - "a coastal town south of Cairns...staging point for many American troops in Australia....it was developed into a major base (Garbutt)....the Townsville area had 90,000 (Allied troops) by the middle of 1943. Many units from both the RAAF and USAAF were based or transited thru the strip", Ibid.

Oct. 6, 44 - Got up at 6 a.m. had roll call at 7:30. Got paid for the trip to here in a.m. Boy, I was sure bawled up on the money here. I got $15.75 but they paid us in Australian money. I saved some of it. Went to Townsville in the afternoon which is about two or three miles. Got a watch strap and two locks. Most the things are cheaper here. There wasn't a cigarette in the whole town and all drinks are scarce. The bars opened up about two hours or less. I met Davis[1] and was coming back to camp so stayed in with him for a while. We had a plane assigned to us in the a.m. but an order came out canceling all B-24's out of here so will go A.T.C. They sell cigarettes for one hour on camp they're so scarce. This field is called Garbutt. Went to bed about 10:30 when I got back from town.

Oct. 7, 44 - Didn't do anything in a.m. Went to canteen for breakfast. Am standing by ready to ship out at any time. Was supposed to go this a.m. but our plane was taken away from us. Laid around in the afternoon and went to town in evening. Saw "Eagle Squadron".

Pass to Townsville

Oct. 8, 44 - Didn't get up until 9 a.m. Met two fellows who had been in the Borneo bomber raid a few days before and came down for more planes. He said every plane was damaged. Wrote letters in p.m. Went to variety show on post in evening and got ready to ship out.

---

1 - Robert Davis - listed under 'My Buddies in the Service' with a notation "went around with him for over six months and a swell friend."

Oct. 9, 44 - Got up at 3:30 a.m. and went down to aerodrome with belongings. Had to weigh them and we took off in C-47 from Garbutt Field at 7:30 a.m. and landed at Nadzab[1] in New Guinea at 1 p.m. Had to leave Raymond and Crockett behind for one day because we had too much baggage. We slept in tents with nets. It is all jungle country and mountains are all around us. A lot of planes are here including fighter planes.

DH
Douglas C-47 "Skytrain"

The C-47 was used primarily for military transport of men and material. It carried a crew of three with no armament. Powered by two Pratt & Whitney engines, it had a range of 1,500 miles, cruise speed of 185 mph, maximum speed of 229 mph and a ceiling of 23,200 feet., Dave Hanson, *American Aircraft of World War II*, September 2004, www.daveswarbirds.com/usplanes.

Oct. 10, 44 - Got ten letters this morning. The first since leaving U.S. They'd been sent directly here and not followed us. Got $10 from home and snapshots from home and Mary Alice (several letters and pictures of her are kept in a separate scrapbook). Wrote letters and moved to another tent.

Oct. 11, 44 - Moved today and wrote letters tonight. Found out that this valley I'm in was the main battleground in New Guinea. Paratroops were landed here. The fellows have steel helmets they found here also.

1 - "Located in the Markam Valley outside of Lae. It was the site of the only Allied paratrooper assault in New Guinea mainland on September 5, 1943. (note 10/11/44 diary entry) Almost immediately, the area was developed into a major forward airfield and later a massive air base and staging area for future operations in the region. The Nadzab airfield complex included five separate airstrips." – Justin Taylan, *Pacific Wrecks*, 2005, www.pacificwrecks.com.

Oct. 12, 44 - Got up at 4 am and went on K.P.[1] until 8 pm. Got a letter from M.A. (Mary Alice Garside) writing letters at night.

Mary Alice Garside

Oct. 13, 44 - Went to school in a.m. and heard lectures, didn't do anything in p.m. and wrote letters at night. Bought some things at PX (Post Exchange - similar to a convenient store). Didn't get any mail.

Oct. 14, 44 - Didn't do anything in a.m. Went to machine gun class in the afternoon. Went to show. It rained at night. Wrote letters.

Oct. 15, 44 - Went to church at nine and didn't do anything else. Slept in p.m.

Oct. 16, 44 - Went to detail formation at 7 a.m. and got paid partial payment of L10 or $32. Put on K.P. for rest of the day. Got one letter from M.A. (Mary Alice). Didn't do anything at night.

---

1 - "Kitchen Police - this was an assignment to assist in work in the kitchen. Usually assigned on a recurring basis. It was not a punishment usually...It was not a fun assignment, peeling potatoes, emptying garbage, washing pots and pans, etc." - Evans, Don in e-mail message to author, 2003.

Oct. 17, 44 - Have off in a.m. & am scheduled to fly at noon. We flew over Leahe (Lae) to come here and only thirty miles from it. MacArthur[1] is stationed only a couple hours ride from here. Everyone that's been here a long time really hates him. The P-38's and P-47's buzz these tents daily and plenty low too. Flew in p.m. and that crazy Faletti tried to out

Lockheed P-38 "Lightning"

This twin tailed, twin engined fighter was extremely fast and maneuverable. It was used as a long range, bomber escort and fighter. It carried 1 - 20-mm cannon and 4 - .50 caliber machine guns. Powered by two Allison engines it had a range of 500 miles, cruise speed of 300 mph, maximum speed of 390 mph and a ceiling of 39,000 feet., Dave Hanson, *American Aircraft of World War II*, September 2004, www.daveswarbirds.com/usplanes

Republic P-47 "Thunderbolt"

Used as a fighter, long range, bomber escort and close ground support. It carried 6 or 8 .50 caliber machine guns. Powered by an Pratt & Whitney engine it had a range of 800 miles (on internal tanks), cruise speed of 300 mph, maximum speed of 467 mph and a ceiling of 43,000 feet., Dave Hanson, *American Aircraft of World War II*, September 2004, www.daveswarbirds.com/usplanes.

---

1 - MacArthur, Douglas (1880-1964), American general, who commanded allied troops in the Pacific during World War II. As supreme commander of the Southwest Pacific, MacArthur led a combined Allied force in a series of victories, gradually retaking the islands seized by Japan at the beginning of the war. The campaign concluded with the retaking of the Philippines (October 1944-July 1945). "Douglas MacArthur," Microsoft® Encarta® Online Encyclopedia 2008 http://encarta.msn.com.

Oct. 17, 44 (cont.) - maneuver a P-47 I guess. It was really a rough ride. We flew around Leahe (Lae)[1] and up to Finchavin (Finschafen),[2] about eight miles away. This is really a huge valley with very high mountains on either side so we can only fly in the valley. In places the trees are dead and the jungle is thinned out where the fighting had taken place here. A lot of planes are cracked up all over the valley and at Leahe (Lae) harbor a Jap ship is sunk. Over 100 ships were unloading at Finchavin (Finschafen). Got one letter from home. Wrote two at night.

Oct. 18, 44 - Got up at 5:00 and went to fly. Flew formation, six planes and plenty close too. Went to church at night and then wrote letters.

Oct. 19, 44 - Went to skeet range in a.m. and shot a round of skeet. Didn't have anything in p.m. Read "The Hostages". Yesterday I got two cartons of cigarettes, the first I could buy since leaving Hawaii. Our rations are 4 cartons a month and all I could get was Raleigh and Old Gold. (brands of cigarettes) No mail.

Oct. 20, 44 - Got five letters today. Rained early morning. Had pistol practice in p.m. and wrote five letters.

Oct. 21, 44 - Had a very interesting lecture on jungle training in a.m. and went out in jungle in p.m. It was fun and very interesting. The growth is very heavy and some places (had) deep mud. Saw banana trees, pineapples, palm, coconuts, tomato plants, corn, cucumbers or resembling. All the plants and things to live on in jungle. Went to a native village and through their gardens (they are) not kept up and (has) very – primitive food, some of it. They wore few if any clothing and most of the women were all dried up. Very fascinating to watch. Was instructed on the character of natives and what not to do. Had a very interesting day and had lecture on natives at 7 p.m. Saw the end of the show "Madam Currie". Suppose to go on my first mission tomorrow.

---

1 - "Major city on New Guinea's northern coast. Allied Forces evacuated Lae on January 22, 1942. Japanese landed in March 1942. The town became a Japanese stronghold and aerodrome. As the war progressed, it was isolated, and efforts to resupply and reinforce the garrison...were thwarted. On September 16, 1943 Australian (forces) entered Lae and found the Japanese there weakened from lack of food and ammunition...(they) abandoned position after position", Justin Taylan, *Pacific Wrecks*, 2005, www.pacificwrecks.com.

2 - "Little remains now of the old town. Japanese occupied this area on March 10, 1942. By October 2nd (of 1943) Australian troops were in control of Finschafen. After occupation....it was developed into an airfield and large base and assembly area", Ibid.

Oct. 22, 44 - I went on my first raid. Got up at 5 a.m. and took off at 7:35. Went to Wewak airfield, which is the Jap held territory of New Guinea.[1] We had a ten plane formation and eight fighters of P-38's and 47's as escort. Our target was some gun emplacement right on the coastline on a narrow strip of land jutting out in the water. Carried 8 - 1000 lb. general purpose bombs and altogether 80,000 lbs. were dropped. Very few bombs hit the target due to a very thick overcast over the target. Couldn't see the hits but a cloud of smoke hung over the target after we circled to come back. No interceptions and no ground action. Bombed at 8,800 ft. and the concussion was very great from there, sounded like flak was being shot at us. After each mission we get 2 oz. of whiskey issued but I didn't go get it. Mission lasted 4 hours and 55 minutes. Had p.m. off, got one letter and went to chapel at night. Am writing letter now.

Oct. 23, 44 - Was put as runner in orderly room but we was called at 8 a.m. to ship out. We went on a B-24 in two full crews and baggage, also four men crew to fly the plane and really had a load. It took five plus hours to get here to Owi Island[2] in the Netherlands East Indies.

CK
Owi Island - George Udelewitz Collection

1 - "Occupied by the Japanese...December 18, 1942...(It) became the largest concentration of Japanese Army troops on mainland New Guinea...Largely neutralized from the air by attacks from the USAAF 5th. Wewak was bypassed by the Allied landings further to the west...At the end of the war, Australian troops...engaged the Japanese...The defenders were starving and without hope of survival, but fought vigorously. In May 1945 Wewak fell to the Allies and the remaining Japanese fled into the hills and high ground inland....The formal surrender took place ....on September 13, 1945 ....Of the 100,000 Japanese troops of the 18th Army, only 13,000 survived the war to surrender.", Justin Taylan, *Pacific Wrecks*, 2005, www.pacificwrecks.com.

2 - "Located just off Biak. Occupied by the Japanese, this island was liberated and became an Allied Airfield.", Ibid.

Oct. 23, 44 (cont.) - Biak[1] is only two miles off shore and quite a big island; Jaepon (Yapen) Island[2] is at our south. Biak still has Japs on and some wild stories goes around about them. One fellow has a Jap general's helmet with holes in. Owi is a very small island with three landing strips not long enough for B-24 to take off with maximum load. There are about fifty planes and three squadrons cover the entire island. It was bombed and strafed by Japs three weeks ago. I was put in the 2nd Bomber Squadron and in the 22nd Bomber Group. (see photos next page) This group is called the Red Raiders. We passed over quite a few islands on the way and the natives lived in huts built up over the ocean on the shores. Flew over Jap held territory. This squadron has been plenty lucky so far only one plane, four enlisted men and one officer have been killed in last year. We bomb the Philippines from here and also Borneo. Ballic Pappins (Balikpapan) oil fields[3] were bombed from here. The trees and brush were just shoved aside here to make room and are strewn all over. It's only an hour's ride from the northern part of New Guinea.

Oct. 24, 44 - We were put in a tent with ordinance men because no other room and we intend to move up closer to Philippines in a little while. Cleaned our .45 pistols and got more ammo in a.m. Was checked out on turrets in p.m. and wrote letters and sent addresses. Had a lecture in a.m. from C.O. (Commanding Officer) and Ops. (Operations) officers.

MF

A vintage WWII .45 caliber pistol

1 - "Large island north of the New Guinea mainland. On May 27, 1944, the US Army 41st Infantry Division landed on Biak and fierce fighting followed as most of the Japanese were entrenched in natural limestone caves and fortifications. A tank versus tank battle occurred on Biak, when Japanese Type 95 Ha Go tanks attempted to attack the beachhead. They were destroyed by US Army M4 Sherman tanks.", Justin Taylan, *Pacific Wrecks*, 2005, www.pacificwrecks.com.

2 - Jaepon (Yapen) - "Large island located to the south of Biak. Occupied by the Japanese until the end of WW II.", Ibid.

3 - Balikpapan Oil Field, Borneo…was a primary target of the B-24's, at this time. It was noted for it's heavy fighter opposition and flak.

RESTRICTED

Symbols:
- WP — Will proceed
- MOCA — By military or commercial aircraft.
- TDN — The travel directed is necessary in the military service.
- EWM — Travel directed is necessary for performance of emergency war mission.
- TCNT — The Transportation Corps will furnish the necessary transportation.
- CGMD — And thence to such other places as the Commanding General may direct.
- OCWR — And on completion of this temporary duty will return to proper station.
- IFRQ — It being impracticable for the Government to furnish rations or quarters in kind.
- MALR — Monetary allowances in lieu of rations as prescribed by.
- D272 — Duties being exceptional a delay in excess of 72 hours is authorized.
- MALRQ — Monetary allowances in lieu of rations and quarters as prescribed by.

HEADQUARTERS
V BOMBER COMMAND
APO 920

SPECIAL ORDERS)

No. 303)   - EXTRACT -   29 October, 1944.

5. Having been asgd and trfd in gr to V Bomber Command per par 1, SO #94, FEAFCB&TC, dtd 20 Oct 44, the VOCG, further assigning and transferring in gr the following named O and EM, to the orgn indicated, APO 920, eff 20 Oct 44, and to report to the CO thereof for asgmt and dy, are hereby confirmed and made of record.

22d Bomb Group

2D LT	JOSEPH E. TINGATE	Cpl	Alfred D. Fulton
2D LT	RICHARD R. WOODS	Cpl	Forrest C. Bricker
2D LT	JOSEPH C. KERNEY	Cpl	Edward O. Schultz
2D LT	DONALD L. SHAVER	Cpl	Clinton S. Tibbotts
2D LT	WALTER K. VAN SCYOC	Cpl	Frederick F. Sperel
2D LT	JERRY S. LIMBERT	Cpl	William B. Potter
2D LT	ALEXANDER C. KOLCZAK	Cpl	Raymond J. Walters
2D LT	JOHN N. THOMAS	Cpl	Arthur J. Frigerio
2D LT	ROBERT B. MILLER	Cpl	Walter E. Bailey
2D LT	ARTHUR F. JACOBS	Cpl	James F. Ward
2D LT	KEITH T. GATES	Cpl	Albert J. Peterson
2D LT	JAMES N. KIEF	Cpl	Horace L. Combs Jr
2D LT	VALENTINO CASTELLINA	Cpl	Willie L. Seay
2D LT	ALFRED B. ANDERSON JR	Cpl	Norval K. Graham
2D LT	GORDON C. MILLS	Cpl	Waldo F. McIntosh
2D LT	WILLIAM N. MacVICAR	Cpl	Joseph F. Hurter
2D LT	WALLACE H. HIMLER	Cpl	Samuel A. Haiga
2D LT	VANCE E. SKARSTEDT	Cpl	Elson B. Freeland
2D LT	FRANCIS W. SHARON	Cpl	Sealy H. Hart
2D LT	THOMAS H. WARREN	Cpl	Charlie Perkins
2D LT	RICHARD J. FALETTI	Cpl	John C. Richards Jr
2D LT	WILLIAM D. COLEMAN	Cpl	Verland D. Bloxson
2D LT	MILFORD W. CROCKETT	Cpl	Charles C. Murphy
2D LT	CAMILLUS A. RAYMOND	Cpl	Daniel L. Fiorese
T Sgt	Mendal E. Hendrickson	Cpl	Robert A. Gardner
T Sgt	Lyle O. Taege	Cpl	Arthur F. Dater
Sgt	Bartholomew A. Carbone	Cpl	Richard E. Schoen
Sgt	Paul E. Perkins	Cpl	Joseph M. Tosto
Cpl	William F. Bridge	Cpl	Jack S. Bates
Cpl	James J. Perry	Pvt	Robert W. Walton

- 3 -

Orders transferring Mr. Bates to the 22nd Bomb Group

HEADQUARTERS
22ND BOMBARDMENT GROUP (H)
APO 920

30 October 1944

SPECIAL ORDERS
NO 124

1. Having been asgd to this Gp per par 5, SO 303, Hqs V Bomber Command, APO 920, dtd 29 Oct 44, the following named O & EM, are further asgd to the orgns indicated, eff 20 Oct 44.

2ND BOMB SQ (H)

2nd Lt RICHARD J. FALETTI,	2nd Lt WILLIAM D. COLEMAN,	
2nd Lt WILFORD W. CROCKETT,	2nd Lt CAMILLUS A. RAYMOND,	
Cpl WILLIAM F. BRIDGE,	Cpl JAMES J. PERRY,	
Cpl ARTHUR F. DETER,	Cpl RICHARD E. SCHOEN,	
Cpl JOSEPH M. TOSTO,	Cpl JACK E. BATES,	32838983

19TH BOMB SQ (H)

2nd Lt ROBERT B. MILLER,	2nd Lt ARTHUR F. JACOBS,
2nd Lt KEITH T. GATES,	2nd Lt JAMES M. KIER,
Sgt PAUL E. PERKINS,	Cpl ALBERT J. PETERSON,
Cpl HORACE E. COMBS Jr.,	Cpl BILLIE E. SEAY,
Cpl NORVAL K. GRAHAM,	Cpl WALDO F. McINTOSH,

33RD BOMB SQ (H)

2nd Lt WALTER K. VAN SCYOC,	O-715875	2nd Lt JERRY E. LUMBERT,
2nd Lt ALEXANDER C. KULCZYK,	O-2060316	2nd Lt JOHN W. THOMAS,
2nd Lt WALLACE H. WHEELER,	O-771182	2nd Lt VANCE E. SKARSTEDT,
2nd Lt FRANCIS W. SHARON,	O-2061064	2nd Lt THOMAS H. WARREN,
Cpl FREDERICK F. SPEGEL,	32951738	Cpl WILLIAM E. PROTTER,
Cpl RAYMOND J. WALTERS,	36814257	Cpl ARTHUR J. FRIGERIO,
Cpl WALTER B. BAILEY,	33764379	Cpl JAMES P. WARD,
Cpl CHARLIE PERKINS,	35805515	Cpl JOHN C. RICHARDS Jr.,
Cpl VERLAND D. BLOXSON,	35540051	Cpl CHARLES C. MURPHY,
Cpl DANIEL L. FIORESE,	32856717	Cpl ROBERT A. GARDNER,

408TH BOMB SQ (H)

2nd Lt JOSEPH E. WINGATE,	2nd Lt RICHARD R. WOODS,
2nd Lt JOSEPH C. WERNER,	2nd Lt DONALD L. SHANVER,
2nd Lt VALENTINO CASTELLINA,	2nd Lt ALFRED B. ANDERSON Jr.
2nd Lt GORDON C. MILLS,	2nd Lt WILLIAM N. MacVICAR,
T/Sgt MENDAL E. HENDRICKSON,	T/Sgt LYLE O. TAEGE,
Sgt BARTHOLOMEW A. CARBONE,	Cpl ALFRED D. FULTON,
Cpl FORREST C. BRICKER,	Cpl EDWARD O. SCHULTZ,

- 1 -

Orders transferring Mr. Bates to the 2nd Bomb Squadron

Oct. 25, 44 - Didn't do much today. It rained last night and leaked through tent. It rains almost every night. Put up a bomb sight for an officer at link trainers and went to parachute shop and had zipper on B-4 bag fixed. A mission was called at 2 a.m. this morning to bomb in the big naval battle on now. One cruiser was hit by bombs. One plane had to ditch on take off in 408th squadron killing five and six got out. Had two bomb bay tanks on a very long mission.[1]

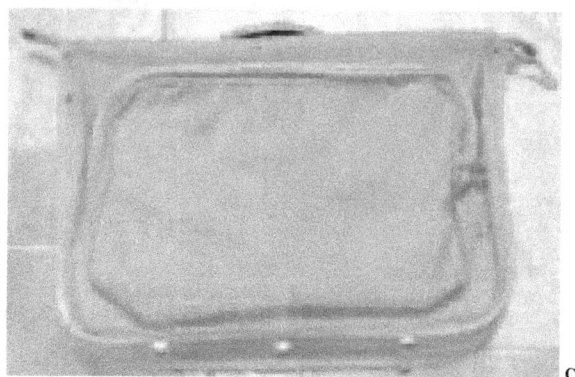

cs

A vintage B-4 bag

Oct. 26, 44 - Another mission went out on that naval battle.[2] Was issued gas mask, steel helmet, mosquito net today. Didn't do much. Coleman and Raymond are on the list to have a mission tomorrow. They have split our crew up for the first few missions to fly with experienced crews.

Oct. 27, 44 - Had to clean shower room this a.m. Went to beach and got some pretty shells. There are about three women on this island it is quite a thing here to even see one. We are going to move in at the Philippines soon.

Oct. 28, 44 - Raymond went on a mission to the Philippines this noon. Went swimming in Pacific in afternoon.

1 - "Six B-24's from the 408th began taking off from Owi Island…Immediately after lifting off, B-24J-175 #44-40726 crashed into the water about a mile beyond the end of the airstrip. Of the eleven crewmen aboard, six were rescued and five were killed. One of the men who was saved apparently died later, although his identity is uncertain, and another required amputation of a leg. The cause of the crash was attributed to mechanical failure.", Lawrence Hickey, The 22nd Bombardment Group in World War II, Volume III, Photo Supplement, ed. Don Evans (Bonsall, California: Alliance Business Services, 2001), 227.

2 - The naval battle mentioned was the climax of the Battle of Leyte Gulf. The "Battle of Samar" was primarily between US Escort Carrier forces and their escorts and Japanese Surface Naval forces comprised of battleships, cruisers and destroyers.

Oct. 29, 44 - Went over to bomb trainers in morning with Coleman and went swimming in afternoon. Went to church at night. Raymond got back from a nineteen hour mission and didn't get any flak or fighters.

Oct. 30, 44 - Didn't do much all day. It rained as usual, went swimming and wrote letters.

Nov. 1, 44 - A Grumman Avenger TBF cracked up just one side of the runway. It was really a wreck. Straightened up my things and went swimming in afternoon. The first day in four it had sunshine. Was put on a crew, Perry, Bridge, Schoen and me. They split crews to fly with experienced men. Wrote letters. Went to show and saw "Summer Storm".

DH

Grumman Avenger TBF

Carried a crew of three. Powered by a Wright engine it had a range of 1,010 miles, cruise speed of 147 mph, maximum speed of 276 mph, a ceiling of 30,100 feet. It had 2 wing mounted .50 cal. machine guns, 1 - .50 cal. dorsal turret mounted machine gun and 1 - .30 cal. ventral mounted machine gun. It could carry a load of up to 2,000 lb. bombs, Dave Hanson, *American Aircraft of World War II*, September 2004, www.daveswarbirds.com/usplanes.

Nov. 2, 44 - Rained most of the day. Was checked out on new turrets in morning. Went swimming. Didn't do much. They are packing the camp and getting ready to move to Philippines. They take cargo to Biak in C-47 only two miles away.

Nov. 3, 44 - Moved to tent across from me, which had a floor. Was put on detail to load C-47 all day. There are four squadrons in our group. We (2nd) are blue, 33rd is Orange, 408th green and 19th is white. Also the 43rd group[1] is on this island and the Jolly Rogers, 90th group[2] is on Biak.

1 - 43rd Bomb Group, 5th A.F - 63rd, 64th 65th and 403rd Bomb Squadrons. Known as Ken's Men . *Kens Men, 5 AAF, 43rd BG*, Site maintained and dedicated to members of 43rd Bomb Group Association, Inc. P.O. Box, 360, Snyder, TX, 2005, www.kensmens.com.

2 - 90th Bomb Group, 5th A.F. - 319th, 320th, 321st and 400th Bomb Squadrons - Bonnie and Jason Dilworth in e-mail to author, May 2005.

Nov. 3, 44 (cont.) - The tail (of our plane) is painted the color (associated with each squadron).[1]

Nov. 4, 44 - Was on same detail but it rained all morning. Was put on crew to go on my first mission here to Philippines and am supposed to brief at 10 o'clock and take off at 12:45. This crew is on as a spare in case of another ships failure to take off so am not definite of going. Coleman, Perry, Bridge and me are on same crew. Coleman went on mission to Philippines four days ago and had to salvo his bombs. He had a lot of flak and saw fighters, which didn't attack.

Nov. 5, 44 - Went to briefing and then went and got a chute and harness. Went to ship and they warmed motors up ready to take off in case of failure of another ship. All took off and we waited twenty minutes but nothing happened so we came back. Was quite excited at prospect of going. Falletti was co-pilot on one ship. They came back at about 4 p.m. the next day and met fighter opposition. One plane had a rudder shot off. I went to show at night. Got writing paper and two bottles of beer at PX but gave the beer away to the fellows in my tent. Very unusual to have beer here.

Nov. 6, 44 - Didn't do much of anything except write. Washed a few clothes out and went in sun to get tan. I went and got my three bottles (beer) off Coleman and passed one around the tent at night.

Nov. 7, 44 - Just laid around and not doing anything much. The first two boats went to Leyte[2] today. There was some destroyers and other large ships just off shore today.

Nov. 8, 44 - Read a book today. Got some tobacco off Paul Shapiro (see page 181 - "The List") in my tent. Didn't do much.

Nov. 9, 44 - Didn't do anything today. Got my first letter today from home. Dated the 21st of October. Wrote letters.

---

1 - The 22nd B. G. was divided into four squadrons. Each had a rectangle with a specific color painted on the tail of each plane in that squadron for easy identification., Lawrence Hickey, The 22nd Bombardment Group in World War II, Volume III, Photo Supplement, ed. Don Evans (Bonsall, California: Alliance Business Services, 2001), 134.

2 - "Island in the southern part of the Philippines, north of Mindanao. First island in the Philippine archipelago to be liberated by American forces...(which landed on October 20, 1944)...MacArthur planned to invade Leyte as the first foothold in the Philippines. The island included seven airfields. Six built by Japanese, one by Americans.", Justin Taylan, *Pacific Wrecks*, 2005, www.pacificwrecks.com.

Nov. 10, 44 - Was on detail a short time this morning. Had new PX supplies and got a lot of gum. Was issued five cartons of cigarettes as months ration. A bombing mission was up and I was on it with Faletti and Bridge from our crew. It was supposed to be to Leyte on the front line, 1000 lbs. bomb probably on Jap pillboxes but at last minute was canceled. I was tail end charlie[1] and take off was about 1 a.m. "Five Graves to Cairo" was the movie tonight.

Nov. 11, 44 - There was a big LST boat out on the dock this a.m. and then left later. Was very hot today and set out on the beach writing letters in the after noon.

LST- 1, Landing Ship Tank

Designed to land soldiers, tanks, supplies and other equipment directly on to the beaches.

Nov. 12, 44 - Didn't do much of anything again today. Was going to church at night found out too late that it was way over in the 43rd Group. Read a book.

Nov. 13, 44 - Finished the book in the morning and did my washing in the afternoon. A mission list is posted the same as the last with Canepa,[2] pilot - Falletti, co-pilot and Bridge with me. They wake us at 0300 and take off is 0555. Hope I go on this one. Am writing letters at night.

---

1 - This refers to the rear aircraft in the formation. Evans, Don in an e-mail message to author, 2003.

2 - Most probably refers to James Canepa member of 2nd Bomb Squadron - deceased. 2nd Squadron Newsletter, December 2001.

Nov. 14, 44 - Got up at 3:30 a.m. briefed at 4:15 and took off at 6:15. Went on my first mission to Mindanao[1] and the target was a runway. It was the southern part of the Philippines. Going over the target we had a lot of flak or ack ack. Was plenty scared and really thought we'd never let the bombs go. It really gave me a funny feeling and not a good one. The flak was extra close and shook the ship. Didn't get any fighters and we had no escort. Three groups went each having 24 bombers with 5 - 1000 lb bombs. Got approximately 11 1/2 hours combat time. Hit the target at 12:15 and to get out of the flak we had to go through the harbor. Can't say I enjoyed it at all. My gun jammed when test firing and had the tail turret. Poor bombing.

Nov. 15, 44 - Rested up in the morning. Was put on detail tearing down mess hall in afternoon.

Nov. 16, 44 - Our boats were to come in and be loaded this morning but they didn't come in. Was getting ready to move and took one bag to orderly to be shipped up on boat.

Nov. 17, 44 - Loaded trucks in morning to put on boats which came in about noon. Was put on boat as checker in afternoon which was easy. I met Joe Benesh who was on the LST boat # 559[2] and was over to # 610 for parts. Was there until 9 p.m. that night with him and he couldn't have off all night. He said he was in a convoy with Roberts (Bates) (next page) boat.[3]

---

1 - "Mindanao is the Southernmost Philippines Island...and southern most part of the country. Occupied by the Japanese in December 1941.... the liberation of Mindanao became the last assault of the Philippines campaign.", Justin Taylan, *Pacific Wrecks*, 2005, www.pacificwrecks.com.

2 - During World War II, LST-559 was assigned to the Asiatic - Pacific theater and participated in the following operations: Capture and occupation of southern Palau Islands - September and October 1944 Leyte landings - October and November 1944 Lingayen Gulf landing - January 1945 assault and occupation of Okinawa Gunto - April 1945 LST-559 earned four battle stars for World War II service, Yarnell and 'Navsource' team, *Navsource Naval History, Photographic History of the U.S. Navy, 2003*, www.navsource.org.

3 - USS Fremont (APA-44). During WW II *Fremont* was assigned to Asiatic-Pacific Theater and participated in the following campaigns: Marianas operation - Capture and occupation of Saipan, 16 to 26 June 1944; Western Caroline operation - Capture and occupation of southern Palau Islands August, 17 September 1944, Ulithi Atoll, 23 September 1944; Leyte operation - Leyte landings, 20 October to 18 November 1944; Luzon operation - Lingayen Gulf landings, 9 to 11 January 1945; Iwo Jima operation - Assault and occupation of Iwo Jima, 19 February 1945, Ibid.

Robert Bates – Mr. Bates brother

Nov. 18, 44 - Went to see Joe (Benesh)[1] early this morning and stayed with (him) until noon. Deter, Coleman and Crockett went up on Joe's boat and I introduced them to Joe so they could tell me if Joes boat was there in Leyte when I arrive by air. Went to show at night and saw "Johnny Come Lately". Moved to another tent as they took six rows (of tents) down.

Nov. 19, 44 - Wrote letter and read all day. Not much doing today.

Nov. 20, 44 - Didn't do much in morning. Went out to the line with Paul Shapiro and Ed. Found out I go on mission tomorrow.

Nov. 21, 44 - Got up at 3:30 and after briefing we took off at 5:30 and bombed gun emplacements on Mindanao close to where I went on my first raid. We had 80% hits on our target, the best. We had flak and were the lead flight in the lead squadron. The 90th and 43rd also went with us. The flak wasn't as heavy on our ship as the first raid but a lot closer just to the right of our ship. One shell burst almost in our wing. We had two holes in our ship when we landed but the crew chief said they were already there. I saw the bombs of all the planes hit and what a mess they made. Two of the 90th ships didn't return. I was a waist gunner and

---

1 - Joe Benesh graduated from Horseheads High in 1942. He lived in Tompkins Corners, NY. He knew Jack Bates well and played sports with him. He attended college for one year and then enlisted in the Navy on July 20, 1943. He attained a rank of Gunner's Mate 1st Class and was discharged in March of 1946. Benesh, Joe in phone interview with author, 2003.

Nov. 21, 44 (cont.) - wore a flak suit (jacket)[1] for the first time. I thought it might be tested too for a while. Was still quite scared when the flak came and so were the old timers this time. One guy went on his last mission with us. One ship dropped its bombs on Davao[2] a city there and that is strictly enforced not to hit any cities. They're trying to find out who it was and it'll go hard. They tell us on every raid not to hit the population. It was either the 19th (Bomb Squadron) or 33rd (Bomb) Squadron. Put in 11:15 combat time. Bridge went.

Nov. 22, 44 - Worked detail (tearing) tents down in morning and filled in some muddy places in afternoon. Wrote letters and went to the show and saw "Janie" at night. Found out that we're not going to Leyte the 25th as was planned because of the Japs trapping our 5th Air Force that is up there or something. It's too hot up there at present anyway and we're staying here for an indefinite period. I'd rather anyway as its longer missions and (we get) more combat hours in. Gave out beer at night.

Nov. 23, 44 - Thanksgiving Day and I'm on K.P. today. We had turkey. K.P. was quite easy. Am up for another mission tomorrow. Had all turkey I wanted. Wrote letters at night. We can mail our letters now. We couldn't for a couple of weeks now.

Nov. 24, 44 - Got up too late to eat and had to hurry for briefing. The mission was to Mindanao, the same place as my last and at ack ack positions. We warmed the motors up and had a break in the oil system so couldn't take off. The spare (airplane) also had a magneto out so only five ships from our squadron went. I would have had more missions than anyone on my crew too.

Nov. 25, 44 - Worked in the afternoon up on the line with Ed. Mostly laid around wrote letters.

Nov. 26, 44 - Laid around in a.m. and had a short detail fixing up mess hall screen in afternoon. The rumor around is that we're going to Palau Island very shortly for our next base. It seems that our Air Force on Leyte is shut off and we're forced out of our base up there. There would be an awful risk going there.

---

1 - "The jackets (flak) consisted of irregularly shaped metal plates stitched between two sheets of canvas to form a vest...They weighed about twenty pounds each. Most veterans decided early on not to wear them, but to put them between their seats and their butts, thus protecting the most important part" - Stephen Ambrose, The Wild Blue, The Men and Boys Who flew the B-24's Over Germany, (New York: Simon and Schuster, 2001), 167.

2 - "Port City and harbor located on the south-east coast of the island." (of Mindanao), Justin Taylan, *Pacific Wrecks*, 2005, www.pacificwrecks.com.

Nov. 27, 44 - Am scheduled for a mission tomorrow. Perry and me (are on one ship), Bridge and Tosto are on another ship. We're lead plane in second flight. It's Perry's first mission. Intend to leave here real soon for Palau. That is straight north from here. A B-24 of the 43rd was lost yesterday, caught fire.

Nov. 28, 44 - Took off at 5:30 and went to Mindanao again. This time we bombed planes that were on the ground. There were huge fires started and we must have got a lot of planes. Also some explosions. It rained just as we came to the target but we had a good view of the target. We had no flak or fighters. The 90th got flak and lost one plane. It was Perry and Tosto's first mission. We had an oil leak on way back but made it OK. Had 18 - 260 lb. fragmentary bombs. We circled the target twice and saw the others bomb. Very good bombing. About fifteen ships were sunk in the harbor there. We got eighteen cans beer that night. I got twenty-five cans but gave it away, most of it.

Nov. 29, 44 - Didn't do anything in a.m. and got a haircut and put some of my things in the B-24 that I'm going to Palau on. Due to typhoons at Leyte we are going to another island about this size; Angowi (Anguar[1]) or something like that in the Palau Islands. Japs were killed there a few days ago. The trees are supposed to be all wrecked from the Navy shelling it, only a couple of months ago, (during) the invasion there. Went to show at night.

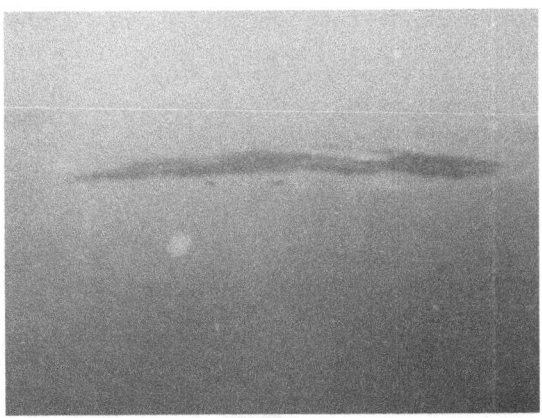

Anguar

1 - "Anguar is the southernmost of the Palau Islands group...which lies about 500 miles east of Mindanao....Anguar and Peleliu were taken from the Japanese by combined Army and Marine forces which were landed on the island on September 17, 1944 and....(on) September 20...the island was announced secure...Construction of the airfield was begun that day.", Justin Taylan, *Pacific Wrecks*, 2005, www.pacificwrecks.com.

Nov. 30, 44 - Didn't do anything all day. At night we went to Seabees (short for C.B. - Construction Battalion) and got a load of lumber to load on plane to Palau. Our electricity was off tonight.

Dec. 1, 44 - Went out to line in a.m. with Karitsky and got writing paper from plane. Read and wrote letters in p.m. Was supposed to leave yesterday but now its tomorrow.

Dec. 2, 44 - Got up at 0330 and took the rest of our things to the plane, bunk and everything. Took off at 0900 and landed on this island in Palau group about one. It is maybe a little bigger than Owi and is already cleaner looking place. They claim there are still a few Japs on it at one end. I'd say its only about two miles long and not that wide. There is a lot of other islands to the north. A few ships are here. The place is just being fixed up runways aren't all complete yet. I fixed up a tent and was put on K.P. in the afternoon. A lot of stone here and they are leveling the ground for tents now. All the trees are either dead or cut in half by the shelling of this island. Maj. Sweeney[1] gave us a talk at night. A new group in the 7th Air Force just from the states are here. They have only been on seven missions and had a lot of tough luck. They think a lot of us because of our record.

Dec. 3, 44 - Worked putting up tents all day. The reason for not going to Leyte was that the runway was always wet and wouldn't hold up a B-24. Deter and Schoen, Coleman and Crockett are still there. Most of the first boat loads that went to Leyte are here now. There was a mission up for tomorrow but it was canceled. There is an Am.(erican) grave yard about 50 yards from my tent with 253 dead. It is beautiful with a small stone chapel.

American cemetery noted above - Eugene A. Andrew Collection - CK

1 - Major James E. Sweeney - Assistant Operations Officer, Lawrence Hickey, The 22nd Bombardment Group in World War II, Volume III, Photo Supplement, ed. Don Evans (Bonsall, California: Alliance Business Services, 2001), 200.

Dec. 4, 44 - Put up tents in morning. Got ten letters at noon, all with new address. Put frame of PX in a tent in p.m. and then wrote letters. Saw some monkeys and birds that look like chickens. There is an infantry outfit here with small tanks. Also a marine (outfit). Our show house was to open tonight but it broke down.

Dec. 5, 44 - Did nothing in a.m. and help put up orderly room in p.m. Am on list for mission tomorrow. Wrote letters. Got one letter.

Dec. 6, 44 - Took off at 8:30 and bombed an airdrome on the island (of) Cebu[1] just the other side of Leyte. We flew over Leyte. It was very bad weather. Had rained most of night and was raining when we took off. Worse I've flown in. We even lost our flight in the clouds. It was excellent bombing and huge fires were burning all over. Large explosions were seen even after we bombed. Our radio operator heard a Jap news broadcast about our raid. They said we hit the city which was close to our bomb run and that we machine gunned the citizens. They're poor liars and we took pictures of our target when and after the bombs hit to prove it. Every ship in front of us had flak but they must have hit the gun pos.(ition) because as we went over they stopped firing. We had four P-38's as escort that we picked up just before we hit the target. There must have been about seventy-five planes on the mission. Got 10 hours combat time. There is an awful lot of islands around Leyte and it has very deep harbors all along the coast. Very hilly but pretty with a lot of farms and such. Saw two towns and city.

Dec. 7, 44 - Helped dig a drain today with a jack hammer in almost solid rock. Some fellows came in from Leyte but not Deter or Schoen. Coleman, Raymond and Crockett are back now.

Dec. 8, 44 - Take off was at 8:00 this morning and we were going to Cebu again. The weather was terrible all the way up and raining all the time almost beyond flying weather. Almost got sick it was so rough. At our rendezvous the visibility was zero and we couldn't find our formation anywhere. We radioed to other planes but couldn't pick up hardly anything. Finally after circling over half hour we headed for target alone met one of our ships coming back alone so we turned around salvoed our bombs in the ocean about 30 minutes from target and headed back figuring that the other plane had gone over target and couldn't see

---

1 - "Cebu Island lies between Leyte to the east and Negros to the west. Cebu City is a large city on the island….well equipped and supplied Japanese troops defended this area. On 03/26/45, Allied troops assaulted the island and city. Abandoning it's defenses the Japanese forces fled to the hills - into caves and pillboxes and continued their resistance until April 1945.", Justin Taylan, *Pacific Wrecks*, 2005, www.pacificwrecks.com.

Dec. 8, 44 (cont.) - to bomb. It was too rough to fly in anyway. We're second ship back and found out the whole area was covered over. The formation that went over the target were made up of all squadrons any one they could find and they were attacked by about ten Zeros but they were in a six ship formation and the Zeros didn't dare attack. If we had of went over the target alone we'd probably be duck soup for all those Zeros. They look for lone ships but won't attack formations. Some fellows came in from Leyte and they said the Japs had landed paratroops way back of our front lines there and have the remains of our Air Force up there trapped. That means Deter and Schoen are in it and in danger of being wiped out. The fellows in our group have made a front line to defend them selves.

Dec. 9, 44 - Fixed up my tent some today. Was on detail for a while. Went to show at night.

Typical set up for movies - screen is stretched between two palm trees. Moviegoers brought their own seats. Photo taken at base in Samar.
Alfred Pavlu Collection - CK

Dec. 10, 44 - Didn't do much all day. Helped Coleman build a shelf. Deter came in last night and he said they sure had it rough with the front lines less than a mile away where the paratroops landed. Schoen is staying up there.

Dec. 11, 44 - Was on detail a short time today. Wrote letters and went to show for a while but didn't stay. It has rained every night since I've been here and water runs through our tent floor.

Dec. 12, 44 - Went all around this island and saw where the Jap caves were and the things the Navy shelled. I never saw so perfect pillboxes as the Japs had. Saw ten American tanks strung all over a complete wreck. A magnesium plant is completely destroyed and a railroad the Japs had. One huge pillbox used as a lookout was battered and torn but still stood up. Nature built the best entrenchment of rocks any army could have here. Remains of the fighting are strung all over. Saw the Jap graveyard. They have a stick on top (of grave as marker).

Dec. 13, 44 - Went on another mission today to Cebu again and the same airdrome. Saw five Jap planes on ground. Hit a lot of bad weather again. No resistance. Saw Barton[1] in 408th. Got 9:45 combat time. Crockett went on first mission.

Dec. 14, 44 - Slept till after nine and haven't done anything so far. The food has been <u>very</u> bad and we have K rations now.

Dec. 15-16, 44 - Didn't do much. Built a floor in our tent. Got three letters. Wrote some letters.

Dec. 17, 44 - Finished the floor and didn't go to chapel. Was put on guard duty at 5 and had 2nd shift, 8 - 10 & 2 - 4.

Dec. 18, 44 - Rained hard today. Just puttered around tent. Got five bottles of beer tonite.

Dec. 19, 44 - Was on detail covering pipe from well to showers in morning. Was on detail in afternoon and wrote letters at night. Went to show.

Dec. 20, 44 - Went on a mission to Negros[2] Island, which is just west of Cebu. It was quite cloudy and some fighters came out of the clouds in the squadron behind us but don't know who they were. Faletti flew as first pilot for the first time. This island is Anguar in the Palau. I never saw so many islands so close together as they are after we got to the

---

1 - Cpl. Beverly Barton trained with Mr. Bates at Fairfield-Suisun, Air Force Base, Cpl. Barton's crew ferried over B-24L #44-41537, from the states to Australia, in the same flight as Mr. Bates. #44-41537 was lost on March 26, 1945 with entire crew., Falletti, Richard in letter to author, January 2001.

2 - "Located to the south of the Visayan Sea, and to the west of Cebu...March 29, 1945 (troops) landed on western Negros...resistance (north of the island) was overrun by late April, and the remaining Japanese fled south...isolated battles continued...until the end of the war.", Justin Taylan, *Pacific Wrecks*, 2005, www.pacificwrecks.com.

Dec. 20, 44 (cont.) - Philippines.[1] Just separated by inlets and such. Got 10 hours and 30 minutes combat time. The primary target was Cebu but we went to secondary which was at the edge of a river and a huge sugar plantation on the other side which wasn't to be hit but some bombs went over there. We found out all of those milk runs we went on with no flak are just about over. We tested the guns and everything getting ready for some rough times around Manila and such they say.

Dec. 20, 1944 mission to Negros Island
Note black explosions in between the two cloud patches
lower center of photo

Photo of #333 "Triple Threat"
Plane Mr. Bates flew on during Dec. 20, 1944 mission

1 - "The Philippine Islands during WW II played a major part in many campaigns and operations by both the Americans and Japanese. Invaded in December of 1941 by a Japanese amphibious force, the islands were captured...American forces liberated the island...at the end of 1944.", Justin Taylan, *Pacific Wrecks*, 2005, www.pacificwrecks.com.

Dec. 21, 44 - Have a bad cold from flying. Nothing much to do today. Went to show and wrote letters. There is a mission to Clark Field[1] near Manila tomorrow. Was glad I wasn't on it. They expect heavy resistance.

Dec. 22, 44 - They came back from raid and only had light flak. One 408th ship got shot up by five Zeros. They had 50 fighter planes as cover and they got two of the Zeros. Everyone landed at Tacloban[2] to refuel in Leyte. There was a mission posted and we had almost our whole crew going together but it was canceled because all our ships didn't come back (from Tacloban). Our officers gave us four quarts (probably whiskey) for Christmas. Barton was on that raid and ship that got holes in it.

Dec. 23, 44 - They had a mission up tonite for Clark Field again and this time I'm on it.

Dec. 24, 44 - Today is the day before Christmas and I'll never forget this day. Went to bed after 11:00 and they called us out at 2 a.m. for the strike. We had a very good briefing at 3:30 and they were figuring it could be rough, giving us the escape routes and all. Took off at 5 a.m. and two amplifiers blew out on number three and four engines on take off after about half the runway and we had to go back. They changed them and we took off about twenty minutes after the rest of our squadron. We picked them up though at our rendezvous which was a small island above Leyte which we got to at 9:30. A little after 10:00 our escort of approximately sixty P-47's came up and we proceeded to the target, which we got to about 11:30. We were to the right of Clark Field and went north way around it and went in to the target from S.W. to N.E. They had 120 mm guns which was a new gun to them and instead of tracking us it was a barrage. The sky got black with the flak and it was very accurate. We no more than turned on the run when the Zeros

---

1 - "Clark Field was first a military outpost in 1902...The outpost was later named "Camp Stotsenburg." In 1917....construction began on a half-mile dirt runway, hangars and other support facilities.....This aerodrome portion of Fort Stotsenburg was completed in 1919 and named Clark Field....This was the largest airfield complex in the Philippines. Over the decades until 1941 it was expanded until it was composed of 12 airfields: Clark 1, 2, 3, 4, 5, Clark North, Clark East, with other fields in the surrounding area including two strips at Angeles, two at Macbalacat and one at Bamban/Bambam. The massive complex was used in the American defense against the Japanese landing in 1942. This was the biggest base of the war for both the US and Japanese....July 4, 1946 the United States granted the Philippines its independence. One of the conditions for the proclamation of Philippine independence however was the acquisition and retention of US military bases in the Philippines including Fort Stotsenburg and Clark Field were combined to create Clark Air Base.", Justin Taylan, *Pacific Wrecks*, 2005, www.pacificwrecks.com.

2 - "Capital of Leyte, site of several airfields built after liberation.", Ibid.

Dec. 24, 44 (cont.) - attacked us and threw phosphorous bombs down at us from above. Nobody had seen the Zeros until after they dropped their bombs and they were plenty close to us and we even flew through the smoke. The P-47's really opened up and everything was confusion from then on with the flak so heavy and rocking the ship and the fighters attacking and dropping the bombs. I saw one Zero go down and blow up. I thought that this must be it and maybe you don't think we did some praying. When the bombs did go I started to watch them fall and see where they hit but a second later there was a stream of phosphorous bombs so thick I actually couldn't see the bombs through it and looked up to see where the fighters were that dropped them and I never did see Clark Field because of the excitement. We were almost too occupied and excited to get scared but there was plenty of reason to be. There were approximately forty Jap planes in all and about ten attacking us. One came close with a P-47 on his tail and those red circles on each wing sure looked big. Due to our formation I only got a chance to shoot about ten rounds at them and then almost hit a B-24. Our bomb run is usually one to two minutes but it was eight minutes today and flak about a minute before and a good two minutes after and it seemed like every minute was an hour. A Jap bomber had come up and picked up our altitude and speed and radioed to the guns so all they had to do was set the fuses and aim and they sure did have both perfect. For 200 feet above and below it was a solid barrage and we really sweated. Our lead ship got a direct hit about a foot back of the waist big enough for two men to go through and holes all over the waist, horizontal and vertical stabilizers and was really a mess. The radio man, Deis,[1] who was on the right waist gun got killed and the left waist was injured. That was # 277 ship. # 318 which Coleman was on got a hole the size of two fists between the fuselage and number three engine opening the two main gas cells and the gas streaming out so you could hardly see the fuselage. They were on our left. Another plane # 333 got a hole in the bombardiers' window and knocked him out but didn't hurt him. Our plane had seven or eight holes in the wing, bomb bay and two holes in the cockpit window next to the pilot. A piece of the window hitting him. Every plane in our squadron was hit and boy we thought this must be it! When we finally got out of it which seemed like (an) eternity we had to slow up and protect # 318

1 - "B-24J-205 #44-41277.....was leading six 2nd Squadron planes...on targets near Clark Field, Luzon...when accurate flak began bursting around them....a probable 120 mm. round....exploded inside, blowing out a huge hole in the right side of the waist gun position....the top turret gunner found the radio operator (Deis) dying from severe injuries and the assistant engineer....with serious wounds in both legs....the pilot made a safe landing at Tacloban......here the casualties were removed. Deis was already dead.", Lawrence Hickey, The 22nd Bombardment Group in World War II, Volume III, Photo Supplement, ed. Don Evans (Bonsall, California: Alliance Business Services, 2001), 227.

Dec. 24, 44 (cont.) - which was bad off. They threw out guns, cameras and everything. They were feeding four engines on the left tank and just made it to Tacloban in Leyte where we all landed. The lead ship going ahead due to the injuries. Three ships came back from Tac.(loban). The amplifiers blew out again on take off and we had to replace it again and picked up a lot of bags of mail there. Schoen is up there now. We had to take three crews in our three ships that came from Tacloban. We were sure tired and got back at 9:30 pm with fifteen hours combat time. Everyone was stinko when we got back.

Phosphorous bombs

#44-41277 in which waist gunner Dies was killed,
just after landing at Tacloban, Letye.
Note the damage just below and to the left of the waist gunner's position.

Dec. 25, 44 - Got one letter today. We had turkey for dinner and pie and cake. Didn't even hear a Christmas carol. Tonite I am on the list for the mission to Clark Field again tomorrow. Don't think I don't dread to go and am really sweating it out already. Perry, Bridge, Tosto and Deter and I were together yesterday and it was their first flak and fighters. I didn't believe the Japs used those bombs (phosphorous) until I saw them. Some were white streamers and some exploded in white clouds with streamers shooting out. The first one I saw I thought it was a fighter which exploded.

Dec. 26, 44 - Got up at 2 a.m., briefed at 3:30 and took off at 5:00. Went to Clark Field, Manila again (see photos next page). We rendezvoused at 9:30 and picked up our P-38 cover this time which was about fifty of them. We hit no. 4 strip or rather the planes around it. Before we had (h)it no. 2 strip. We came into the bomb run from a sharp angle and had a fairly short run. The flak was again terrific, not quite as bad as the last one. We got one flak hole. The 408th squadron got hit bad, two killed and one wounded. We broke to our left and no sooner got out of flak when the Zeros came in. I was at the left waist and the first one came in level at 9 o'clock. I started to fire when another came up from the tail less than 50 yards away so I switched to this one and just as I fired it went in a spin in flames. Perry, our tail gunner had shot it. I watched it go down in flames and the pilot bail out. A P-38 was also on its tail. It had got caught in our slip stream and it was firing at us from the tail. We had two bullet holes in our wing and bomb bay which took off our fuel selector valve and broke our hydraulic lines. There were about six Zeros that attacked us. The nose gunner in 408th got hit in the head by a (bullet from a) Zero and killed.[1] Our squadron was credited with five Zeros. We had to feather no. 1 engine just after the Zeros attacked and came in to Tacloban on three engines. A Zero attacked one P-38 with only one engine and the P-38 came in our formation for cover. We landed at Tacloban with two chutes at the waist window ready to pull if the brakes didn't hold. They tried to fix No. 1 engine and we took off for our base but got a half hour out and had to turn back. We stayed in Leyte all night and I had my first experience at being bombed that night. The bombs hit quite a ways off. Saw my first Filipinos and their homes which were just shambles around there. It rained and we were soaked. Didn't get much to eat that day.

1 - "a Ki-84 Frank fighter...attacked the lead element...The nose turret gunner in the plane on the right wing was killed....the fighter (then) dove between the lead aircraft and left wing plane...it raked the belly and tail of the lead plane...killing the right waist gunner and badly wounding the radio operator,", Lawrence Hickey, The 22nd Bombardment Group in World War II, Volume III, Photo Supplement, ed. Don Evans (Bonsall, California: Alliance Business Services, 2001), 227 & 228.

Picture of the damage done to Clark Field during bombing runs by the B-24's

Dec. 27, 44 - Stayed in Leyte all day and night. They couldn't find the trouble (with our plane) and had the Navy and Marines trying to figure it out. The super charger was the trouble but nobody could fix it. Rained all day and night again.

Dec. 28, 44 - Didn't get it fixed again so at 4 p.m. we took off with a 408th crew and came back to Anguar late that night. Was even on the mission list tomorrow but someone had crossed my name off. They sure don't plan on giving me a rest. If I go on many missions like the last two they'll be putting me to rest I'm afraid.

Dec. 29, 44 - I slept about all morning and I sure was tired. Took it easy all day.

Dec. 30, 44 - They have crews ready on the alert to take off for that convoy around Mindoro[1] the Japs brought in. Our pilot Canepa had operations take me off the alert list yesterday because we had been flying so much and was tired. Didn't do anything but rest up. Can feel that these rough missions are taking a lot out of me. Am being bothered with my left ear. It never seems to clear.

Dec. 31, 44 - Got up and went to chapel today. Wrote letters and had a few drinks at night. There is a mission to Clark tomorrow but for a change I'm not on it.

---

1 - "Located to the south-west of Luzon. Liberated by American forces...By December 23rd, two strips were in operation on the island, and provided air support for the liberation of Luzon...", Justin Taylan, *Pacific Wrecks*, 2005, www.pacificwrecks.com.

Jan. 1, 45 - Slept about all morning. Was on detail to get ready for inspection in afternoon. This 7th Air Force outfit who has island regulations are really making it rough on us with the orders they put out. Was on guard at night which is another of their orders. You would hardly think they were overseas and a war is going on the way they act. Got a letter from Robert tonight and found he was here at Anguar at one time. Wrote him a letter. There were a lot of bags of mail come in late tonite.

Jan. 2, 45 - Helped sort mail in the morning got fifteen letters - eight from home. Went to show at night. Am on mission tomorrow probably to Clark again. Am flying for first time with whole crew except Coleman and Schoen who (are) at Leyte.

Jan. 3, 45 - Called at 1:45 am. Briefed at 3 a.m. and took off at 4:15. Went to Clark Field and bombed the revetments at the very north end of the field. The flak wasn't as much as the first two times but close. Had P-47's as cover, two squadrons but no Zeros showed up. Faletti flew very poor. Had a scare over the target. Went into a bank and dive as a flak burst in front of no. 4 engine. I thought we were hit and going down for a minute. Got 14:30 combat time. I looked Robert up and found he was out in the harbor at Tacloban where he refueled. A sailor said he'd look him up.

Jan. 4, 45 - Had a lot of mail today. Rested up and wrote letters.

Jan. 5, 45 - Had an inspection today. Wrote letters and got a lot of mail. Went to show.

Jan. 6, 45 - Got letters today and also wrote a lot. Was on detail in afternoon. Found out we are moving very soon to Samar[1] in Philippines.

Jan. 7, 45 - Went to chapel in morning. Got a picture of mom in mail and also a package with moccasins, t-shirt, candy and such. Had letters and wrote at night. Got first 'Eclipse News'.[2] Played officers in softball at night but it rained before we finished. Did pretty good too. Am up for a mission tomorrow, they say to get Jap shipping.

---

1 - "Located adjacent to Leyte Island.", Justin Taylan, *Pacific Wrecks*, 2005, www.pacificwrecks.com.

2 - The 'Eclipse News' was a company newsletter put out by Mr. Bates former employer.

78

Jan. 8, 45 - Called at 1:15, briefed at 2:30 and take off was at 4 but at 3:45 they canceled the mission. It rained or poured all night and we got soaking wet. The runway wasn't serviceable they said but there was a front the whole East Philippines. Helped sort mail in afternoon and had three letters. It rained all night and I'm up for a mission again tomorrow.

Jan. 9, 45 - Took off at 4:00 this time and the weather was still bad. We had a bomb bay tank leak and salvoed the tank with 400 gallons of gas. Went to the end strip on Clark Field. The flak was quite heavy and we had two holes, one under Falletti's seat and one that cracked the bombardiers window just ten seconds before Coleman dropped his bombs and was he scared. He said it was like a firecracker going off. They fired flak even after we made a 180 degree turn. The one near Falletti cut six wires and damaged others. Perry has the flak piece. We landed at Tacloban and refueled. When we took off the weather was terrible. The rain and clouds were so bad we was afraid we had gone past the island. We were really sweating it out. The only clear place in the Pacific was just over the field and we never thought anything was better than those lights. We were really in a bad way for a while. Took 8 - 500 lbs. and had 14:30 hours. Balacap[1] was the name of the strip.

CK

Nose art on #42-109978 "Baybee"
Mr. Bates flew on this plane during Jan. 9, 1945 mission
Charles Shawver collection

1 - "one of two Japanese airfields located near and part of the Clark Field complex named Macbalacat", Justin Taylan, *Pacific Wrecks*, 2005, www.pacificwrecks.com.

Jan. 10, 45 - Slept all morning and went to a flak lecture at 1 p.m. Was quite interesting. They believe the Japs are using radar at Clark Field on their guns. I always thought they did as the flak was always accurate. Today they sent a ship equipped with radar finding in it to make sure and we have a few planes with radar jamming equipment on it to use in the future.

Jan. 11, 45 - Wrote letters during the day. Played ball with squadron enlisted men against the officers. Really did good and had a double. Also some good plays. Helped sort mail at night and got seven letters. Also got four papers, the first yet. Faletti is leaving for Nadzab tomorrow (as pilot instructor).

Jan. 12, 45 - Got a haircut today. Faletti left at 1 p.m. Sure hated to see him go. We had steak for supper and was it hard to cut. Some left for Samar in C-47 today but nobody from our squadron. That mission on Jan. 9 was the day Luzon[1] was invaded, just to the northwest of Clark Field. We saw fires over there which could have been on the invasion. We also had the 13th Air Force and strafers in on that mission. Sure hope they take Clark Field and Manila[2] soon as it will probably make the missions easier. We are planning on being based at Clark Field soon.

Jan. 13, 45 - Helped sort mail and got four letters. Didn't do much today. Read a book. There was a mission today, north of Clark Field, a barracks area and the first time they didn't get flak in a long time.

Jan. 14, 45 - Went to chapel with Coleman in a.m. Washed socks in afternoon and sent laundry in a.m. First bunch left for Samar and first bunch came back from Sydney today. Am up for a mission tomorrow and am expecting an easy one for a change.

---

1 - "Luzon is the largest Philippine island...Some areas of Luzon were occupied (by the Japanese) until the end of the war.....", Justin Taylan, *Pacific Wrecks*, 2005, www.pacificwrecks.com.

2 - "Manila was a beautiful city prior to the war...Declared an open city by MacArthur on December 26, 1941 in hopes of saving it from bombing and destruction....Despite this, Japanese bombers did hit the city, and on January 2, 1942 Manila fell....The people of Manila suffered a long and brutal Japanese occupation...After the American landings at Lingayen Gulf...the city of Manila became a battlefield from February 4 to March 3, 1945...Although MacArthur banned air strikes against the city, artillery was used to pound resistance. MacArthur (prematurely) declared the city liberated on February 6th, and returned to Manila on February 7....The battle for the city lasted for a month....where fanatical Japanese defended until the end.", Ibid.

Jan. 15, 45 - Wow, what a day. Last night they called us at 9 p.m. after the show and briefed us. We had to go pack our bags and I (got) through at 11:30. They called us at 12:45 a.m. so we didn't go to bed. Briefed and took off at 3:15 with toilet articles, writing paper and such. Went to Clark Field and bombed the end no. 1 runway, Stotsenburg Barracks (Ft. Stotsenburg) (see diary entry 12/21/44) which was big area. Instead of going far to the right of Manila we went just off shore to the left and had a good view of Manila, Corregidor[1], and Bataan.[2] There was only approximately ten bursts of phosphorous flak and to show how accurate and close they always come, we had one plane hit in the wings and our plane could have been, one burst just outside our plane. I was in a 90th group plane which had a radar jamming unit in. Could almost see our troops which were about 40 miles away. We didn't come back to Anguar but circled about two hours over Samar strip to land. We stayed here and the first thing we had to contend with was mud. After we got situated and ate they had us go out and load bombs for a mission tomorrow. It was 11 p.m. when we finished and I hadn't had any sleep for two days. When landing we fly just over a small town at the edge of the water. There are an awful lot of small islands all around here and coral reefs. We are close to the water with a big cliff bordering one side. We are close to the town but nobody is allowed in. The Filipinos are very interesting people to watch. Most can't speak English to understand but they are all over around our tents wanting to work for us. The women do laundry and come to tents with it. They seem to live a nice clean life and can really make dresses fit well with what few they have. They are all short of clothes and do anything for you to get them.

---

1 - "Island at the entrance to Manila Harbor. Also know as Fort Mills, and later as "The Rock". The HQ for US Naval Defense forces on 21 December 1941...On May 5, 1942 a force of 2,000 Japanese... assaulted the island...Despite determined American resistance, the island surrendered on May 6, 1942....the site of the greatest surrender of US forces ever. After the battle, only one Japanese reinforced company remained on the island (300 men), with approximately 500 POW, mostly Americans to repair the island's installations, and cleanup the island and collect scrap for shipment to Japan. The POWs remained on the island until shortly before liberation. As American forces approached, approximately 6,000 Japanese troops occupied the island, mostly Navy. After extensive aerial bombardment, naval bombardment....Americans assaulted the island on February 15, 1945.....The Japanese fought from caves, and launched banzai charges... The liberation resulted in 225 KIA and MIAs, 645 WIA. Nearly all the defenders were killed, 4,500 in battle, 20 captured, 500 buried alive in caves, 200 killed trying to swim away. Today, Corregidor is a protected national park.", Justin Taylan, *Pacific Wrecks*, 2005, www.pacificwrecks.com.

2 - "Located at the southern tip of Bataan peninsula. American and Filipino defensive line after Japanese attack on Luzon. MacArthur....was evacuated to Bataan on December 24, 1941.", Ibid.

Jan. 16, 45 - Got up at 9 and went and put up our tent. A Filipino cleared away a piece of jungle for us. They all have big knives with them. We gave him two undershirts and two pesos for all mornings work and he helped set up tent. They said the Japs treated them very bad and killed a lot off, took their clothes and made them work with no pay. Had six letters my first day here. Took our shower from a shower truck at the side of the road with the women passing us all the time. They aren't bothered by this. I am up for a mission tomorrow again and there's a good chance it's our first one to Formosa. Today's mission was supposed to (go to Formosa) but a Corsair crack up made a late take off and couldn't meet our fighters so they went to Luzon near Clark and hit a town. Am going to squadron briefing at 9:30 tonight. The trees are all dense palm and look beautiful; the mud is really bad in places. We have no clothes with us but what we wore.

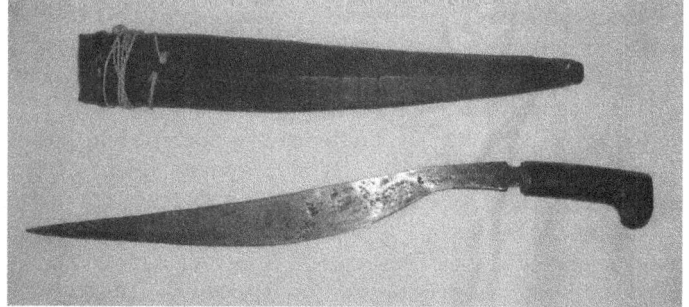

Example of bolo knives carried by Filipino's. This is Mr. Bates personal knife. This knife and the one shown on page one hundred and six have wooden sheaths and are approximately fifteen to sixteen inches long.

Vought F4 "Corsair"

Powered by a Pratt & Whitney engine it had a range of 1,005 miles, maximum speed of 446 mph and a ceiling of 41,500 feet. It had 6 - .50 cal. machine guns and could carry bombs, rockets and napalm., Dave Hanson, *American Aircraft of World War II*, September 2004, www.daveswarbirds.com/usplanes.

Jan. 17, 45 - Called at 5:00 and we took off at 7 a.m. Went to bomb Bambam/Bamban (see footnote on diary entry 12/21/44) at the end of Clark but after going to the Manila Gulf we turned back due to a thick overcast and went to secondary which was Legaspy (Legaspi)[1] a town at the southern part of Luzon. Bombed railroad yards. We made three bomb runs. Our plane was that Jolly Rogers ship with radar and we had 6 – 1000 lb. bombs while the rest had only five. Got back after one for my shortest mission(s). It seemed like bankers hours. There was no resistance. Got 6:10 combat time. Fixed up tent in afternoon - with a Filipino helping me. At night we had a talk by Major Sweeney and then mail call. There was a lot (of mail) and I got six letters. There was an air raid just as we were going to bed but I don't think planes came. It rained all night and the mud is real bad. Cars are stuck and (the mud is) over our shoes. There is no lights here and our tent is way back in the jungle and hard to find. Schoen was here when I came. He'd came from Leyte and it was first time I saw him in a couple of months since Owi.

Bombing mission to Legaspy (Legaspi) - Jan. 17, 1945
Note the bomb explosions at the lower right hand corner of the photo
At the extreme lower right hand corner is a black burst of flak

Jan. 18, 45 - Helped put up mess hall all day. Tosto and Deter made Sergeant but the rest of us aren't even in so we won't get it for a while. Don't know why Faletti didn't put us all in. He should have.

---

1 - "Site of Japanese landings on the SE tip of Luzon (Philippines) on December 11/12, 1941.", Justin Taylan, *Pacific Wrecks*, 2005, www.pacificwrecks.com.

Jan. 19, 45 - Was helping put up the mess hall in the morning. It rained all night and got soaking wet when the tent leaked. Boy, the mud is really wicked around here. Had to change clothes twice and was a mess. Helped in the mail room in the afternoon. There are a lot of Typhus cases in the other units and 40% are fatal. Also malaria. There is as much to worry about diseases around here as there is casualties. Am up for a mission tomorrow.

Example of tents at the 22nd Bomb Squadron base in Samar.
Eugene A. Andrew Collection – CK

Jan. 20, 45 - Was called at 4:45 and briefed at 6. Took off at 8:00 and was to go to Bamban/Bambam at the end of Clark Field. Got twenty minutes from it and the weather was so bad we went to the secondary which was the west central part of Negros island at the edge of a town. It was a supply area. Made three runs over the target and the second bomb hung up a second (and caused us) to miss the target. There were two strips (air fields) there but no planes came up. There was no flak. The weather was bad and it rained just before take off. Three planes went to primary and bombed it. They said the clouds were open over it. They went over the target three times with intense flak every time. One plane was hit. The lead ships bomb bay doors wouldn't open. Got 7:30 combat time. Our troops were twelve miles from target.

Jan. 21, 45 - Worked throwing coral around the operations where the mud was bad. The mud is terrible bad. They had mission to Formosa[1]

---

1 - "250 mile long, densely populated island off China. Occupied by the Japanese...It contained approximately fifty wartime airfields. (Including Kagi, Takao, Toshien, Toyohama, Koshun, Shinchiku, Matsuyama, Taichu, Tainan, Kiirun, Taihoku – see maps on pages 36 and 38)) At the end of the war it came under direct air attack from Allied aircraft.", Justin Taylan, *Pacific Wrecks*, 2005, www.pacificwrecks.com.

Jan. 21, 45 (cont.) - again the third time now and didn't make it this time. The other two were due to bad weather. This morning the lead ship (#44-40860) of the group, 19th (Bomb) Squadron was taking off and its wing tip hit a Corsair.[1] Only 120 feet between planes to go along the runway. It kept going and hit a bulldozer at the end of runway and the gas caught fire. It exploded the 1000 lb. bombs from heat and four out of five of the bombs went off. Everyone was killed including the group commander, Colonel Robinson. They only found a piece of one body. That canceled the mission.

Pyre of smoke indicates place where Colonel Robinson's plane exploded killing everyone aboard.

Jan. 22, 45 - Worked in the mail room in the afternoon. Had off all morning. There was a lot of mail came in at night. Every day we've been here there has been a wreck of Corsairs or B-24's. # 333 or 'Triple Threat' hit a C-47 and killed the 47 pilot. They finally got off to Formosa today. They said there was flak but inaccurate. Everyone was scared because of the jinx this Formosa raid caused.

1 - "Liberators from the 22nd B.G. were scheduled to depart from Guiuan Strip...*Our Honey* was...to be the first plane to take off...a flight of four US Marine Corsairs....were at the far end of the strip preparing to depart...*Our Honey* began it's take off.....The plane made a long take off roll, then lifted off....The left wing clipped a spinning prop on one of the Marine fighters...shearing away six-and-a-half feet of the wing....then hit a piece of heavy construction equipment....immediately crashed and burst into flames. About five minutes later, three of the four bombs (exploded), destroying what remained of the wreckage. The mission was aborted and the next day the remains of the eleven crewman, plus the driver of the Sea Bee carry-all, were taken...to Tacloban, where they were interred in the American military cemetery.", Lawrence Hickey, The 22nd Bombardment Group in World War II, Volume III, Photo Supplement, ed. Don Evans (Bonsall, California: Alliance Business Services, 2001), 228.

An example of how close the planes were along the runways. Wing tip to wing tip. Contributing to the crash of "Our Honey". Frank McLeish Collection

Nose art from #44-40860 "OUR HONEY"

Jan. 23, 45 - Worked in mail room again. It is better than detail work in the mud so I only work when I want to. Another wreck today with three killed and five injured by Corsair. Started eating in our mess hall a couple of days ago. Schoen went to hospital with 101 fever. He hasn't went on a mission yet.

Jan. 24, 45 - Mailroom again today. Took off early and wrote letters. My mail has come quite regular here and a lot of it to. Tosto went to hospital two nights ago.

Jan. 25, 45 - Mailroom again. We moved in to end of mess hall with PX next door. Had a cigarette issue last night and also PX opened. Got snaps (pictures) from Mary Alice. Last night was first night it hasn't

Jan. 25, 45 (cont.) - rained. We've had seven alerts, air raid, but no planes. They raid(ed) Tacloban Tuesday. Perry and Coleman went on a mission to Luzon, Baggio (Baguio)[1] and bombed General Yamashita's home in the mountains. He's a Jap in charge of Filipino operation and the guerrillas told us about him. They strafed and had 100% hits. It was beautiful place and they said we intended going there on rest leave when we take it.

Jan. 26, 45 - Am behind in my diary. Worked in mailroom. Hauled lumber for our tent floor. Had a couple of letters. We are almost definite to go on the point system now instead of the 300 hours. Have to have 100 points. Get one point for every five hours, one point for a ship in the squadron being holed by flak, one point for fighter interception with cover and three points if no cover. Also points for parachuting out, ditching, getting lost, and crack ups and crash landings which I'm not sure of. This town close to here is Guiuan. We're on the farthest southeast tip of Samar. Had an alert tonite again.

Jan. 27, 45 - Worked in mail room in morning. Helped put up Chaplains tent in the afternoon. It has rained every nite but one or two since I came here. Schoen has been evacuated to Australia they said. He has yellow jaundice. Hasn't had a mission yet. Am up for a mission tomorrow.

Jan. 28, 45 - Was called at 4:45. It was raining and we didn't take off until 7:15. Was supposed to (take off) at 6:30. Went to Grande Island[2] which is a small island in the middle of the mouth of a gulf just northwest of Manila. We hit two - 14" gun positions there. Very poor bombing and none were knocked out. Bombed at 7,000 feet too. Made three bomb runs and circled about six times. Our secondary was Corregidor. There were A-20's, B-25's (see photos next page), Corsairs and two groups of B-24's up around there. Fires were around Manila and huge smoke clouds. We are figuring on moving in a week or

---

1 - "Located in the mountains to the west of La Union Province. Situated at nearly 6,000' altitude....April 27, 1945 (a) US force...liberated the town. Until the end of the war, Japanese resistance persisted to the west and north of Baguio. Japanese forces officially surrendered in Baguio on September 3, 1945....", Justin Taylan, *Pacific Wrecks*, 2005, www.pacificwrecks.com.

2 - "Subic Bay was an American military base before the war. Occupied by the Japanese Navy, and then recaptured January 30, 1945 by the 38th Division. During the war 27 known ships were sunk in the bay, including those both scuttled and sunk....Grande Island guards the entrance to Subic Bay with gun emplacements remaining to this day.", Ibid.

Jan. 28, 45 (cont.) - two. It is up by Lingayen Gulf.[1] They are thinking of only operating out of there and still be based here until we move in to Clark Field. We can't yet because we have to knock all the planes out of Formosa so they won't bomb Clark. The concrete runways are all good yet. We are supposed to be in Stotenburg (Ft. Stotsenburg) barracks the very ones we bombed once but didn't hit.

Douglas A-20 "Havoc"

Used as an attack bomber it carried a crew of three, an armament of seven, .50 cal. machine guns and carried up to 4,000 lbs of bombs. Powered by two Wright engines it had a range of 945 miles, cruise speed of 256 mph, maximum speed of 317 mph and a ceiling of 23,700 feet., Dave Hanson, *American Aircraft of World War II*, September 2004, www.daveswarbirds.com/usplanes

North American B-25 "Mitchell"

A "medium" bomber it carried a crew of five and from two to eighteen .50 cal machine guns as well as up to 3,000 lbs. of bombs. Powered by two Wright engines it had a range of 1,200 miles, cruise speed of 230 mph, maximum speed of 275 mph and a ceiling of 25,000 feet., Dave Hanson, *American Aircraft of World War II*, September 2004, www.daveswarbirds.com/usplanes.

1 - "Site of both the Japanese (1941) and American (1945) landings....After the American landing at Lingayen on January 9, 1945, this strip (Lingayen Aerodrome) was hastily constructed right on the beach....", Justin Taylan, *Pacific Wrecks*, 2005, www.pacificwrecks.com.

Jan. 29, 45 - Was on detail today helping put the lights in the tents. We got ours wired up also. Got a few letters. Got some guerrilla money from Filipinos.

Jan. 30, 45 - Had all day off. Fixed up tent. It rained for two days now. Our tent leaked it rained so much. Got all wet last night. We put lubing (a type of grease to prevent further leaks) all over it. Two missions have been canceled the last two days due to it (the rain).

Jan. 31, 45 - Got paid today. Got 488 pesos or 244 dollars for five months pay. A month was held up on our flying pay which will get on going home. Rained about six times today. Had an alert tonight. The news sure sounds good now. The last mission I went on was Grande Island in Subic Bay and that is in the center of the mouth of the bay. We knocked out the guns and the next day they made a landing in that same bay.

Feb. 1, 45 - Slept about all morning. Read all afternoon and got two letters from home and a valentine. It rained all last night and about five times today. The mud is bad as ever. Bought a straw hat off the natives here. Also got a Marauder.[1] (see photo next page)

Feb. 2, 45 - Read all morning, got four letters. Rained twice. Raid on Corregidor. Got my $100 check or money order and sent it home. Am up on mission tomorrow and first call is 4 a.m. to Corregidor again.

Feb. 3, 45 - Was called at 4 a.m. Went to planes and take off was at 6:45 to Corregidor. We warmed up and as we were going to take off a plane way up front had a flat tire. Believe it or not but the mission was canceled due to it. We had to be away from the target by 10 a.m. as other groups were coming over. The place is so small to park planes that the planes have to take turns taxing out as they are in back of each other. The front plane was held up so that we couldn't make the target in time. Got one letter. Had cigarette ration. Made another $50 money order to send home. 7th Air Force that was with us at Anguar landed and are going with us on a mission tomorrow. (I am) Also up for it.

Feb. 4, 45 - Was called at 4 a.m. Was supposed to take off at 6:45 but the rain came and we took off at 7:30. Couldn't find our formation at rendezvous so went to target alone. We bombed a gun emplacement

---

1 - "it is a history of the 22nd bomb group published in 1944 and inscribed by Sgt. Leonard Eastman of the 2nd Squadron.", Klimesh, Cyril in e-mail to author, 2005.

Marauder

Feb. 4, 45 (cont.) - shore battery on Caballo Island.[1] Had the best view of Corregidor yet and flew directly over twice. Also had a good view of Bataan. There is a small mock ship in very center of the mouth of Manila Gulf called Fort Drum.[2] It is man made of concrete and has four guns on (it), looks very impressive from air. Corregidor has what may be factories or barracks at the wide end very long and big with large building all along mostly in rows. The southeast end gets narrower all the time. It has a very high cliff of stone all around and there is caves from shoreline of cliffs to all parts of island. Has a dock at about middle of island on north east side. It looks very impressive from air and except for the buildings it would be very formidable to bomb. It is all coral rock and rugged land all over. It had four anti-aircraft guns but they have only fired three times at planes. It has small fighter strip at the very tip of the narrow end. One end is very close to the mainland of Bataan and it too has a strip near the end of Bataan by Corregidor. There is a large mountain at end of Bataan peninsula. You can seem to vision the path those people on the place took when the Japs came. We had 6 - 1000 lb. bombs. We missed the narrow target by 200 feet landing in the water. On the way back, south of Manila about ten minutes flying we saw what seemed like our front lines. A fire was there and saw tanks and convoy coming up a good road. There were fields where artillery holes were overlapping each other they were so close. Had 6:30 hours combat time. There are very beautiful towns all along the Luzon coast. Large factory building and modern. I saw what I think is the most beautiful and largest church in my life up there. The country is very nice. Went to chapel at 7:15 at night. From all indications the Navy must be going to go in Manila Bay. The past week we've went on a raid almost every day to knock out gun or shore positions on Corregidor and vicinity. The 5th Air Force was made a sucker out of those missions we sent to on Grande Island in Subic Bay. We went on about three missions to there and knocked out all the large navy guns. Then the Navy came in and took the island and made landings in bay. They found out the Japs had evacuated the island a good two weeks before we even bombed it.

Feb. 5, 45 - Didn't do much today. Wrote letters and got one. Read a book "30 Seconds Over Tokyo" it was real good.

---

1 - "a former US Army coastal defense post, located inside Manila Bay....including two massive 14" coastal guns and four 12" mortars...visible from nearby Corregidor Island.", Justin Taylan, *Pacific Wrecks*, 2005, www.pacificwrecks.com.

2 - "Small island developed into a fortress, shaped like a battleship guarding the southern entrance of Manila Harbor...", Ibid.

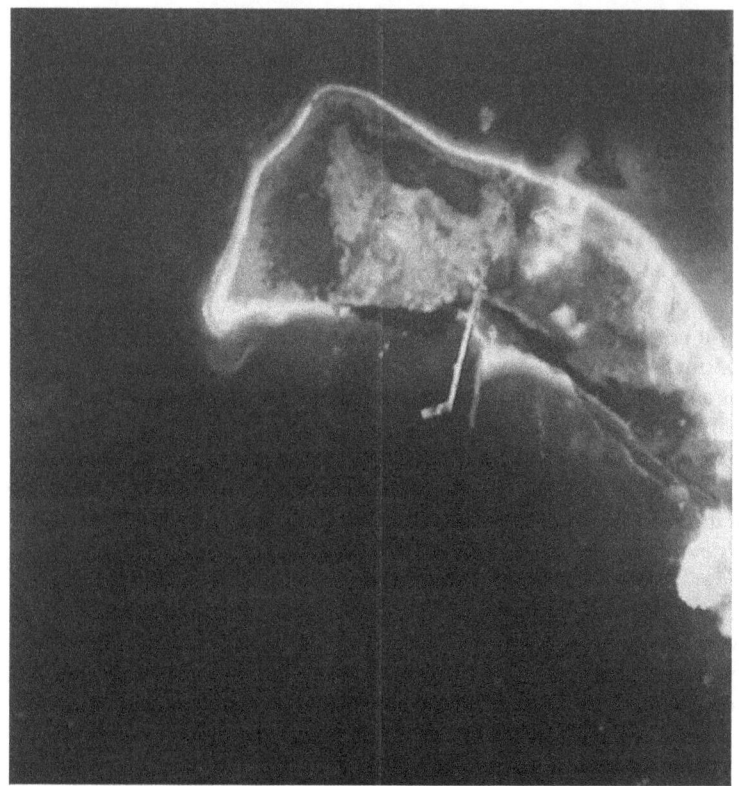

Aerial photo of Caballo Island - February 4, 1945

Feb. 6, 45 - Was put up for mission tonight but was canceled. Inspection tomorrow. Played cards at night until 2 a.m. I mailed $50 home last night in a money order.

Feb. 7, 45 - Got up at 9:30, had inspection at 10:00 and about 10:15 they called us for a mission. Ate at 10:30 and was scheduled to take off at 1 p.m. or before if possible and go to Mindanao right next to Davao[1] and bomb personnel. They didn't get the bombs loaded until after one so it was changed to Cebu Island. We bombed a town, Bogo[2] and had 21 - 250 lb. bombs. Boy, there was fires galore and smoke higher than 10,000 feet. Jap personnel were suppose to be there. It was an unusual kind of raid and the shortest one I've gone on, 3:55 (combat time).

1 - "Port city and harbor located on the south-east coast of the island (Mindanao). Location of wartime airfield", Justin Taylan, *Pacific Wrecks*, 2005, www.pacificwrecks.com.

2 - Town in the north east portion of the island of Cebu.

Bogo - Cebu Island - Feb. 7, 1945 mission
Note bomb blasts in the lower center/right of the photo.

Feb. 8, 45 - Rested up today. Had a lot of letters and wrote also. Sent some guerrilla, Jap invasion (see photos next several pages) and Australian money home. Tried to hunt a tube for radio but couldn't (find one).

This booklet was found in the memorabilia collected by Mr. Bates. It seems to be a "commercially made" item that contained samples of Japanese currency and is probably the Japanese money that is referred to in the Feb. 8th diary entry. It carried the following inscription: "Collection of war notes circulated by the Japanese government in the Philippines from January 1942 to February 4, 1945 when Manila was captured by the invincible American forces of liberation. May God Bless America and the Philippines forever."

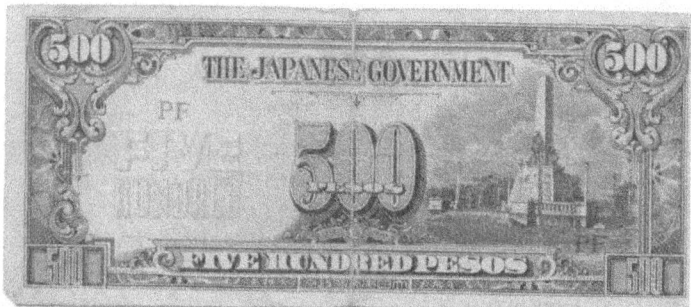

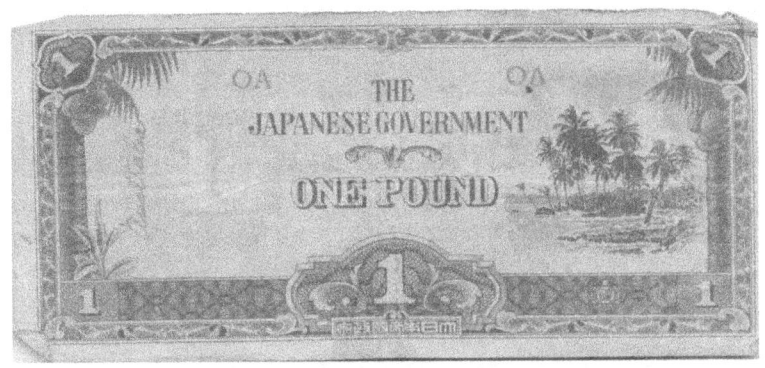

Feb. 9, 45 - Got some papers and a lot of mail today. Had two 'Eclipse News'. Wrote letters.

Feb. 10, 45 - Helped put up the bakers shop today. It was very hot. Had eight letters. Found out how I can get off and go to Tacloban but will wait until my next mission. Our (light) bulb burned out so we went to mess hall and stayed for a while watching big card games.

Feb. 11, 45 - Had a Filipino girl, Rosita (see photos next page) take our laundry and do it. She wasn't bad for a girl here. Went to chapel at night. Found out I could go on three day pass to look Robert (Bates), (Gordon) Ridenour[1] and Mann up tomorrow.

---

1 - Gordon M. Ridenour, formerly of Main St., Horseheads, NY. He volunteered with the American Red Cross and served 40 months in the Pacific. He died June 23, 1970 - 'Ridneour' exhibit - Horseheads Historical Society, Horseheads, New York.

Millie and Rosita (L to R) squadron tailors

Feb. 12, 45 - Up at 6 a.m. and went to operations and got pass. Took off in C-47 and went to Tacloban strip. Made a bad landing, went to Red Cross canteen and then to 59th Service Group to look up (Gordon) Ridenour at Red Cross. Got to wrong outfit and went in Tacloban to what was supposed to been 15th Strategical Hospital but turned out to be 13th (Strategical Hospital). They couldn't locate it so went to Red Cross and found Ridenour. We had a long talk and I went to Navy headquarters to find Robert (Bates) and was sent to port control. Found out he wasn't there and that (Joe) Benesh was. Waited for boat to go out but decided it was too late so went to M. P. (Military Police) post where I met a swell M. P. who took me to his outfit to eat. Then went to hotel which was a bare room with only a straw mat to sleep on and mosquito barrier but clean. Met a Army man who was on boat and a Filipino in his army there. We talked late and went to this Filipino house about two blocks away. He was about 50 years old and had lived in Brooklyn (NY) for about fifteen years (and worked) in ship yards. Served coffee and talked. Went to bed about 1:30 a.m. The Filipino was at Davao and captured there in (the) army. Was at Cebu, Negros and Luzon where I bombed and knew each place. His cousin only two weeks ago went to Negros in big boat after sugar and Japs near where we bombed the sugar plantation took his boat. There are a few good looking building there in Tacloban. The capitol especially. The jail, hospital and theatre. The streets had no sidewalks and had mud very deep all over. Old houses. Girls were real good looking compared to Samar here. Japs lived in all (the) house(s) with civilians, each house had garden and chickens. The Japs made them have. No stores but few coffee and donut shops.

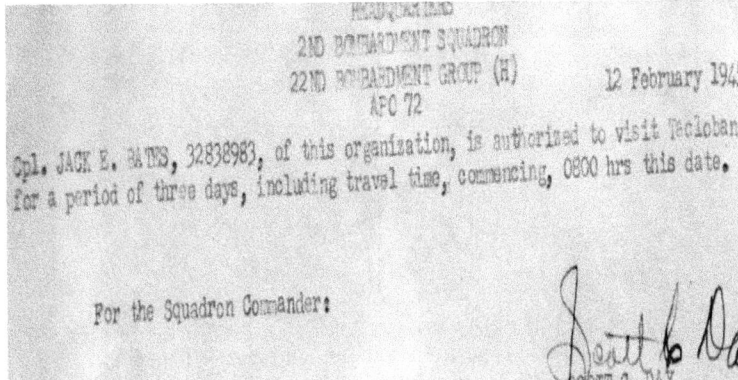

Pass to Tacloban

Feb. 13 - 14, 45 - Got up at 8 a.m. went and ate at the Filipino place and went to see Mr. Ridenour. Took an Army boat out and couldn't get to Joe's (Benesh) ship so came back and waited until 1:30 and took the Navy ship. Joe was in town getting mail but soon came. Everyone wanted to know about flying. I couldn't get a boat back so stayed all night and slept with Joe out on the top deck. It was my first night on a boat. Waited around all morning and finally Joe and the rest went in town at noon. They landed me at the airstrip. I went over to operations and couldn't get a plane. Saw a 33rd ship come in so went over and got a ride on that. It was getting mail and I had no chute. Got back at 6 p.m. and had twenty-five letters, mostly old ones. Was up for K.P. for three days like all details are for now.

Feb. 15 - 17, 45 - Was on Kitchen Patrol all three days. Not hard and only had to work one meal with pans. Didn't write a letter all week long. Pike[1] is off flying now with over 100 points. A ship of ours got hit by flak in engine today on raid to Formosa, Heito. A 43rd ship got shot down. There have been only seven times our squadron have been intercepted by fighters and we've been on two of them. In Europe only 1% casualties and here it is 5% so it's a lot harder here.

1 - Most probably Clinton T. Pike - gunner - a member of 2nd Bomb Squadron listed as living in Salisbury, MA. - 2nd Squadron Newsletter, December 2001.

Clinton Pike (on the left) with captured Japanese flag
Found on Wakde Island Carl H. Friddle Collection

Feb. 18, 45 - Didn't write a letter all last week. Got up and went to chapel in morning. Had steak for supper. Two 90th group planes got shot down in flame over the target today in Formosa (research indicates that B-24 # 44-49432 of the 90th Bomb Group was lost on this day). A 19th (Bomb) Squadron plane went down and a 43rd. We didn't get holed.

Column of smoke indicates where # 44-49432 piloted by CO Milton
Porter was lost with her entire crew on February 18, 45 mission to Formosa

Feb. 19, 45 - Didn't do anything today. Got a carton of cigarettes, no mail, wrote letters. Had apple pie and we had a whole pie (that) Joe (Benesh) brought. Sent in laundry. We take a shower from a five gallon can here. Only two planes got flak today on mission to Formosa. The 90th and 43rd went in ahead of us and went straight through flak. We turned off after hitting target. They must be either crazy or after a lot of quick points.

Feb. 20, 45 - Today I was in the Army two years. My Sergeants rating came out today also. Paul Shapiro came back from Owi to get his orders. He's going home now his orders came in. Wrote five letters.

Feb. 21, 45 - A ship of the 19th (Bomb Squadron)[1] cracked up upon landing today. Two broken legs resulted. Went to show and saw "Ministry of Fear". Am up for mission tomorrow.

Feb. 22, 45 - First call at 6 a.m. and take off at 9 a.m. We were late due to one of our ships blowing the nose wheel out on take off. They were at flying speed but stayed down and tore the front of plane up but nobody got hurt.[2] We took off about 9:20 and after flying for almost an hour found we had a gas leak in carburetor and turned back. I came about the closest ever to being in a crash on landing. The wing almost hit the ground due to a crosswind and we hit on one wheel and still bounced almost half of runway on one wheel. Couldn't get our nose wheel down. Went to USO show at night. "Hells a Poppin". It was grand and after not seeing women in so long. The actresses looked very nice. I had a swell time. They were going under a movie contract when they got back. I got 1 hour 45 minutes flying time but they said we wouldn't get credit for anything.

The results of "blowing the nose wheel"

1 - "The 19th Squadron lost 42-10019, one of its original B-24Js, on Feb. 21, 1945, when (it)..hit a crosswind while landing at Samar...The plane ran off the runway, sheared off it's landing gear and wrecked, badly injuring two of the crewman on board..." Lawrence Hickey, The 22nd Bombardment Group in World War II, Volume III, Photo Supplement, ed. Don Evans (Bonsall, California: Alliance Business Services, 2001), 184.

2 - "During take off from Samar.....on Feb, 22, 1945, this aircraft (#42-109978) blew the tire on its nose wheel, which collapsed the strut, dropping the nose of the 2nd Squadron plane to the runway. No one on the crew of 2/Lt. Richard E. Barron was injured. The plane had 61 red mission markers and a Red Raiders insignia on its port side nose, and the artwork known as BAYBEE on the starboard side., Ibid, 184.

Feb. 23, 45 - Didn't do much today. Wrote letters, got two letters, a Filipino wrote a letter to Mom and he let me read (it) today.

Feb. 24, 45 - Got up late, no mail, wrote letters. A mission is up for tomorrow, everyone on crew is flying but me. A raid went to Formosa today and got a point for flak. One plane landed with no. 3 and 4 engines only. Pike and Owens[1] went. They had 102 points and twenty hours so we don't know when we're going home now. Our intelligence officers and such are responsible and could be a lot better all around.

Feb. 25, 45 - Went to chapel in morning. Got eight or nine 'Stars'[2] and about ten envelopes of newspapers, sports books and news. Got a very good picture 8 x 10 of Mary Alice. Had an alert at night. Got a cold and sore throat.

Feb. 26, 45 - A list of those through flying came out today (there are) about a dozen (on the list) and one fellow has only ten months overseas. All have to get 105 points to ensure going home. Got two letters from home and a card. Wrote letters at night. Cold was worse today. Was on detail helping carpenter.

Feb. 27, 45 - No mail came in. Plane was grounded in Tacloban. Wrote letters. Had steak for supper, very tough. Read sport stories.

Feb. 28, 45 - Got paid today. Got 134 pesos or $67. Got twelve bottles of beer issue costing $1, Deter got his pictures of Dec. 24 on mission developed. Rained hard last night and also showers through day. Sent two Marauder books in the mail.

Mar. 1, 45 - Read most of the day. Rained most of the day. Had cigarette issue. Got five letters, two Christmas cards and three 'Eclipse News'.

Mar. 2, 45 - Am a few days behind in this diary. Didn't do much of anything Friday or Saturday. Found out they grounded me all this time due to my nerves.

Mar. 3, 45 - no entry

Mar. 4, 45 - Went to chapel at night. Didn't get up very early. Had inspection in afternoon. We expect to move the 8th to Clark Field.

---

1 - Most probably Graham Owen a radio operator/gunner of the 2nd Bomb Squadron, deceased., 2nd Squadron Newsletter, December 2001.

2 - Probably refers to the "Stars & Stripes" a newspaper for servicemen.

Mar. 5, 45 - Briefed at 7 a.m. and take off at 8:30. Went just southeast a couple miles from outskirts of Manila and our target was Jap personnel in support of our ground troops. The Japs were lobbing mortar shells in Manila and after our bombing with 22 - 250 lb. bombs at 11:45 a.m. the ground troops were to move in. An estimated 3,000 Japs were in the area. The ground sent up an urgent message to us not to drop bombs as we made our run. I was going to drop bombs for Coleman but we held ours. "A" flight dropped theirs on the target as their radio was out. We had made three runs on target and was bombing at 6,000 ft. so had a very good view of Manila which we flew directly over. It was a pitiful sight to see with blocks on blocks of just shambles, no sign of even where buildings were, even smooth they were destroyed so. Other places cement buildings still stood in ruins. The northern outskirts looked very good. I saw field artillery moving up against Japs. There were C-47, fighters and other planes on the ground near three fields on the very outskirts of Manila, one runway they use was just a macadam road our planes used. The fields were in ruin with Jap planes in wreckage. Ships were sunk in Manila harbor. We had a very poor pilot who had just checked out from co-pilot and all of us hollered about him. Got 6:50 (combat time).

Mar. 6, 45 - Had meeting in mess hall and got low down on what to expect at Clark. Sounds pretty nice too. Got laundry and cigarette issue.

Some of the damage done in Manila

Mar. 7 - 8, 45 - Didn't much happen lately. A 13th (Bomb) squadron plane dropped a 1000 lb. bomb on one of their own ships underneath them. Getting things packed and sending by C-46, C-47 and B-24 to Clark.

Mar. 9, 45 - Got a ronson lighter (butane based cigarette lighter) from Gamble[1] for 25 pesos. Deter and Tosto went to Clark Field as engineer and r. m. (radio man) to take a load of things up. There was a C-46 cracked up a short distance from them and a Jap asked an infantry man where the fuel dump was. He was dressed in Filipino clothes and when they hollered at him he ran. They shot him only a couple hundred yards away from them.

DH

Curtiss C-46 "Commando"

Used primarily as a transport ship carrying cargo, troops and equipment. It carried a crew of three with no armament. Powered by two Pratt & Whitney engines - range 1,200 miles, cruise speed 183 mph, maximum speed 269 mph and a ceiling of 27,600 feet, Dave Hanson, *American Aircraft of World War II*, September 2004, www.daveswarbirds.com/usplanes.

Mar. 10, 45 - Went on mission as ground support up to Manila and bombed Jap personnel closed in by ground men on all sides in a small area. 6 x 1000 lb. bomb load. Got 7:05 (combat time), saw Manila good, had some bad weather. Secondary was very northern tip of Luzon. A dam was at one end of primary which wasn't to be hit. We had 100% hits. The last mission, when we salvoed our bombs in ocean it was because the Japs got hold of our radio stuff and called us up to hold our bombs so we wouldn't hit them. Told us to bomb a town a short distance away that probably had our own troops in.

---

1 - John M. Gamble a member of 2nd Bomb Squadron listed as residing in Baltimore, MD., 2nd Squadron Newsletter, December 2001.

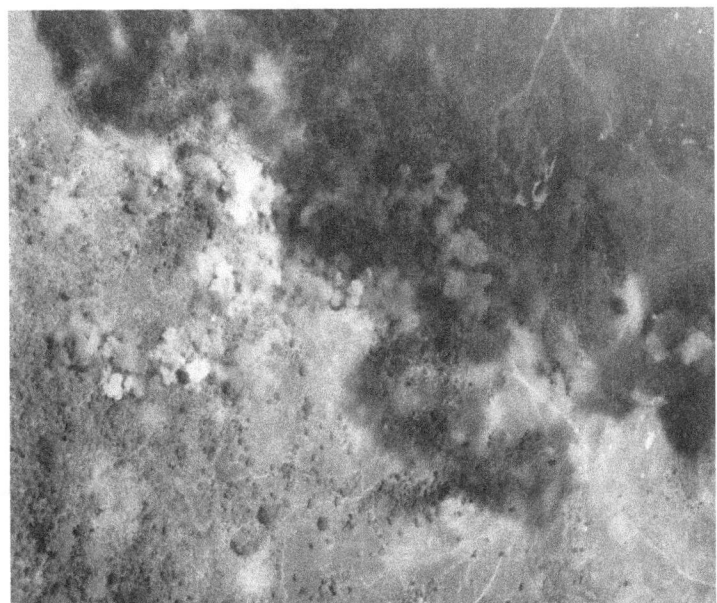

Bomb run in support of ground troops - Mar. 10, 1945
IPO Dam

Mar. 11, 45 - Stayed in bed all morning, went to chapel at night but they didn't have services. About half the squadron is moving by plane to Clark Field tomorrow. Our crew is going on rear echelon by LST, which will be quite a while yet. Coleman went to Formosa today with 19th (Bomb Squadron) and got eleven hours.

Mar. 12, 45 - Took our tent down and moved two tents over from ours in a better tent. A lot left for Clark today. The wind blows hard all the time and it rained today. There isn't any lights here anymore.

Mar. 13, 45 - Am up for K.P. tomorrow. Another bunch left for Clark today. About half of squadron is left. Wrote letters. The wind blows hard and rains hard.

Mar. 14, 45 - Had K.P. today. Was very easy and Filipinos did all the work. Found out today that the reason we came back from Dec. 26 mission on three engines was, they found a bullet in it. We couldn't see it so they had to change engines. Only a few are left here and we expect to stay any length of time before the boat gets in. The squadron went up to Formosa from Clark yesterday, the northern part and had a lot of accurate flak. Five men got hit by flak. They made two runs on the target is why.

Mar. 15, 45 - My second and last day of K.P. Schoen finally got back from hospital at Leyte. Been gone a long time. He's going up to Clark on next plane and hasn't flew yet. Bought a bolo knife off a Filipino for ten pesos today. Also a carton of cigarettes for one peso. Rained all day off and on.

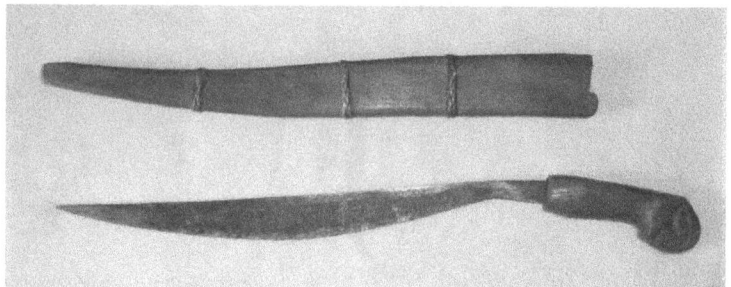

Mr. Bates had two bolo knives. The one on page eighty-two is worn from use. This one is more of a ceremonial type and in better condition

Mar. 16, 45 - Very hot today. Went to show at nite down to CB (Construction Battalion) outfit. We have no lights or shows here. The whole outfit is up at Clark, planes and everything except about sixty men and all but thirty-two will go by air. I'm on boat echelon[1] and don't know when we'll go. We're the only crew to my knowledge that they held back.

Mar. 17, 45 - More crews went up to Clark. They say our boat is supposed to be here in two weeks. Got mail for last time since mailman has gone.

Mar. 18, 45 - Got up to go to church but our group had no services. Was supposed to move down near the orderly room but didn't as we move to group tomorrow.

Mar. 19, 45 - Worked on the medic tent of group which is where we move to. Nailed screen on in morning and moved in that afternoon. Sixteen men in here. Deter and Tosto went to Clark today. They came down after them.

Mar. 20, 45 - They sent us down mail and got four letters one from Mom.

Mar. 21, 45 - Was in charge of some Filipinos and tore down the intelligence building and cleaned up area. Finished "Kings Row".

1 - This involved moving the heavier equipment that couldn't go by plane by sea., Evans, Don in an e-mail to the author, 2005.

Mar. 22, 45 - Got two letters today. Also newspaper. Rained in afternoon. Building leaks and had to put covering over the bed. The show "This is the Army" is showing last night, tonight and twice tomorrow night. Was going tonight but it rained. It's a stage show with Erving Berlin.

Mar. 23, 45 - Was up for detail but got off as I'm on C.Q.[1] tonight from 6 - 12. Got a carton of cig. (cigarettes) while on C.Q. They made ice cream for six of us, chocolate and it was pretty good.

Mar. 24, 45 - Made a writing box for stationary. Was put on C.Q. again tonight as the fellow that was on got a pass.

Mar. 25, 45 - Slept all morning. Went for ride in jeep up past Marudes about nine miles and a good trip. On way back stopped in to a rooster fight. First time I saw them. It was quite interesting. Stayed all afternoon and they had one fight after another with big bets. They (the roosters) have long blades about two inches long on the back of legs and sharp as razors. Went to show at night to 33rd C.B.'s saw "Winged Victory" which was pretty good. The first day I really enjoyed myself here.

Mar. 26, 45 - Everyone putting all equipment, lumber, etc. on vehicles ready to move on the LST when it arrives. The rumor is either the 1st or 10th of next month. War news is really good in Europe. Lt. Cohen's crew is missing from our squadron on a raid over Formosa.[2] Am glad I stayed here now. Had a beer issue at night.

Mar. 27, 45 - Had fifteen letters today. Wrote at night. Rained a lot today. Went to show at night.

Mar. 28, 45 - We had a (word) problem Scudder showed us and we were working on it all day long. It rained. Wrote letters also. Nobody could get it (the word problem) but there is a way to do it.

---

1 - Charge of Quarters - assignment given on a rotating basis to act as the senior enlisted man in the absence of the usual senior man., Evans, Don in an e-mail to author, 2005.

2 - "....six B-24's from the 2nd Squadron took off from Clark Field....to bomb the strategic town of Takao, in southwestern Formosa....Somewhere along this route B-24L-10 #44-49698...disappeared...No radio contact was made with the plane after take off...it most likely crashed into mountains on the island of Luzon...no trace of the aircraft was found....all members of the crew were declared dead in 1946", Lawrence Hickey, The 22nd Bombardment Group in World War II, Volume III, Photo Supplement, ed. Don Evans (Bonsall, California: Alliance Business Services, 2001), 229.

Mar. 29, 45 - Up at 6:30, had eggs for breakfast. Tried to get that (word) problem all morning. Read in afternoon, it rained part of the day. A typhoon was expected to hit here between 12 at night and 6 this morning but it broke up. The planes had thousand lb. bombs on to hold them down. Went to show at night saw "Street of Chance". Today made it six months overseas.

Mar. 30, 45 - Up at 7:00 a.m. Read most of the morning. Wrote one letter. Played Cassino (a card game) with Brock and got beat. On C.Q. at six at group orderly room. Typed letter until 11:30 p.m. Called guard at 1 a.m. and went to sleep. Set alarm for 4:30 to wake cooks but didn't hear it. They got up anyway.

Mar. 31, 45 - Up at 6:30. Got off C.Q. at 7:15 and slept rest of morning. Rained in morning and afternoon. Got two letters from home, one from Jackie Horton in L.A. Got some Sunday papers and Reporter (hometown newspaper entitled "Chemung Valley Reporter") in mail dated October. Played Brock in Cassino and went to show "Arsenic & Old Lace". B-29's due in early in morning from states.

Boeing B-29 "Super Fortress"

A long range, high altitude, "heavy bomber" with a crew of 10 and up to 11 - .50 cal. machine guns. It could carry up to 20,000 lbs. of bombs. Powered by four Wright engines it had a range of 3,250 miles, cruise speed of 230 mph, maximum speed of 358 mph and a ceiling of 31,850 feet., Dave Hanson, *American Aircraft of World War II*, September 2004, www.daveswarbirds.com/usplanes.

Apr. 1, 45 - Easter - up at 7:15. Had eggs for breakfast. Went to chapel in morning to Navy but couldn't find it on time. Got six letters today dated from October to December. Loaded cement bags in B-24 to go to Clark in afternoon. Went to Navy chapel at night and had communion. Got Easter Lily.

Apr. 2, 45 - Up at 7 a.m. Had meeting at 10 a.m. of our rear echelon about loading LST. Got paid in envelope brought from Clark. Got seven letters. Read rest of "Chad Hanna", had ice cream for supper.

Apr. 3, 45 - Up at 7:15. Hot cakes for breakfast, went to Navy post office and got fifty air mail stamps in the morning. Went with Perry for ride all around area. Talked to Filipino family. Wrote Jr. (Mr. Bates brother Wellington Jr.) As Perry is duty Sgt. he has a jeep. Saw "Bachelor's Wife" at C.B.'s. Made ice cream afterward. Had cake mixture and used water.

Apr. 4, 45 – up at 7 a.m. Went back to bed all morning. Went for ride in the afternoon. Got laundry. Went to stage show at CB's, very poor two men and two women, one girl could sing. Saw "Till We Meet Again" for the second time. Made ice cream again and had ice cream mix instead of canned milk. Wrote home. Had cola syrup but used water with it.

Apr. 5, 45 - Wrote letters in morning. Read book in afternoon. On at group at 6 p.m. Made ice cream after the show and it was good. Had coke syrup with water. Steak for supper. Eggs for breakfast. Typed letters (while) on C.Q. They say a few of us are going to Clark in a day or so by plane.

Apr. 6, 45 - Slept in morning. We washed and sprayed oil on all the trucks we take on ship tomorrow (this protects the metal from the salt water). Had meeting at night, went to show. Murphy came down from Clark and said the last three days our group has hit Hong Kong,[1] China (they were) intercepted and (had) flak the first day. Packed and put on truck all my stuff. Murphy said I made Staff Sergeant. Made ice cream.

Mr. Bates Staff Sergeant Stripes

1 - "Includes Hong Kong Island, Lantau Island and a small portion of mainland China. A British colony prior to the war.....", Justin Taylan, *Pacific Wrecks*, 2005, www.pacificwrecks.com.

Apr. 7, 45 - Called at 5 a.m. Went to dock at 8 and had all trucks loaded by 11. Ate on the LST we are taking, 573[1] is the number. Didn't move in the afternoon and we went out and anchored at night. Food is extra good. Only sixty of us.

LST-573 beached at Morotai, Western New Guinea, 30 May 1945, while trucks of the Australian Army's 2/16 Transport Platoon are being guided up LST-573's ramp.

Apr. 8, 45 - In morning we moved over by Leyte, Tacloban and down to Tanawan[2] were we stayed all night. We saw a lot of destroyers, aircraft carriers and such there.

1 - USS LST-573 Commissioned, 21 June 1944 and assigned to the Asiatic-Pacific Theater and participated in the: Leyte operation - Leyte landings, October and November 1944; Luzon operation - Mindoro landings, December 1944; Consolidation and occupation of Southern Philippines - Visayan Island landings, March and April 1945 and Mindanao Island landings, March 1945. Specifications: (as reported by Office of Naval Intelligence-1945) Ship Complement - 7 officers, 104 enlisted; Troop Accommodations - 16 officers, 147 enlisted   Typical loads - One Landing Craft Tank (LCT), tanks, wheeled and tracked vehicles, artillery, construction equipment and military supplies. A ramp or elevator forward allowed vehicles access to tank deck from main deck. Additional capacity included sectional pontoons carried on each side of vessel amidships, to either build Rhino Barges or use as causeways. Married to the bow ramp, the causeways would enable payloads to be delivered ashore from deeper water or where a beachhead would not allow the vessel to be grounded forward after ballasting Armament (varied with availability when each vessel was outfitted. Retro-fitting was accomplished throughout WW II.) The ultimate armament design for United States vessels was 2 - Twin 40MM gun mounts w/Mk. 51 directors; 4 - Single 40MM gun mounts; 12 single 20MM gun mounts.   Yarnell and 'Navsource' team, *Navsource Naval History, Photographic History of the U.S. Navy, 2003* www.navsource.org.

2 - Located south east of Manila, Philippines.

Apr. 9, 45 - Started for Manila in a about forty-five ship convoy heading south of Leyte. There is a APA ship either # 43 or 53 in front of us. All kinds of ships in convoy. Had life boat drill. On guard at night. We got thirty-five Australians on board last night.

Apr. 10, 45 - Went around Letye today and up the west coast. Weather has been good, no trouble. Played cards about all day. On guard again tonight.

Apr. 11, 45 - Past Mindoro and a large port there. A few of our convoy went there. We have about forty-five ships kept moving all day.

AP - 54, USS Hermitage, Troop Transport   PC

A typical example of an AP troop transport it had an approximate capacity of 6,000 men. It had an approximate speed of 20 knots with a crew of 700+. It's armament consisted of 4 single 5"/38 guns, dual purpose gun mounts for 3"/50 guns and 8-.50 cal. machine guns. Yarnell and 'Navsource' team, *Navsource Naval History, Photographic History of the U.S. Navy, 2003* www.navsource.org.

Apr. 12, 45 - Came in Manila harbor in afternoon, passed close to Corregidor and saw parachutes where troops landed. Passed Fort Drum, a cement, man made, island with 14" Navy guns on. Also Caballo Island where I bombed once. (see Feb. 4, 45 entry and photo) Lot of sunken ships all over.

Apr. 13, 45 - Docked in morning. We had to turn to get out of the way of all the Jap ships in the docks. Saw at least fifty and all types. Really a sight one won't forget. We went through Manila in truck convoy and what a sight. Restaurants with good food, white girls with high heeled shoes and lip stick. The first time on a cement pavement in six months. Shell holes all over and pill boxes in concrete at end of roads. New cars of the latest type with new white sidewall tires. Went to Clark Field sixty miles away with cement highway all the way. About thirty bridges we passed, all newly constructed as the old ones were bombed. I saw a 500 lb. bomb of ours beside one that never went off. Very flat country

April 13, 45 (cont.) - with rice fields, hardly any trees. Railroad tracks with train on and telephone wires strung up. Really a sight. Most people have pony and cart to ride on. Very hot in the day and camp was dirty. Fixing the camp for quite a permanent base. First thing I saw was a lot of Jap planes strung all over a field here. Deter, Tosto and Schoen were here. A field of Jap planes over fifty yards away. An estimated 2,000 are here. One new "George" Jap plane we never knew they had. Some are serviceable, about two hundred. There are also B-17's, Spitfires, Navy B-24 (PB4Y2 - Privateer) with one tail and other planes. A lot of bamboo is around here. Played softball at night against officers. Had a armful of papers, two packages and about fifteen letters. Sent laundry.

Japanese planes remains at Clark Field, Philippines CK

PB4Y-2 Privateer DH

It was distinguished from the B-24 by having a new tail unit (with a tall single tail fin and rudder), a lengthened forward fuselage, changes in armament (two Martin dorsal turrets, an Erco nose ball turret and Erco two-gun 'teardrop' blisters on each side of the fuselage), and different engines (which had round instead of oval cowlings). It carried twelve .50 cal machine guns, up to 12,800 lbs. of bombs, had a of range of 2,800 miles, cruise speed of 140 mph, max. speed of 237 mph and ceiling of 20,700 feet., Dave Hanson, *American Aircraft of World War II*, September 2004, www.daveswarbirds.com/usplanes.

Apr. 14, 45 - Read newspapers, looked at the Jap planes, wrote letters. The dust is very bad. It rained towards night. Chow is quite bad but the Filipinos come through area with bananas, melons, watermelons and fried fish, chicken and such. The 19th (Bomb Squadron)[1] got a ship shot up bad today at Formosa, Deter and Tosto went. They also saw a B-24 go down a while back on one of the missions to Formosa. It is really a tough target with ships shot up everyday. We lost a ship while I was at Samar due to bad weather here on Luzon somewhere. They never found a trace of it. Dawson[2] was in it, whom I went through armor school with, a swell friend.

Cpl. Edward A. Dawson - second from right - front row
Thomas Cadder Collection - CK

Apr. 15, 45 - Got up early and went to church. Chaplain spoke of Roosevelt's death.[3] Perry, Bridge, Tosto and Deter went to Formosa today. All but Bridge saw a 33rd plane (Patient Kitten - see photo next page) blow up completely over the target.[4] One of our planes were holed. Our rescue is a submarine, B-17 with boats attached, PBY. Got

---

1 - #42-100174 'Tempermental Lady' - Over ran runway and was wrecked due to damage over Tainan Airdrome, Formosa - it had over 70 missions., Cyril Klimesh, *22nd Bomb Group*, 2001, www.redraider22bg.com.

2 - Cpl. Edward Dawson - aerial gunner was on the crew which flew plane #44-421537 'Modest Maiden' overseas.

3 - Franklin D. Roosevelt, 32nd President of the U. S. Served from 1933-1945. Died April 12, 1945, The White House, 2005, www.whitehouse.gov/about/presidents.

4 - "...the 22nd was participating in a coordinated strike....the plane in the #3 position....was apparently hit in the fuel tanks by a large AA round...#44-41031 (Patient Kitten)...exploded in a blinding flash...immediately disintegrated and the debris showered to the ground 10,000 feet below....No chutes were observed and there was no chance of survivors, Lawrence Hickey, The 22nd Bombardment Group in World War II, Volume III, Photo Supplement, ed. Don Evans (Bonsall, California: Alliance Business Services, 2001), 229.

Apr. 15. 45 (cont.) - seven letters and newspapers today. Am up for mission tomorrow to roughest target in Formosa, most guns there and we've only hit it once and was shot up. All but Crockett are going on same ship. Looked like a bad time ahead. None of the missions are easy any more. Faletti is in Sydney where he went from Nadzab, New Guinea and is suppose to be here now but is over due.

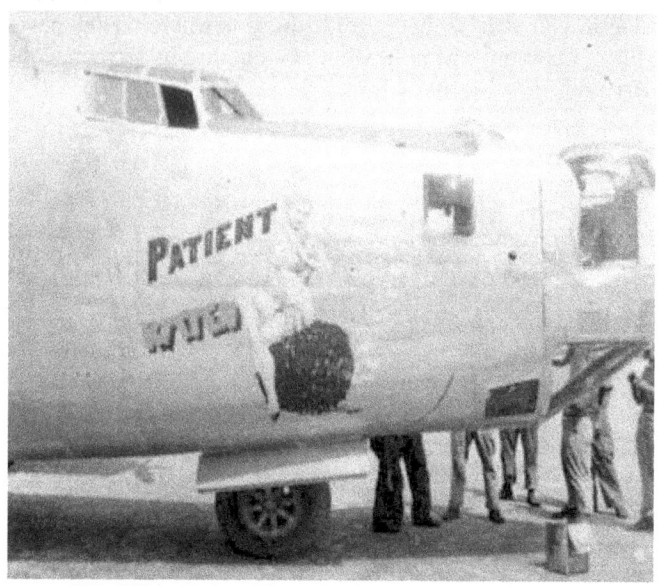

#44-41031 - Patient Kitten (see footnote #4 on previous page)

Apr. 16, 45 - Got up for mission at 5:45. We had a 19th (Bomb Squadron) ship to fly but they came over and took it so we had 365 (#44-40365), our squadron ship and was to fly it in 19th (Bomb) Squadron but the hydraulic system was bad and we didn't take off. I was glad as we had a very rough target. Yesterday, instead of our group losing one plane, they lost two planes and the 43rd group which had same target also lost two. Things look bad on every mission. We were hitting China which has been easier than Formosa. The reason for hitting Formosa all the time believe it or not is just because that so called <u>British</u> Navy that just came here got shot up a bit going through the Formosa Straits.[1] So now we're knocking out everything. Am up again for mission. Played ball at night.

---

1 - "Shallow channel of water, approximately 100 miles wide, that separates the island of Formosa (Tawain) and mainland China.", Justin Taylan, *Pacific Wrecks*, 2005, www.pacificwrecks.com.

Apr. 17, 45 - Up at 5:45, briefed at 7:00 and take off was at 8:30. We went to Shinchiku airdrome at northern end of Formosa. Our target was at the edge of the ocean and we expected a very rough time as we lost a ship over there before. We were lucky and had only moderate ack ack by heavy radar guns.   Used plenty of evasive action   too.   Had frag(mentation) bombs. Got 9:45 hours combat time. Schoen saw a rubber life boat on the water just off shore so some plane must have gone down. Saw a B-17 and Catalina which was part of our rescue. We flew up the whole coast of Formosa which is just covered with airdromes on the east coast. I'm up for a mission again tomorrow which again is expected to be very rough.

Picture taken of Shinchiku airdrome raid on April 17, 45 from the belly of plane Mr. Bates occupied during the mission - #42-100157. Note the many explosions from the fragmentation bombs on the lower center and right of the runway. Also note the revetments to the top left of the runway. Revetments were meant to protect aircraft or anti-aircraft guns on the ground. In the center right and upper right are craters from bombs dropped some time earlier.

Boeing - B-17 "Flying Fortress"

A "heavy" bomber it had a crew of 10 with 13 - .50 cal. machine guns. It could carry up to 17,600 lbs. bomb load. Powered by four Wright engines it had a range of 1,850 miles, cruise speed of 170 mph, maximum speed of 300 mph and a ceiling of 35,000 feet., Dave Hanson, *American Aircraft of World War II*, September 2004, www.daveswarbirds.com/usplanes.

Consolidated - PBY "Catalina"

A multi-purpose craft it carried a crew of seven, 2 - 50 cal. machine guns and 3 - 30 cal. machine guns and up to 4,000 lb. bomb load. Powered by two Pratt & Whitney engines it had a range of 2,545 miles, cruise speed of 117 mph, maximum speed of 179 mph and a ceiling of 14,700 feet., Dave Hanson, *American Aircraft of World War II*, September 2004, www.daveswarbirds.com/usplanes.

 # 42-100157 - Pleasure Bent
This is the plane that Mr. Bates flew on during 04/17/45 mission - Richard Faletti

Apr. 18, 45 - First call at 5:15 and take off at 8. Our primary was at the capitol of Formosa (Taipei), a very rough target. The squadrons broke up to come in at different points to act as a surprise. The whole target was 10-10 covered by clouds so we went to our secondary which was on west coast. That was about 8-10's cloud coverage and after making two bomb runs we gave up and went to Tainan, a city in southeast tip of Formosa and then we were going to make a "mickey" run (radar run) if necessary. It was wide open and in we went. The flak was about the most anyone has had in Formosa yet. Two ships were hit, one had six holes and one had two large ones. Our ship had tin foil (small strips of tin foil, in large amounts, were dropped from the bombers to confuse the radar used by the Japanese anti-aircraft gun – see photo next page) to use on the radar guns they had. That made the fourth target and third bomb run. We threw it out and had just enough. Two squadrons had already dropped their bombs so a squadron went in ahead of us and dropped. In these missions at Clark they have used ten ships to a squadron instead of six and only five of ours got to the target, some turned back due to trouble. We had six P-51's as our cover and they had plenty of flak. We had barely enough gas to get back and almost didn't get to Tainan but drop(ped) them (our bombs) elsewhere on Formosa and head(ed) back. Ship # 157 which I flew yesterday had one engine out and another ready to go out. It landed in northern Luzon. We were sure lucky today. I have fifty points now. Got 10:10 hours (combat time) and dropped frag bombs.

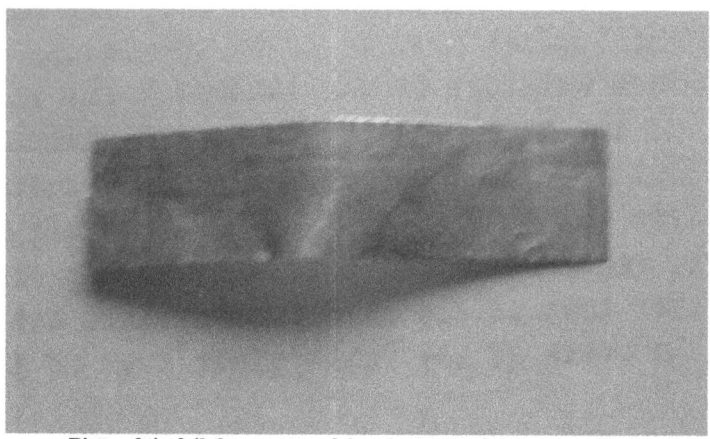
Piece of tin foil thrown out of bomber to confuse enemy radar.

Apr. 19, 45 - Rested up today, played softball at night and beat 408th squadron. Wrote letters. Faletti is back from Sydney, Australia.

Apr. 20, 45 - Didn't do much today. At 4 p.m. they called our crew and told us we were flying tonite on a night recon mission over Formosa. Played ball at night, came back, took a shower and hurried over to briefing at 8 p.m. We were scheduled with the whole crew. The first time since Wewak mission but group said Faletti (h)asn't enough experience to fly alone. They gave us another pilot and copilot and rest of crew flew. Ours was only ship scheduled from our squadron. Each squadron sends one plane a night, taking off at one hour difference as a nuisance raid to keep Japs up all night. We took off about nine o'clock and hit target about 1:30 a.m. We hit Taihoku (Taipei) which is the capitol (of Formosa/Taiwan) and most ack ack up there. The target was the center of the city of 650,000 and bombs were 12 - 500 lb. incendiary. It was about 9/10 overcast and they threw six searchlights up at us which were radar controlled. I waited until they had the(m) on for a minute and they started to pick us (up), then I threw tin foil out and the searchlights were going all over then. They couldn't track us. One would have got us but we went over a cloud. It would be bad if they ever spotted us and then the flak would really come.

Apr. 21, 45 - We got back from mission about 6:30 a.m. and got 10 hours (combat) time. We bombed by mickey which is by radar and hit our target. It was my first long night ride and reminded me of that saying, bombers moon. Waited two hours for trucks to pick us up. Got interrogated and slept all afternoon. Played ball at night. Made big fires on target. Got three letters. Got fifty-two points now.

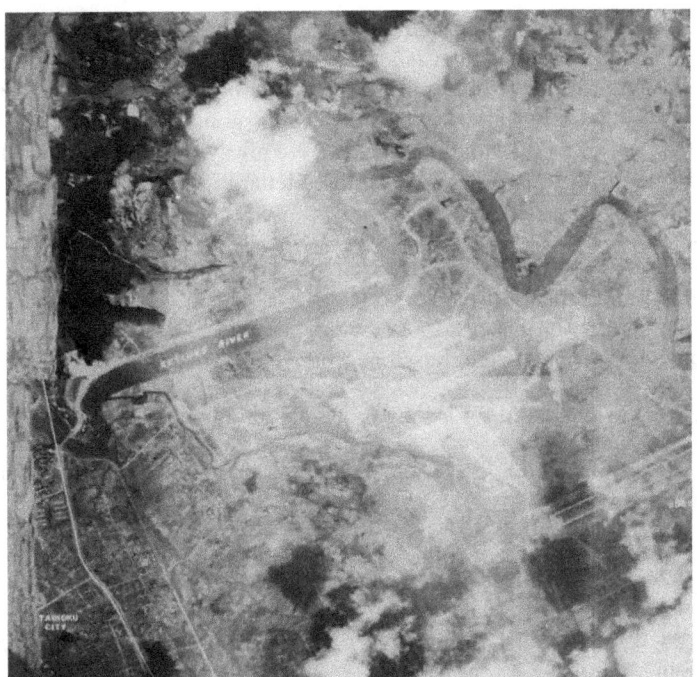
Taihoku/Matsuyama Airfield - Apr. 20, 1945 mission

Apr. 22, 45 - Got up early to go out to line and learn about engineering but nobody to work with out there. Had a cigarette issue one carton. Had real good chicken tonite and banana pie. Went to chapel service at night. Am up for mission tomorrow to Taihoku, capital of Formosa, first call at 4:15 a.m. Got two khaki pants and fatigue pants at supply.

Apr. 23, 45 - Take off was at 7:15 and we were Archer 4 (a planes radio call sign) and our target was Matsuyama airdrome just out of Taihoku (Taipei) the capital. Went up west coast of Formosa cut in just north of Shinchiku where the(y) fired flak at us at their extreme range. We then made a large circle at Matsuyama to get away from Taihoku and got flak from another base. The flak over the target was very intense the worst yet on Formosa and we see the squadron ahead of us go in and boy we started sweating it. Was really bad but we used a lot of evasive action. Coleman got hit in the head by a piece coming in the blister window. He was watching the bombs drop. It didn't pierce the skin though. We came off the target and the(y) started firing again which was quite close. Then as we went through Formosa to get out to sea they fired again at (us from) a town. Boy, five times we had flak in one mission. We got 9:20 combat time and have fifty-five points now. The

Apr. 23, 45 (cont.) - Japs have been using planes on Formosa to use against us at Okayama[1] that island nearer Japan we're fighting on now. Our whole crew flew our first mission together since Wewak. Faletti flew pretty good but almost passed out after going over the target. We were at over 12,000 ft. and no oxygen. We always bomb between 10,000 and 13,000 ft. with no oxygen. Got three letters.

Apr. 24, 45 - The dust is terrible here and the sun always shines and is really hot. Got four letters. Fixed the tent up. Had a meeting this morning, all combat on the strike report. Coleman got the Purple Heart for that scratch on his head. Perry got his papers for air medal on his Zero he got on Clark Field mission. Played 408th in softball.

Apr. 25, 45 - On detail for awhile today. Nothing much doing.

Apr. 26, 45 - Helped in mailroom today. Wrote letters. Got papers and two letters.

Apr. 27, 45 - Had a ten dollar money order made out for flowers on Mother's Day. Had two letters. Helped in mailroom.

Apr. 28, 45 - Not much doing. Got newspapers. Walked our laundry girl home in afternoon. Wrote letters.

Apr. 29, 45 - Went to chapel in morning. Layed around.

Apr. 30, 45 - Got paid in afternoon, 227 pesos, got the $10 money order and mailed it. Had meeting about house in Manila for squadron. Paid seven pesos for Filipinos help and house for squadron. Got two letters. Up for mission.

May 1, 45 - First call at 5:45 a.m., took off at 9 a.m. and went to Formosa. Primary was Krgei (Kagi),[2] a third up western coast. The weather got very bad at Formosa and rained hard. Couldn't reach primary so went to Tainan the secondary which was closed in also 9/10 coverage. Couldn't fly formation due to clouds and we had (the) only radar in lead ship. We saw target through clouds but only bombed by guess. Salvoed bombs which - hit on beach; carried 12 – 500 lb. incendiary. Got 8:50 combat time. Had a couple burst of flak way off not accurate. All but Coleman flew together. He's checking out as lead

---

1 - Although, there is an Okayama, Japan Mr. Bates is most probably referring to Okinawa an island just south of Japan and scene of heavy fighting during World War II.

2 - Probably Kagi - "a large, town in central Formosa with a rail marshaling yard.", Justin Taylan, *Pacific Wrecks*, 2005, www.pacificwrecks.com.

May 1, 45 (cont.) - bombardier. Had leaflets (see photos this and next page) to drop over target to people but held on to them. Had medical lecture and lecture on Jap shipping after (coming) back.

PS
#42-100318 – Titian Temptress – unidentified crewman
Mr. Bates flew on this plane during the May 1, 45 mission - Richard Faletti

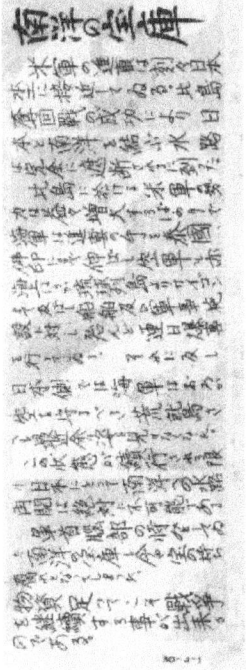

CK

Example of leaflets thrown from B-24's during various missions and mentioned in May 1, 45 diary entry.

Example of leaflets, mentioned in May 1st diary entry, written in Japanese.

This particular document, written in Chinese, refers to the "Cairo Declaration". Translation and information concerning this document courtesy of Yan Ei Chen

President Roosevelt, Generalissimo Chiang Kai-shek and Prime Minister Mr. Churchill, together with their respective military and diplomatic advisers, have completed a conference in North Africa. The following general statement was issued:

"The several military missions have agreed upon future military operations against Japan. The Three Great Allies expressed their resolve to bring unrelenting pressure against their brutal enemies by sea, land, and air. This pressure is already rising.

The Three Great Allies are fighting this war to restrain and punish the aggression of Japan. They covet no gain for themselves and have no thought of territorial expansion. It is their purpose that Japan shall be stripped of all the islands in the Pacific which she has seized or occupied since the beginning of the first World War in 1914, and that all the territories Japan has stolen from the Chinese, such as Manchuria, Formosa, and The Pescadores, shall be restored to the Republic of China. Japan will also be expelled from all other territories which she has taken by violence and greed. The aforesaid three great powers, mindful of the enslavement of the people of Korea, are determined that in due course Korea shall become free and independent.

With these objects in view the three Allies, in harmony with those of the United Nations at war with Japan, will continue to persevere in the serious and prolonged operations necessary to procure the unconditional surrender of Japan."

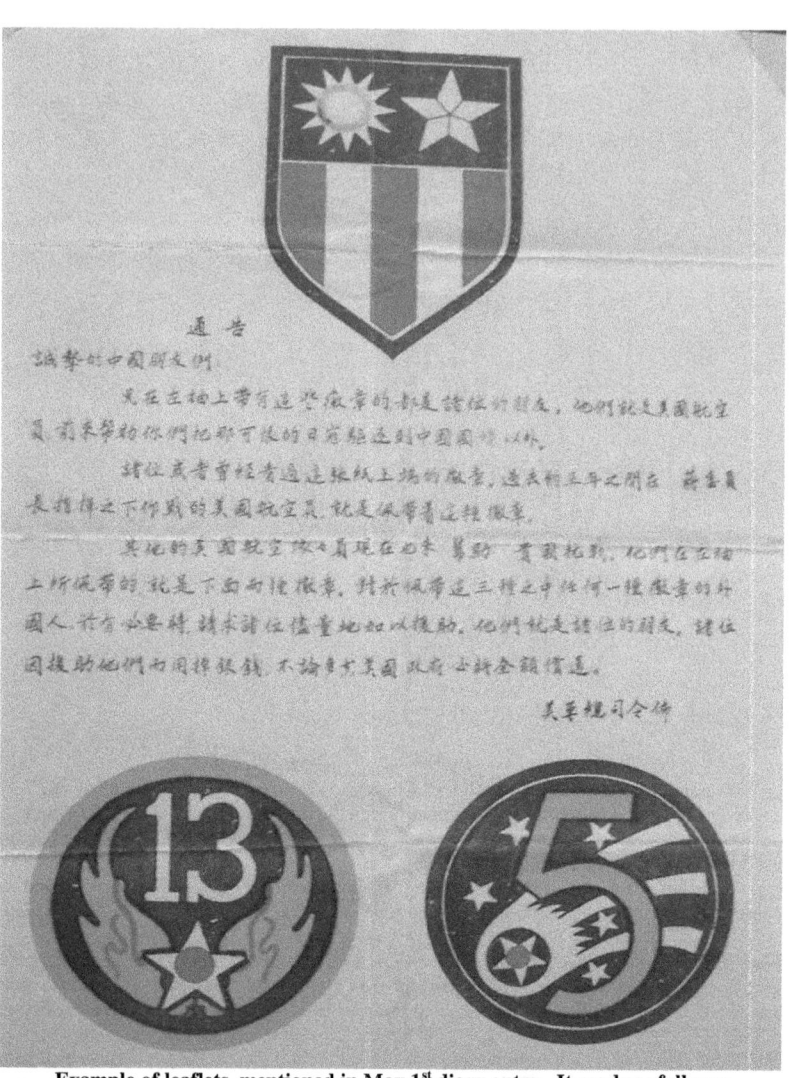

Example of leaflets, mentioned in May 1st diary entry. It reads as follows:

Attention…..Dear Chinese friends. Whoever has this emblem on the left sleeve is your friend. They are members of the American Air Force, who are here to help you repel the despicable Japan thieves and rid of them from China. Maybe you have seen the emblem above before. About five years ago, under Chiang President's military directions, the American Air Force members have this emblem on them. Other American Air Force members are now helping your country fight the war. These members have the below emblems on their left sleeves. Those foreigners having anyone of these emblems, if necessary, please assist them as much as possible. They are your friends. If you spent money in the course of assisting them, no matter how much, American government will pay you in full. American Commander Publication - translation courtesy of Yan Ei Chan

May 2, 45 - Am having trouble with my right ear. Have to go to medics twice a day. Got two shots today. Was very sick from them and arm very sore. Went to bed early. News sound(s) good.

May 3, 45 - Got a $100 money order and made (it) out in Angeles (part of the Clark Field airfield complex) today and sent it home. Went to medics four times today and think I'm grounded for a while. Had ditching drill in morning. Played Navy (in softball) at night and beat them. Did pretty good and got on every time. Ear hurts.

May 4 - 5, 45 - They grounded me for a while as my ear got worse. Didn't do anything. Went to medics twice a day.

May 6, 45 - Went to chapel service in morning. Not much doing.

May 7, 45 - Played ball at night, wrote letters and worked detail part of the day. They get us out every morning to go to police up the whole area and going to have us drill. Had teeth checked in morning.

May 8, 45 - All but Coleman and me went on a ground support mission to northern Luzon. The weather got bad and Faletti crashed after hitting the runway at 105 mph and turned in a ditch.[1] No. 1 engine and prop were badly damaged, both landing gear and nose wheel. The ship was badly damaged but no one was hurt bad. Perry got a couple of bandages on. Got two packages, one from home and Aunt Dovey. Picture frame. Played ball.

1 - "....#44-4182, ran into bad weather during the return trip from a mission to Tuguegaro, Luzon..with 2/Lt. Richard J. Faletti piloting. Touching down....the aircraft....landed to one side with its left wheel off the runway. Faletti subsequently lost control of the plane, which veered off the hardtop and ran into a ditch, breaking it's back. The crew suffered only minor scratches.", Lawrence Hickey, The 22nd Bombardment Group in World War II, Volume III, Photo Supplement, ed. Don Evans (Bonsall, California: Alliance Business Services, 2001), 197.

Photos of B-24 #44-4182 mentioned in May 8, 1945 diary entry
Piloted by 2/Lt. Richard Faletti

May 9, 45 - All those that crashed up yesterday flew today with Capt. Benson[1] as co-pilot. Faletti made a very good landing. Got another mosquito bar today. Played 33rd and won.

May 10, 45 - On detail for a while. Fell out all this week at 7:30 for police up of area. Got package with ball hat and lighter from Gary (Gary Garzinski - known as 'Uncle Charlie' by Mr. Bates family - Ken Bates). Played 19th (Bomb Squadron) and won.

May 11, 45 - Today I was 22 years old. Got a couple of birthday cards. Wrote letters.

May 12, 45 - Played ball and lost 1 - 0 to another enlisted man's team. Should have won. Got 'Sporting News' (a monthly magazine dedicated to assorted sporting events - football, baseball, etc.).

May 13, 45 - Mother's Day - went to chapel in morning and heard a good service. Wrote letters most of the day. Got two 'Sporting News' in the mail. Nice and cool today as it was cloudy. Am up to fly tomorrow. Rest of crew went to town.

May 14, 45 - First call 5:15 and take off at 8:20. Went to Toshien, Formosa,[2] our secondary and a mickey run with 10-10 cloud coverage. Bombs hit close to water and in it, one hitting a sunken ship. Went through Formosa from east coast and had flak from town as we turned in. Very inaccurate. Got 8:30 (combat) time. Threw tin foil out.

1 - Most probably Cameron Benson - listed as living in Augusta, Ga. - 2nd Squadron Newsletter, December 2001.

2 - City on western coast of Formosa about one quarter the way up the coast.

May 14, 1945 bombing run on Toshien, Formosa

May 15, 45 - Raymond got word his wife had a 6 lb. 8 oz. baby girl. Was scheduled for mission tomorrow. Scheduled to receive air medal by general today but was canceled. Made out points for discharge in morning and had 52 so far.

May 16, 45 - First call was 4:15 and was going about 2/3 up Formosa west coast. Just as we neared the runway to take off we blew the left tire. It was very loud and a fire flash went past tunnel guns so we thought an engine exploded and really started to get out fast. Gave us a bad scare. Was lucky it didn't happen a couple minutes later as we'd have taken off. Didn't do much during the day. Went to officers tent at night and celebrated Raymond's baby by having champagne. Had good time.

May, 17, 45 - Went out in afternoon with a bunch who got medals. Had the air medal (see photo next page) pinned on by Brig. General Crabb of V B.C.[1] along with Perry, Coleman and Raymond. Took pictures of us. Am up for mission tomorrow at Tainan, Formosa.

1 - Brigadier General Jimmy Crabb of the V Bomber Command., Lawrence Hickey, The 22nd Bombardment Group in World War II, Volume III, Photo Supplement, ed. Don Evans (Bonsall, California: Alliance Business Services, 2001), 139.

Air Medal
"Given for a certain amount of combat missions or combat hours, varies between combat areas." - TW

May 18, 45 - First call at 4:15 and take off at 7:30. Went to Tainan airdrome and bombed planes with 12 - 500 lb. frag. clusters. We have Lt. Cunningham as our regular pilot now and since the crack up Faletti is a co-pilot. We had flak and used a lot of evasive action before going on bomb run. Got a point as one ship got hit. 43rd Bomb Group lost three ships today up there and two more very badly damaged. One blew up, one went down over target and one ditched at sea. Some were very close bursts at us. Went after planes. Got 8:05 (combat) time. Had package from Mary Alice sent at Christmas. Played officers in ball and won. Had four letters.

May 19, 45 - Early this morning one of our ships[1] that took off broke a landing gear on take off going off the end of the runway. They circled for a long time and then bailed out over the field. They were pretty high up. A large crowd were sweating them out. The fighters shot the plane down after all had bailed out, nobody was hurt. Schoen went on mission and all got two points for losing ship. Got newspapers at night and three letters. Read where I got my air medal. Played 43rd in ball and got beat bad. Big fire was on the strip at night. A plane (caught) fire and all ammunition went off.

---

1 - #42-10075 - Faletti, Richard in correspondence with author, 2003

May 20, 45 - Heard a very good Filipino speaker in chapel service at night on Filipino costumes. Suppose to have a Chinese plague shot this morning but didn't take it. Had eight packages last week.

May 21, 45 - On detail a while in morning. Very hot today. Wrote letters. Am out of cigarettes. They are hard to get here due to the black market.

May 22, 45 - Went over to see Barton in 408th and Dean.[1] Too hot to do much work. Went after two loads of sand for our club house. Wrote letters.

May 23, 45 - Heard a good talk on escapes and evasion in China, Formosa and Hainan (island south of China and considered a Chinese province). Formosa is impossible to escape and very heavily fortified with no help from people. China is very good chance to escape from most sections. Wrote letters, got papers in mail. Played ball.

May 24, 45 - Went to school on the new kind of sight and its usage in morning. Got cigarette issue yesterday. No missions for the past two days. Had three letters last night. Played ball.

May 25, 45 - Went to skeet range in morning. Its new they just finished it. We are starting to have gunnery school here now. Got fifteen out of twenty-five in skeet. Every morning we file out at 7:15 for police up our area. Everyone is bitching of how bad its getting here. Had meeting tonight in mess hall on the seventh war loan. I signed up for a bond but a lot of them didn't just because of the bad treatment. You'd hardly think a war was on and we stick our necks out for some pricks like they got here.

May 26, 45 - Had inspection today. Also meeting in mess hall. Played ball and won at night. Had a lot of papers came. No letters. Won a 90 peso watch at PX and its pretty good. Had a lot of supplies in PX today and bought some.

May 27, 45 - Went to chapel in morning. Very hot today. Had meeting in mess hall on club house. Heard rumor of moving from here in about six weeks. They say we have only 2,000 lb. bombs here and haven't gone on any long missions lately, only night recon (reconnaissance).

May 28, 45 - Very hot today. Played officers in ball and won. Got papers from home. Up for mission tomorrow.

---

1 - Jack F. Dean, Engineer. Trained with Mr. Bates at Tonopah in the States. Dean was assigned to the 408th., Faletti, Richard in correspondence with author, January 2001.

May 29, 45 - First call at 5:00. Take off at 7:45. Got a China patch (see next page) in case we're forced down, had an oxygen mask issued as we expected to go to 16,000 ft. for bad weather. Went to Kiirun, big naval base on northeast Formosa and hit repair dumps and other installations. Had 8 - 1000 lb. bombs. Made two dry run passes but turned away before bomb run due to clouds. Went in on third run and had flak. I flew the tail and had a couple of close bursts. We got hit in right wing, an extra point. Joe Tosto has 96 points now. I have 65 points. Am up for mission again tomorrow. One letter from Robert (Bates).

May 30, 45 - First call at 4:00 and take off at 6:45. Target was ack ack positions at Takao (On the western coast of Formosa, south of Toshien and Tainan) which is the heaviest defended area in Formosa. Really expected a bad time. Went over target at 16,000 which is highest yet and first time we used oxygen. Made two runs and had flak on the second one. Threw out propaganda leaflets. (We led) the group in group formation and 43rd came in target in opposite direction. They had quite a bit of flak and one man killed. Yesterday the 33rd had one killed.[1] Nobody got hit so we didn't get a point. Cunningham (see 5/18/45 entry) our pilot went on his last mission. Got 8:30 (combat) time, had 32 – 250 lb. frag. bombs. Played 43rd in ball and won. Got two hits and good game. Had three letters and papers, one package.

"Slightly Dangerous - #44-40366"

1 - "Cpl. Robert N. Simon was the nose turret gunner aboard "Slightly Dangerous" #44-40366…Just after the plane left the rendezvous point….Simon entered his turret...the crew noticed a hum on the plane interphone set….During a check of the crew members, it was discovered...(Simon) was slumped over his guns...apparently...as he leaned over to begin loading the ammo belts... (he) was hit in the back of the neck by the gun sight cradle which crushed his head." Lawrence Hickey, The 22nd Bombardment Group in World War II, Volume III, Photo Supplement, ed. Don Evans (Bonsall, California: Alliance Business Services, 2001), 229.

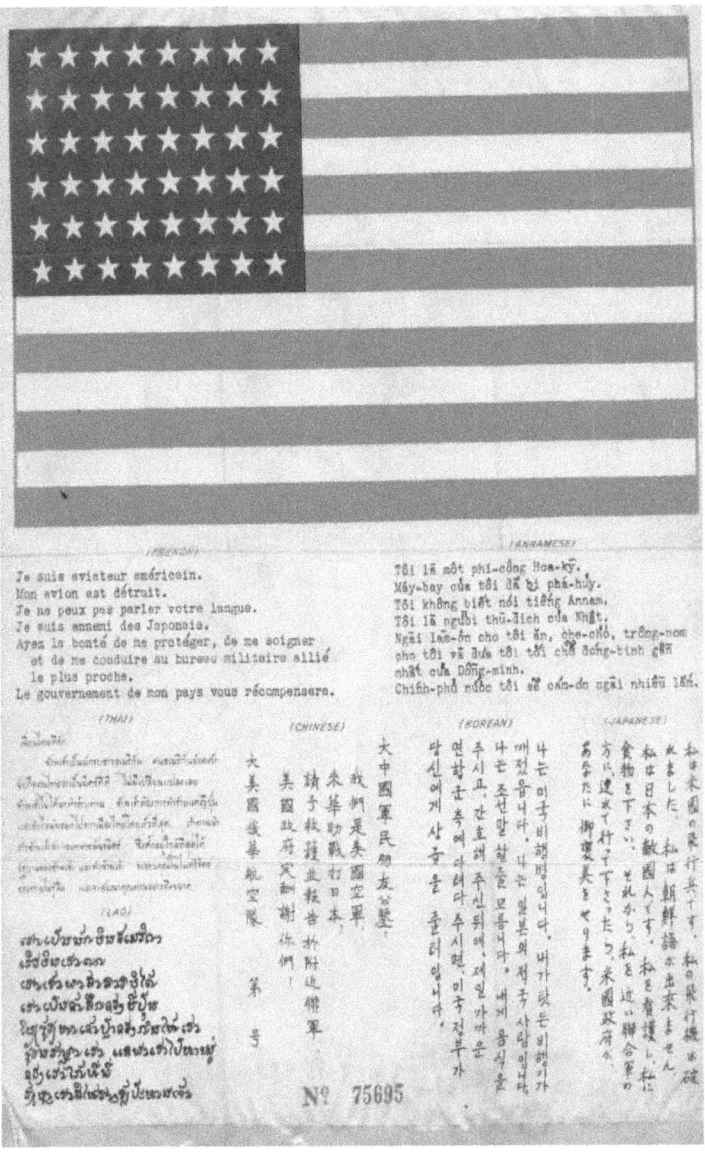

The above "China Patch" was worn on the inside of an aviators jacket as shown in the illustration on the next page. It is written in several languages including French, Japanese, Chinese, Thai, Korean, Lao and Annamese. The Chinese translation reads: Great China Military People Friend Public Notice: We are American Air Force, come to China to assist China fight against Japan: Please help and report to the nearest Allied forces, United States government will compensate and thank you! Great United States China Assistance Air Force. Translation courtesy of Yang Ei Chan.

Mr. Bates called the above "China Patch" (noted in 05/29/45 diary entry). It was more popularly known as a "Blood Chit". Worn by the crew members during missions to China – asking for assistance for the downed flyer. Note the patch shown on the previous page is shown worn inside the jacket in this example. It reads: Assist Allied Country Air Force. They are your friends. Pay attention to these emblems. Translation courtesy of Yang Ei Chen.

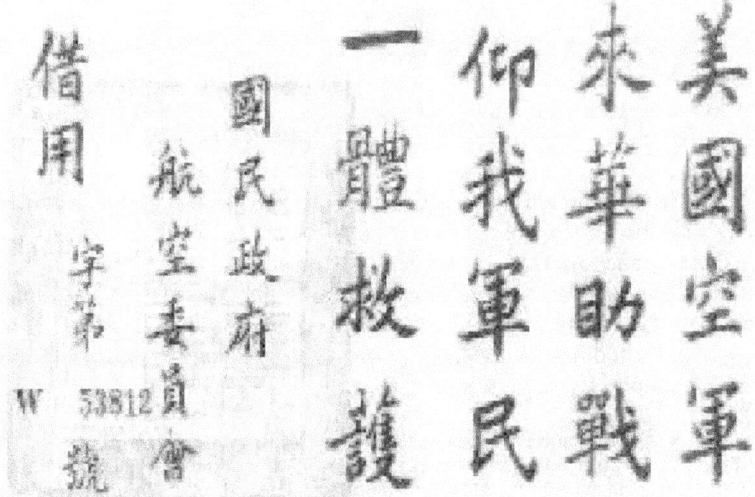

Another document carried by the crew members. It reads: American Air Force. Come to assist China in war. May my militia and people together will help protect. Republic of China government Air Force member. Translation courtesy of Yang Ei Chen.

May 31, 45 - First call at 5:00, take off at 7:45 to the capital of Formosa, Taihoku. A few clouds covered Formosa but the target was clear. We bombed Japanese business district, the very heart of the city, hitting the capitol building. Very large fires were seen. Had very accurate flak with a lot of phosphorous flak too. We got hit in the wing and two other planes hit. Got flak, a lot of it from a town getting out of Formosa after leaving the target. We expected a rough time and were sweating it out before the target. Threw out a whole box of tape (radar jamming tape). The 19th (Bomb Squadron) lost two planes at ditching and one landed at north Luzon. I saw one going to ditch. Got 10:10 hours (combat time) had 8 - 1000 lb. bombs. Got paid at night 242 pesos. Up to fly tomorrow a weather recon. Had three letters.

"Miss Leading" [1] - #42-100204
Charles Critchfield Collection – CK

June 1, 45 - First call at 4:00, no briefing and take off at 6:00 a.m. Went on weather recon to China, only ship and no cover. No bombs and a bomb bay tank. First sight of China, and the scenery is very beautiful, reminds one of a technicolor picture with rice paddies and hills, etc. Forests look something like the states. A lot of rivers, mud color and many islands on the coast. We went to or near Canton (also known as Guangzhu) and Amoy (also known as Xiamen) and other places I didn't know. Didn't go near flak positions. Flew with operations officer, three captains. Got 11:45 (combat) time and the fourth straight day, my 31(st) mission. Played ball (against) our officers at night and won in eight innings. Am up to fly again tomorrow.

1 - "Hit by A/A fire on a bomb run over Formosa, MISS LEADING, B-24J #42-100204 had come in on two engines, minus hydraulics, flown by the severely wounded co-pilot, Lt. Robert Morgan. In the pilot's seat, Lt. Robert S. Edgar, the bombardier, helped by providing additional pressure to the controls. Lt. Charles E. Critchfield, the pilot, had suffered severe fractures to his right arm and leg from the same burst that had hit Morgan.....With no brakes, parachutes were used to slow down the plane which had stopped just short of the end of the runway at Laog Strip in northern Luzon.", Cyril Klimesh, *22nd Bomb Group*, 2001, www.redraider22bg.com.

June 2, 45 - First call at 3:30 and take off at 6:15. Went to Kiirun naval base again and was to bomb in the inner harbor, same buildings. I was sweating it out most of the way as we expected a lot of flak. The target was covered over 10-10 clouds and we made an H2X or mickey run by radar. Had only a couple bursts of flak through the clouds. Had P-51 cover (see photo next page). We have always had fighter cover on Formosa missions. Had 8-1000 lb. bombs. Got 10:00 hours (combat) time and Tosto finished flying today. Had eight letters.

Kiirun Naval Base area.

The arrows and numbers indicate the areas where six of the 22nd B.G. bombers bomb loads landed.   #'s 845 - # 44 – 41845; 365 - #44-40365; 240 - #44-42240; 427 - #44-40427; 126 - #44-41126, 228 - # 44 - 42228

DH
North American P-51 "Mustang"

Introduced as a fighter, long range bomber escort it carried 6 - .50 cal. machine guns. Powered by a Rolls Royce/Packard engine it had a range of 1,000 miles, cruise speed of 275 mph, maximum speed of 437 mph and ceiling of 41,900 feet., Dave Hanson, *American Aircraft of World War II*, September 2004, www.daveswarbirds.com/usplanes.

PS
#44-42240
Mr. Bates flew on this plane during 06/02/45 mission

June 3, 45 - Went to chapel in morning. Had a new chaplain. Am up for three day pass to Manila tomorrow, all the enlisted men.

June 4, 45 - Left for Manila at 10 a.m. Our (whole) crew went. Fifteen men were at the (squadron) house (see Apr. 30th and June 5th entry. It seems that some of the squadron got together and rented a house where they could gather away from the field and relax, etc.) which is on the edge of Manila, next to Grace Park[1] airfield where a lot of Jap planes are smashed, hid all around the houses and yards, even away from the field. Ate early supper just after arriving and Soeder (William)[2] took

---

1 - "Wartime airfield located in the suburbs of Manila.", Justin Taylan, *Pacific Wrecks*, 2005, www.pacificwrecks.com.

2 - Probably Bill Soeder, member of 2nd Squadron, listed as living in Glendale, AZ. – 2nd Squadron Newsletter, December 2001.

June 4, 45 (cont.) - us to town. Went over a lot of Manila and saw its wreckage which is worth seeing. Went to a few clubs and ended up in the Casa Loma night club which is best place I found in Manila, reserved seats, orchestra girls as hostesses to dance, drinks and a ritzy place. Deter and I were together and had a good time, had two nice women. They close all places at 10:30 and no electricity in town but place had their own (generating) system. The other four guys had girls at the house. Spent over 100 pesos today.

Pass to Manila – note the notation on bottom left "Staying at Honeymoon Hotel"

June 5, 45 - Up quite early though we didn't have to. Had bacon, eggs for breakfast. Paid 40 pesos for house and meals which is cheapest there is. It's our squadron house. Steak for dinner. Had two (illegible) girls at house in afternoon. Went to 'Tropic' night club at night. 30 pesos for quart of whiskey. Walked around with Deter before going back for the night.

June 6, 45 - Rode around in jeep. Laid around. Had swell meals. Went to 'International' night club with Deter and two girls. Nina and Nati. (see photos next page) Had swell time. Saw the number one actor of Philippines before war in the club. Had a party at house afterwards with the girls too. Tosto is staying at the house to help the squadron. A very good deal to be able to stay here.

June 7, 45 - Got up early and went to town with Schoen and Deter. Rode around before breakfast. Went back to camp at 2 p.m. Had the best time since coming overseas the last three days. Got two packages and three letters, a bunch of papers. Played ball at 403rd and won but did poorly. Went to bed early as I was very tired. Rained at night.

Nati in Phillipino custom dress

Nina

June 8, 45 - Tent was a mess with dust and everything. Cleaned it up. Read papers, got laundry back. Had one letter. Rained all day and in night.

June 9, 45 - Played ball at night and it rained. Got two letters. Didn't do much. Cleaned pistol. One of our squadron ships crashed on an island about 30 miles north of Luzon, held by Japs and all but three were killed. (Raymond) Riddle, an old man (it is not clear whether Mr. Bates is referring to Riddle's age or his time of service) here was killed. A new crew was flying and the(y) ran out of gas. It happened last Tuesday while I was on pass. They shouldn't have gone on mission as one engine stuck at 2400 rpm and that used too much gas. Their tanks couldn't have been full either. One (man) is back in squadron and the (other) two they sent guerrillas (out) as search party but couldn't find them. A Cat(alina) was following them but they didn't bail out as they should or go to emergency strip only thirty miles away.[1]

June 10, 45 - Went to church in morning with Coleman. Am on guard today, second shift, two hours on, four off. Wrote letters.

June 11, 45 - Had all day off as I was on guard duty yesterday and until six this morning. Slept all morning. Sent laundry in afternoon. Played ball at night. Am up for mission tomorrow.

June 12, 45 - First call at 4 a.m. Was going to Hong Kong and bomb small shipping in harbor. The city is really an island by itself. Had 390 lb. gasoline drums filled with gas and rubber, a new type of bomb and on experiment stage. We couldn't smoke (while the) bombs were in ship. Had no. 2 engine throwing oil and vibrating so on take off we had to feather it and go to Lingayen Gulf where we dropped bombs, two went off and came back. Landed with three engines and got almost two hours flying time but didn't get credit for any as we didn't go past bomb line. Perry and Deter went, got three points to(o). Deters almost finished.

1 - "June 5...shortly after take off from Borax Strip, Clark Field.... B-24J #44-41126 had it's #2 prop stick at 2400 rpm. Without notifying anyone else....the pilot adjusted the power setting on the other engines to match and continued with the mission. Bad weather prevented a strike against both the primary and secondary targets, so the formation broke up and the 2nd squadron conducted a radar-guided bomb drop from 10,000 feet near the town of Taito. After leaving the target area, Lt. Allmon notified the Squadron Leader of the problem and indicated that he was running low on gas....later he radioed that he intended to make a....landing....on Japanese-held Fuga Island....After making contact with a rescue Catalina, (he) set the Liberator down....the plane skidded into the side of a hill, where it broke up....Four crewman....were apparently killed when the top turret crashed forward, crushing them. Four other crewman were braced with their backs against the bomb bay bulkhead, and three of them died when the plane split apart....the other man, Riddle, was severely injured and died later. Three men survived the crash although two of them were severely injured. With the aid of friendly Filipino civilians...(they) evaded capture....they succeeded in signaling a Catalina...(which) rescued them...", Lawrence Hickey, The 22nd Bombardment Group in World War II, Volume III, Photo Supplement, ed. Don Evans (Bonsall, California: Alliance Business Services, 2001), 229 & 230.

June 13, 45 - Was up for mission again today. First call at 4 a.m. take off at 6:45, was going to Takao inner harbor and bomb shipping with new bombs again. (This was a type of 'fire bomb' – used to start fires at the target. They were most effective against Japanese homes as most of the houses were made of only wood and built very close together – these bombs were intended to ignite the homes, causing large, uncontrollable fires and thereby doing as much damage as possible) Encountered very bad weather after getting to rendezvous and had to break up formation on route to target. Radar ship only one to bomb target. We went to a small town on south coast of Formosa where no guns and dropped them on town. Got 8:15 minutes (combat) time. Faletti was pilot for first time in quite a while, since crack up. Deter has one more mission to go. Strong rumors are that we are moving to China or Okinawa very soon. Am sweating out to finish before going as we'll hit main Jap islands and be very rough. Another rumor is that we put in bomb bay tanks and go to southern Jap island and land at Okinawa to refuel which I hope doesn't happen. Am up to fly tomorrow.

**Daisy Mae (With a Little Persuasion)
Mr. Bates flew on this plane on 6/13/45 mission
B-24M #44-41845**

June 14, 45 - Mission was canceled late last night due to bad weather. Am up to fly again tomorrow. Played ball at night.

June 15, 45 - First call at 3:45 and take off at 2:20 with 32-260 lb. frag bombs. Berry (2/Lt. Lawrence R. – see June 24, 45 entry) was pilot and target was ack ack positions at Taichu, about half way up Formosa and inland. We were Braggard - 4 which is (our) call sign and first group of four to go over. The others went in after trainer planes being repaired to go to Okinawa. On first run our bombardier put racks in select and all but twelve bombs dropped. We then went off the run and got plenty of flak near town. Circled around town and went back in on single ship run. Other ships were going over and all getting flak. We went in and sighted on a battery of four guns that we saw firing at us and supposedly hit them. Got phosphorous flak, a few real close. Got holed in wing, three ships were hit, one a big hole. Deters last mission too with 102 points. Got 9:25 (combat time) and extra point. 77 points now. Played officers with them getting sore at us. Got two letters. Had a card from Dick Saunders and he tried to find me. He's near at same A.P.O. (Army Post Office)

June 16, 45 - Had inspection. Cleaned pistol, went to look up Dick Saunders and called at operations but couldn't get him though I found out where he is. Squadron went to Kiirun today and # 228 got hit bad. Jim Ar.....rt (illegible) got hit in face and eye bad. He had 76 missions and kept flying. He lives in Bradford and wants to wait and go home with me. Has a girl he wants to marry in Sydney. They had a shell go through left wing that didn't explode. Barrett,[1] the radio man got it in hand for his second purple heart. Raymond got a purple heart with a scratch on his hand. Had 90 holes in ship and had to junk it.

June 17, 45 - Went to chapel in morning. Very hot today. Went over to Navy with squadron team but didn't play. Am up for mission tomorrow. Was up to fly today but they scratched me.

June 18, 45 - Went to Kiirun on mission. First call at 3:15 and take off at 6:20. Had 8-1000 lb. bombs. Coleman was lead "A" bombardier. I was A-2 and we were Braggar 1. Had intense flak and I counted up to fifty-two bursts which wasn't all. Had the nose turret. Poor bombing. One ship had a big hole in nose. 19th (Bomb Squadron) got jumped by fighters dropping chains with explosives. Got 9:15 (combat) time and extra point. Berry was pilot. Six of our crew was scheduled to fly in all different ships. Up to fly tomorrow. Played 5th Fighter Command and lost 1 - 0.

---

1 - Most probably refers to William Barrett - deceased., 2nd Squadron Newsletter, December 2001.

June 19, 45 - First call at 3:30 and target was Kiirun again. Had 8-1000 lb. bombs. Flew B-1 and Braggar 4. Peterson[1] was pilot. Flew nose. Got 9:40 (combat) time. Went over target and had close flak but didn't drop bombs. Made a circle to go on another run and flew over an airfield where we had a lot of flak. Only one other ship went on second run and went in at same altitude and heading. They really got our range and our pilot and co-pilot both were hit. Pilot on his arm which paralyzed it for a while though didn't go through the skin and co-pilot got hit on top of head and got the purple heart. Got six holes and one went through waist window but Perry and Schoen were throwing out leaflets which was lucky for them. We hit residential district and they said it was our last mission to there. Have got 83 points now. Played a league game tonite, (against) 33rd and won in thirteen innings 1-0. Am up to fly again. One letter. One squadron got jumped today. Had P-51 cover. P-38's were really showing off coming up valley from Lingayen, flying all over us. Really a swell ship.

June 20, 45 - First call at 3:00. Take off was scheduled at 5:40 but General Arnold[2] was here in a C-54 and he wanted to take off at 6:15 and was afraid our group would hold him up so they held the whole mission up for 3/4 of an hour while the General waited to take off. That is the best I've seen yet. We went to Shinchiku and Faletti was my pilot, the only one on crew that flew with me. The Japs brought fourteen fighters in to this place and we went after them. There was very dense 10-10 cloud coverage underneath us about 2,000 feet. We bombed at 14,000 and had H2X on radar run. Had P-51 as cover and they went in below the clouds and said we hit two planes. One squadron got jumped by fighters. We didn't get any flak due to clouds. Had 12-500 lb. clusters of bombs. Got 9:40 (combat) time, Braggar 3 Faletti flew real good.

June 21, 45 - Found out there is twelve crews and nine ships going down to Morotai Saturday and stay for one week, pulling six missions to Borneo and Java where the Aussies (Australians) are, (for) ground support. Am going down, me and Schoen. Perry and Bridge have too many points to go. Our mission is supposed to be to Balikpapan at oil fields. I have 85 points now. Played ball at night and got beat. Played ball every night this week. Had stage show at theatre and saw some of it. Am up for mission tomorrow.

---

1 - Most probably Harold Peterson – deceased., 2nd Squadron Newsletter, December 2001.

2 - Major General Henry Arnold, Commanding General of the Army Air Forces.

June 22, 45 - First call at 4:30, take off was at 7:00. Flew with one of the newest pilots and it will be the last time to(o). Target was Toshien and after ack ack positions. Went above the city and island. We followed B-1 in and made evasive action opposite them which turned us right over their flak. We really got hit and hit bad. Were hit in both wings, fuselage and rudders. Two large holes in right wing bigger than fists and over a foot hole in waist. About two inches from left wing main tank one hit. Almost hit a tire and don't know how many holes in it. Flak burst so close that one piece stayed in ship. All the rest went clear through. They were taking it to Morotai but now it's going to service squadron and they say it's washed out as too badly damaged. Have to put a new wing on. Schoen was flying in another ship that the main spar on wing was hit and plane is going over to service squadron. Everyone that saw our ship sure said we were lucky. It was mostly the pilots fault. Got 88 points now. On bomb run, which was long, the pilot hollered to bombardier to let the bombs go as we were hit in no. 3 engine. Closest flak I've had yet and most holes. They were all large holes and all over. Played ball over to UBC and got beat 4-1. Now they had to cancel going to Morotai until Sunday so as to fix the planes up. We only have six ships working now. Need five new engines and can't get them. B-32's went over a town, Heito just ahead of us. Deter is in Manila and rest of crew had party at night as Schoen and I is going to Morotai and Tosto will probably be gone by time we get back. They had a wild time about twenty of them but Perry and me went over to see officers and didn't drink.

June 23, 45 - They put up a list of crews to go to Morotai and I'm on with Raymond and Coleman. After yesterdays mission we only have six ships. Had a meeting at 2 p.m. packed and had baggage ready to ship at five. Had twenty-three men to plane but they got two planes from 43rd group and put engines on one of our planes so we have nine now. Yesterday the 408th lost a plane.[1] Hedge,[2] on Barton's crew we were with at Tonopah and came over with, was on it. Briefed at six a.m. and was told probable targets down there. They expect an invasion we will help on. Wrote two letters.

---

1 - "B-24L-10, #44-41647...disappeared after taking off from Borax Strip, Clark Field, Luzon..was not seen or heard from again...The Squadron Leader...saw a large concentration of black and gray smoke...along the flight path to the rendezvous point...indicating the possibility that the missing plane experienced a mid-air explosion....it's fate remains unknown.", Lawrence Hickey, The 22nd Bombardment Group in World War II, Volume III, Photo Supplement, ed. Don Evans (Bonsall, California: Alliance Business Services, 2001) 230.

2 - Refers to Tellie H. Hedge, Jr. – Armor Gunner. Faletti, Richard in correspondence to author, January 2001.

June 24, 45 - First call at 4 a.m. and we left at 7 a.m. Had lunches we ate in plane and flew through some bad weather. Got to Morotai at a little after two and circled around in formation for a while. There is a big Navy convoy out here, a lot of small islands surrounding us with some Japs on. Red Cross nurse met us at plane with doughnuts and drinks. 13th Air Force stationed here. An awful lot of British Spitfires, Beaufighters and Mosquito bombers (see photo below and next page) are here. They briefed at night 6:30 for mission next day. I'm not on it. They said under no circumstances to fly over the next island, just a few miles away as there are Jap ack ack positions there and a plane was shot down two days ago. Went to show at night and saw "The Clock" which was good. We're staying in a transient camp all set up but not very good tents. It's all jungle here and a lot of Aussies (Australians).

JT

Supermarine "Spitfire"

Powered by a single Rolls-Royce Merlin engine. Maximum speed of 408 mph, range 660 miles, ceiling of 44,000 ft. It's armament consisted of 2-20 mm cannon and 4--.303 machine guns., Bill Gunston, The Illustrated Directory of Fighting Aircraft of World War II, (Salamander Books Ltd., London, 2002), 54 & 58

JT

Bristol "Beaufighter"

Carried a crew of two, armed with four 20 mm Hispano cannon, six .303 machine guns and one .303 in. Vickers machine gun. It could also carry a torpedo/bombs/rockets. Powered by two Bristol Hercules engines, maximum speed of 330 mph, range of 1,540 miles, ceiling of 26,500 feet., Bill Gunston, The Illustrated Directory of Fighting Aircraft of World War II, (Salamander Books Ltd., London, 2002), 26

JT

De Havilland "Mosquito"

A bomber/fighter powered by two Rolls-Royce Merlin engines, max. speed 410 mph, ceiling of 34,500 feet and a range of 1,860 miles. It carried a crew of two. It's armament consisted of four 20 mm Hispano cannon and four .303 Browning machine guns in the nose., Bill Gunston, The Illustrated Directory of Fighting Aircraft of World War II, (Salamander Books Ltd., London, 2002), 30 & 32

June 25, 45 - Slept in as I was tired. Looked the camp over. Those that went on mission today got jumped by fighters. One of our planes are missing,[1] probably shot down and another one was hit in engine and left tire. They shot the other tire and came in on the hub of the wheel.[2] Geltz[3] who plays ball on squadron team with me was in the (missing) plane. It was lost over the target. Our squadron shot one Jap plane down. I had to go out and help load bombs at night. Had beer issue in afternoon. Up to fly tomorrow.

1 - On June 25, 1945 "six planes... took off...on a strike against the airdromes at Mandai on Celebes Island. The 2nd squadron…encountered heavy flak. The formation was also attacked by Oscar fighters, one of which was reported shot down...B-24M-30 #44-42431 was apparently experiencing mechanical difficulties....no one...saw the plane crash...but several crew members of the trailing 408th Squadron saw a large column of smoke rising from a fire at the probable crash site...After the war, further investigation.....revealed that the B-24 crashed near the village of Maros. Natives buried Lt. Shellington, identified by the name in his hat...six other crewman had been buried by natives at the crash site....four crewman were captured..two days after the crash.....(then) were executed at the local headquarters for the Japanese Navy...The remains of the crew were returned to the US for burial in 1952.", Lawrence Hickey, The 22nd Bombardment Group in World War II, Volume III, Photo Supplement, ed. Don Evans (Bonsall, California: Alliance Business Services, 2001) 230 (2/Lt. Lawrence R. Berry was the pilot - see 06/15/45 entry)

2 - # 44-42240 - "Attacked by three fighters while approaching target, her gunners took care of two of them but not before they had inflicted severe damage. Limping home, (the pilot) Fairies belly landed the Liberator on a field on Moratai. ….", Cyril Klimesh, 22nd Bomb Group, 2001, www.redraiders22bg.com.

3 - Wayne J. Geltz - A.G. - lost on June 25, 1945 mission (see reference 1 this page), Lawrence Hickey, The 22nd Bombardment Group in World War II, Volume III, Photo Supplement, ed. Don Evans (Bonsall, California: Alliance Business Services, 2001), 230

#44-40427 - Mr. Bates flew in this plane during 06/25 mission (unidentified crewman)

June 26, 45 - First call at 3:45 and briefing was last night so we took the trucks at five. Started engines at 5:45 and took off at 6. Had bomb bay tank filled to look for the ship that was lost yesterday. Most (of) the land we flew over were jungle with some fields. Went to Celebes,[1] south western tip of Borneo. Flying with Bax[2] in B-1 and flew on bomb run. I saw a fighter go in at 408th just ahead of us. Lost track of him and next thing I knew he was only a few feet from us coming in. He barrel rolled over our plane coming down in a dive and the wings smoking where he was firing. Really came close and I couldn't get my guns on him in time (Mr. Bates occupied the nose turret on this mission). Then we didn't drop bombs so made another run and a fighter came in again which I didn't see. We had no cover so got three points. Got five points in all. Had 11:15 (combat) time. Circled to look for the lost ship (from 6/25 mission) but didn't see it. Just off this island there is a big invasion fleet just starting out as we came back. We started to fly over but they sent up a barrage of flak and we turned away. They probably are hitting Borneo and the reason for us coming down here. Went to movie at night. Primary today was Limboeng air strip[3] (see photo next page), just south of Mandai which was yesterdays target.

1 - Island just east and south of Borneo

2 - Probably Elmer Bax - Pilot - deceased., 2nd Squadron Newsletter, December 2001

3 - Located on the extreme south and west of the island of Celebes

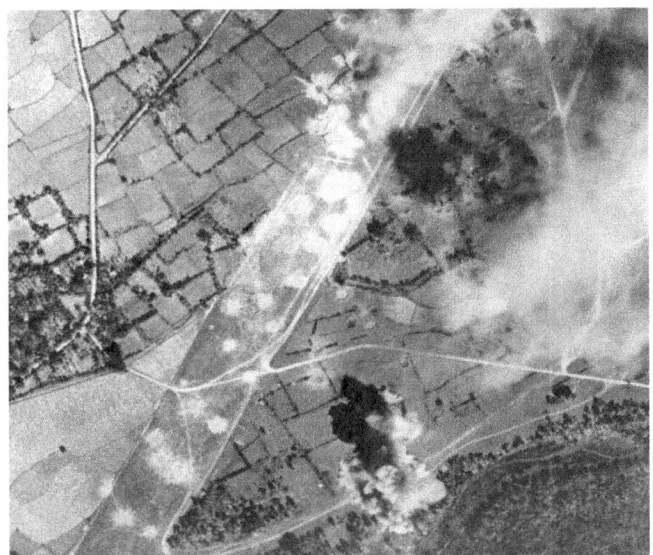
Limboeng airstrip - 06/26

June 27, 45 - Wrote a letter in the morning home. Mission today was target yesterday. They got intercepted. Am up to fly tomorrow. Target is Borneo and have 3,000 gallons of gas. Went to show at night. Was bothered all night with ants in our beds and didn't sleep much at all. 408th lost a plane today.

June 28, 45 - First call at 3:30. Started engines at 5:45 and still dark. They figured we'd have to sweat gas before we got back. We hit very bad weather on way down and at rendezvous which was southeast tip of Borneo. It was really socked in. We never did see any other planes and after circling to climb over the weather we were getting very low on gas so salvoed (dropped our) bombs and headed back. Hit some bad weather starting back and Raymond, who was only one on my crew flying with me, plotted our course and figured up how we could come out with gas from the reading. According to the gas reading we couldn't make it back to Morotai and were really sweating. Put power settings to lowest possible and pilot had us throw out all ammunition. Which helped a lot. Raymond was over a hundred points then as he only needed one more on mission. We had 5-1000 lb. bombs. Got back about 7 p.m. and very dark. Hit bad weather around field. That was a happy bunch that saw the field tonite and they had their mae west, harnesses and one had his chute on. We had a lot more gas than it registered and got back ok. I figured after Raymond told us, we'd probably make it, but the rest were sweating out the time and even made me put on my stuff. They had

June 28, 45 (cont.) - rescue equipment out to(o). It made number forty mission for me and got 96 points. Coleman, Raymond, Deter and Tosto are finished and Perry, Bridge have 98 and 97 back at Clark. Schoen has 90. Was dead tired when we got back and went to bed early. Got 13:45 (combat time). Two planes hit target. Southeast part of Borneo was target.

June 29, 45 - The mission (today) was just above ours yesterday at Borneo. That invasion force should land the first. They had fighters today. Packed my things. Went to show at night but didn't stay. Bought some Aussie beer to bring back. I figure I have 96 points now.

June 30, 45 - Got up at 4:30 to start back to camp. Really had a close call on take off. The engineer pulled up the wheels before we got off the ground and they scraped the dirt. The plane hit the runway, the radar dome in the waist hit and got a hole in it. We really thought we'd crash. Took off about 7:30 and got back at about 2:30. Got paid 242 pesos at night. They had our enlisted mens club open and last night had WAC's (Women's Army Corp) (visit). Got five letters.

July 1, 45 - Went to chapel with Coleman. Joe Tosto left at noon for home. Had my points checked and have twenty extra points and 389 hours. I need eleven hours more and am up for mission tomorrow. So far Tosto, Deter, Coleman and Raymond are finished. Perry and me hope to finish tomorrow.

July 2, 45 - First call was at 3:45 and we took off at 6:30 for Toyohara, Formosa after planes with 40-100 lb. frag.(ment) clusters. Perry and I both finished up today. We had flak, not so much but close and was really sweating. On take off we almost slurred off the runway twice. It was quite a scare. The big scare was on the bomb run. Our plane didn't drop its bombs when the lead ship did and the lead plane rocked over at us and it was the closest call to being hit I had. We kept on straight until we dropped our bombs. It was almost too close. We had two small holes and lead ship had a big one. Got 9:25 hours (combat time) which makes me now really 400 combat hours and twenty-one extra points. Had four hours over a hundred points. It sure feels great not to sweat any more. I played ball with officers and enlisted men at night and we won against a colored team. Tosto had forty-two missions and Deter forty-three. I have forty-one.

July 3, 45 - Went out for police up (clean up) in morning. Read papers most of the day and straightened up tent. Operations counted only 98 points that I had, so I checked over my record and was sweating it out.

July 4, 45 - Went to operations early and checked my records with Caplin[1] and found out I had a hundred points and they had added wrong. I have 397:50 according to them and my books show 401:55 time. Called up Dick Saunders from operations and am suppose to get with him on the phone at 11:30 again. Wrote letters.

July 5, 45 - Got a pass in the morning and went to see Dick Saunders. He's about twenty-five miles away and at Florida Blanca strip.[2] Found him quite easily, ate up there and he came back with me and stayed for awhile. Gave him some hair oil I had as I plan to go home. Had a letter from Mary Alice. She got one of her letters returned that she wrote to me and it said missing in action. She had this letter addressed to me and Deter both and she said she wasn't going to believe it until she got real word. (see photos next page)

July 6, 45 - On guard duty today which isn't bad. Had three more letters today from Mary Alice. Wrote a letter. They are sending my orders in tomorrow.

July 7, 45 - Got off guard duty at 8 a.m. and slept all morning. They had a meeting of combat men in afternoon and have did away with the point system. Its up to the discretion of the C.O. (Commanding Officer) how much you fly and they bounced our orders back and we don't know what is the score now except that all of us that are finished flying are going to refuse to fly if they try to make us. I wouldn't fly again even if I had to sweat the war to end here.

July 8, 45 - Went to church at night. Slept all morning. They say seventeen crews have to come in group before any of us leave. Operations says they aren't going to fly us until they get orders to or they have to. There is strong talk of moving and a lot of outfits have moved to Okinawa.[3]

---

1 - possibly Albert Kaplan - see "List" - page 179.

2 - "Located about 10 miles south of Clark Field and 5 miles west of San Fernando. An American base for B-17's before the war. Used by the Japanese as a satellite of Clark Field. After American liberation, it was enlarged and improved, and again based American heavy bombers......", Justin Taylan, *Pacific Wrecks*, 2005, www.pacificwrecks.com.

3 - "Located 700 miles north of Philippines and only 300 miles from the tip of Japanese home islands. Attacked on April 1, 1945, it was the site of an 83 day battle that lasted until June 22nd and resulted in 40,000 US casualties (7,600 dead or missing) Of the 120,00 Japanese defenders, only 10,000 surrendered, the rest fought to the death....." Ibid.

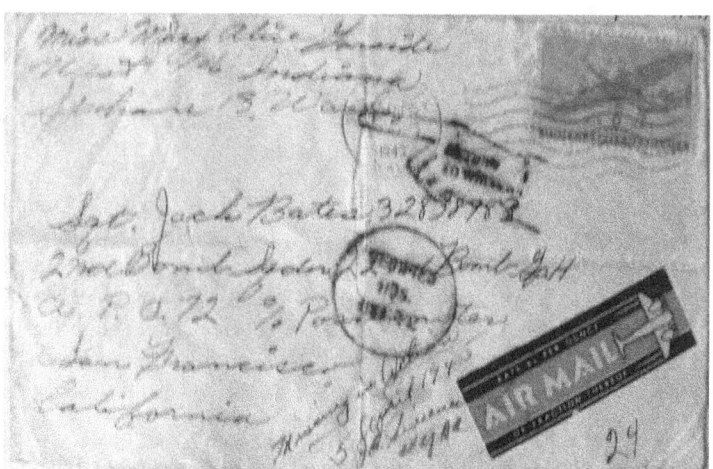

Letter from Mary Alice Garside to Mr. Bates that was returned to her with the notation 'Missing in Action' April 5, 1945 (center, bottom of envelope)

Second letter sent by Mary Alice after she was informed Mr. Bates was 'missing in action'. Notice "or Arthur Deter" second addressee

July 9, 45 - Am half a week behind in my diary. Nothing much has happened. We expect to stay here quite a while as there is no sign of crews to come in. Art Deter went home yesterday afternoon. Goes to Neilson Field (Manila, Philippines). I have got some bombing photos, silk escape map, etc. from operations to take home. Tried to get a new B-4 bag but couldn't.

July 10, 45 - Deter and Tosto both left on a boat today. They said from Manila. The other squadron (the) 19th (Bomb Squadron) keeps on flying their men.

July 11, 45 - Got a job in the mail room to help Montepart out so I won't have any details or fall out for police up in the morning. Dick Saunders stopped in to see me tonite. Went over to Fort Stotsenburg at hospital after a fellow. That place is really built up over there with cement buildings, good roads and everything. They took this area off of combat area so they make everyone salute over there and in towns now. Dick stayed late.

Montepart – mail clerk

July 12, 45 - Went and got mail at Angeles today. Went to play ball at Stotsenberg but after we got out in first inning it rained and got soaking wet before getting back. Last night Baker and I went to some girls that work in our tailor shops house, very nice girls and it rained so hard that we stayed all night. We had a swell party. The neighbors called us in with eats. Every time you visit you have to eat there. This morning I came back and was suppose to be in a formation that Bridge and Perry were in to get two air medals clusters. Nothing became of it though.

July 13, 45 - Thought I had a three day pass to Manila but didn't. Perry, Bridge and Schoen had it fixed up so they went. Demb(s)[1] and Brundshuk (see "List" page 176) only ones left from another crew gone home here with us now. So there are five in our tent. We sprayed our tent to prevent leaks today. It is the rainy season and rains every night. Got five letters and first 'Time' magazine. Mom says Robert (Mr. Bates brother) is home now.

1 - Probably refers to Henry Dembs, listed as living in Webster, NY., 2nd Squadron Newsletter, December 2001.

July 14, 45 - Got two new crews in today but still we're not up to strength. One fellow Strickland is in our tent. We have six men now. Sprayed our tent in the morning, me and Brunshuk. It really works too and now it doesn't leak around me. Went after mail in Angeles in the afternoon and sorted it. Went to see Rosie at night.

July 15, 45 - Went to chapel in morning and then slept til noon. Played 1st baseball (prior games were softball) game this afternoon with two teams in squadron. Didn't do too bad and had lot of fun. Went to Rosie's at night. It rains every night here now. They shot a .45 (caliber) pistol in club tonight and hit someone in the leg.

July 16, 45 - Would have went to Manila but they didn't find me in time. Bridge and Schoen came back but Perry stayed down there. Went after mail. Went to see Rosie again. She works in tailor shop and is very nice for a Filipino.

July 17, 45 - Went to mail room in morning and then slept a while. Helped sort mail, got two letters and some mag. (magazines) too. Had case of beer issue tonight. Read book "Billie Mitchell".

July 18, 45 - Slept most of morning. Went after mail in afternoon and sorted it. Went over to Ft. Stotsenburg to play ball but the other team was restricted. Most outfits are moving from here. Had a lecture on diseases at Okinawa. Some combat fellows are moving up there (Okinawa) on D.S. in just a couple of days. There is hardly any room up there to move in to. Went to see Rosie.

July 19, 45 - It has rained every day for almost two weeks. Bridges orders went in. Perry is still in Manila. I could go (to Manila) but told them I didn't want to. I work in the mail room every afternoon and every other day go get mail in town. List is up to go to Okinawa and go on just one mission. It (trip to Okinawa) was canceled for tomorrow. Borrowed Bill Soeder's camera 118 and took some pictures.

July 20, 45 - Again the trip to Okinawa was canceled due to a typhoon north of Formosa. Had a case of beer issued to us. Had a party at the club tonite with WAC's from Manila there but I didn't go as there were only about twenty-five of them and all were taken. Worked in mail room and played ball at ack-ack (anti-aircraft) outfit and won.

July 21, 45 - Had a bad wind storm that blew some tents over about noon. Went to a good show at night. "Valley of Decision" with Greer Garson. Got my laundry.

July 22, 45 - Am up for M. P. duty in town tomorrow. They left for Okinawa today. Schoen went. I have 69 points toward discharge now. List is on board. Wrote letters in afternoon. It rained as usual today.

July 23, 45 - Played ball at night. Worked in mail room. Conrad, a young Filipino boy whose a relative of those (that work) in the tailor shop got killed by a truck at school. I went and saw him (the funeral services) at night. The fellows that went to Okinawa couldn't go on a mission today because of the weather. They were suppose to go up to Honshu and bomb a Jap carrier, two battleships and two cruisers with 2,000 lb. bombs and they estimated we'd have 25% casualties. They were in a small harbor up there with flak all over the area.

July 24, 45 - Monte(part) went on pass and I ran the mail room today. Took him out to the strip in jeep and rode around. No mail for three days now.

July 25, 45 - Took some pictures today, two of the 120 mm Jap guns out by the bomb dump that fired at us here. They went on mission to Shanghai from Okinawa. A crew came in, a new one.

Pictures of 120 mm anti-aircraft guns

July 26, 45 - Got seven letters today. Took some pictures. Practiced baseball at night. Got 'Time' magazine. Slept all morning.

July 27, 45 - Read in morning. Played baseball at another outfit, ack-ack in afternoon. We had a pretty good squadron team of officers with us. I played short and went two for three, stole two bases and had double play, won 3-2 and good game. Got a sun burn on face and arms.

July 28, 45 - Had inspection in a.m. Helped in mail room most of day. Had a U.S.O. (United Service Organization - provided recreational and entertainment to armed forces) show at night but not so good and saw "The Brighton Strangler" picture afterwards. Went to club for a while.

July 29, 45 - Went to chapel service in morning and then to get mail with Monte at APO 74 in Angeles. Got one letter. First few men were going to Okinawa by boat today but it didn't come in at Subic Bay. They had detail to load (LST) last night. They are all getting ready to move now. My orders won't go in until after the move now so will have to go north. Practiced ball in afternoon.

July 30, 45 - Am behind in my diary. Went over to see Rosie at night and we went up to where Flora lived, about twenty miles in Jim's truck. They gave us a farewell party and Rosie almost cried cause we're leaving. Got back at two in the morning.

July 31, 45 - About all the buildings are down now and moved mail room in club house. They're taking loads of things to Subic everyday and night. Got paid at night, drew 242 pesos. They had a dance and party over by Rosie's and they took us.

Aug. 1, 45 - They moved the tailor shop out now. Had meeting at night and LST is ready to dock. Found out I'm going on first echelon by boat. Got a picture and hanky Rosie made me. They are working all night tonight packing things up. Our bags are packed. Went over to Rosie's house for a while at night. Didn't go to bed until after two. Leaving tomorrow.

Aug. 2, 45 - Helped at mail room and found out I'm mail clerk up north. Took my bags down to the trucks. All the tents went down. Bridge is staying and going home from here. Schoen is staying to fly up. Perry and I are going on boat. Rosie came over to say goodbye. Can only take up to $25 up there which is in American money. Sent $90 home by P.T.T. (Postal Telegraph and Telephone) and got $50 money order with me. We started in truck convoy at 4:00 a.m. and got to Subic Bay at around 7:30 a.m. Had to buy our meals as no place to feed us. Slept in our trucks all night and some loaded LST 1019 (see photo next page).

Aug. 3, 45 - Stayed at trucks all morning and had nothing to eat. Sure hate to leave the Philippines to go north. Loaded trucks in afternoon and had the LST loaded by 3 p.m. I was very lucky as almost everyone has worked all the time. Went on board after loading and ate supper there. Am on upper deck. Had show at night but I slept through it - right next to the screen too.

USS LST-1019

Commissioned, 17 May 1944....was assigned to the European theater and participated in the invasion of southern France in August and September 1944. Later transferred to the Asiatic-Pacific theater, *LST-1019* engaged in the assault and occupation of Okinawa Gunto in May and June 1945., Yarnell and 'Navsource' team, *Navsource Naval History, Photographic History of the U.S. Navy, 2003* www.navsource.org.

Aug. 4, 45 - Pulled out of the shore and anchored just off shore. Good meals on board. Straightened my pictures and things out in morning. Nothing to do here. Grande Island, which I bombed is just to one side of us.

Aug. 5, 45 - Laid in port all day and night. Quite a few ships here. Nothing much happened. Very good food. Wrote letters.

Aug. 6, 45 - Pulled out in a convoy in the morning. About thirty ships are with us. Read a while. We hit some bad weather toward night. It rained and a lot of us got sea sick. I didn't feel too good and had to lay down. Didn't eat any supper.

Aug. 7, 45 - They test fired their guns on the ship today. They really threw up a barrage of flak too. The weather was a lot better today. Am sleeping below deck with Raymond, Coleman and Faletti. The ship is quite crowded. Passed a lot of islands off of northern Luzon.

Aug. 8, 45 - They had more target practice today and the 40 mm twin guns here really sound off. It started to rain and I slept below again. We

Aug. 8, 45 (cont.) - were woke up at 12:30 a.m. at night by an alert. It was a submarine the radar picked up right ahead of us. A destroyer threw eight depth charges over and they didn't know if they sank it or not. Really got a scare at first. Those Navy fellows were really working fast then.

NS

DD-629 USS Abbott

A typical example of destroyers it carried a crew of 273 and had a maximum speed of 38 knots. It's armament consisted of 5 - 5"/38 AA gun mounts, 4 - 1.1" AA gun mounts, 4 - 20 mm AA gun mounts and 10 - 21" TT., Yarnell and 'Navsource' team, *Navsource Naval History, Photographic History of the U.S. Navy, 2003* www.navsource.org.

Aug. 9, 45 - We got word that Japan had asked to surrender. Also about the new bomb (atomic bomb) we have. Everyone sure was excited over this possibility and some celebrated a little at night. Am taking care of our mail on board ship.

Aug. 10, 45 - We had another alert today in the afternoon. It was a plane which we found out later was ours that didn't have its IFF (Identification Friend or Foe - used on American airplanes to identify them from enemy airplanes) on. They were really ready for it too and we expected some excitement. Everyone is talking of the possibility of Jap surrender and our chances of going home. Had four carriers as escort in afternoon.

Aug. 11, 45 - Came in to Okinawa in morning. It is a beautiful place from a distance and we passed other small and rocky islands. Pulled in to port and was going to go ashore with our mail but didn't. Don't intend to dock for a couple of days. There are a lot of ships here. Also planes. Saw B-29 - 24 - 25 - 32's and just about everything else too. Had six bottles of beer issued tonight. They have a movie on board tonight.

Aug. 12, 45 - More news about the Jap surrender but my opinion is that it will be a long time yet. Helped sort mail and went over to another LST with the ships mail man and mailed our letters. We just lay out in harbor

Aug. 12, 45 (cont.) - here and they think we will for awhile. They say if the war ends we will dock, unload this ship and it will take occupational troops to Japan. At 9 p.m. we had an air raid alert. It was quite an experience as every ship let out a smoke screen which was thicker than fog. It was a clear night too. Saw a lot of night fighters go out. Later we found out a Jap plane was picked up on radar 88 miles out and was shot down by fighters about forty miles out. That was quite a record I'd say. We were all expecting trouble and were prepared. The Navy sure works fast on its alerts.

Aug. 13, 45 - This morning we were woke up by the alert again. At 4 a.m. it was and again they laid down a smoke screen and fighters went out. It did not last long and they say the Jap plane turned back. It scared us a little being awakened like that and we did hear shooting way off in the distance. They say the destroyers act as our outer defense by circling the island. Slept all morning below and very hot. Got mail ready and had Navy guy take it today. They didn't show any movies on top deck tonight. I finished reading a very good book "Valley of Decision" today. We moved our ship about a mile and still in the harbor. They told me I'd go in to try and get mail tomorrow though I think it's useless as there is no road to our area, a lot of Japs near there and they say forty miles away from here without any transportation. At 8:45 tonight we had an alert which lasted until 9:45. A lot of planes, mostly B-24's fly over about this time, probably coming back from Tokyo. A heavy smoke screen was laid.

Aug. 14, 45 - I took Sgt. James and we went ashore early at 8:30 a.m. and hitch hiked from just above Naha[1] clear up past Motabu, about 40 some miles. The roads were good but got worse as we went north. A really good trip, we saw a large number of pillboxes and caves near Naha where the worst fighting was. Talked with a Marine who came here on D-Day. Saw a long line of the Jap natives here. They don't know any English but say "Huba Huba" which the Marines were teaching them. They don't seem bitter at us. Went to V B.C. (Fifth Bomber Command) and there found where our area is. Our strip isn't finished, our area is next to a L-5 (see photo next page) strip where two cracked up in less than half an hour. Went after mail but only a few packages were at our area. A few of our squadron were there. Our LST had moved up to where we were so then we went aboard. A big rumor is that they're

---

1 - Largest city on the island (of Okinawa). At the end of the first day of the Marine landing, 60,000 troops had landed on the beach 10 miles from Naha., Justin Taylan, *Pacific Wrecks*, 2005, www.pacificwrecks.com.

Aug. 14, 45 (cont.) - waiting for Truman[1] to broadcast the Jap surrender. We had an alert at dusk. I went to bed early and at 11:00 pm we were awakened by another alert. Nobody knows what to think of the peace settlement now.

DH

Stinson L-5

With its short runway capabilities it was used in a variety of ways - reconnaissance, delivery of supplies and air ambulance. It carried a crew of two with no armament. Powered by a Lycoming engine it had a range of 420 miles, a maximum speed of 130 mph and a ceiling of 15,800 ft., Dave Hanson, *American Aircraft of World War II*, September 2004, www.daveswarbirds.com/usplanes.

Aug. 15, 45 - This morning Truman announced that peace was over the world. It is hard to believe here after last night and I expect we might have more alerts. I sorted and got the mail ready and we were going ashore, the 1st Sgt. and I, but then they got orders to move LST in to beach. Everything is all snafu now. All our orders are not coming through and nobody knows anything of what we are to do. I saw Lt. Gen. Whitehead (Commander of 5th Air Force Advanced Echelon) yesterday. We were told by the Fifth Air Force that he said we were the first Air Force to go in Japan. Am afraid now I'll have to stay here a lot longer. We are still on LST just off Motabu or north of it on Okinawa. A liberty party of crew on boat went ashore but outside of that the peace hasn't affected most of them here. No shouting but a lot of talking. Went ashore at 3:30, mailed our letters, got stamps and envelopes for squadron and went to our squadron area. Got back at 5:30 with those on liberty. Sold the stamps. At 7:30 p.m. we are alerted, the same day

---

1 - Harry S. Truman, 33rd President of the United States - took over Presidency on April 12, 1945 after the death of Franklin D. Roosevelt served from 1945-1953 Born: May 8, 1884 in Lamar, Missouri Died: December 26, 1972 in Independence, Mo – *The White House, 2005*, www.whitehouse.gov/about/presidents.

Aug. 15, 45 (cont.) - Truman said there was peace. We found out the cruiser "Indianapolis" was sunk last night.[1] The alert just ended at 9:30 p.m. and there were Jap planes in the area. Two crashed south of us and they say there were a lot in the area.

USS Indianapolis

Aug. 16, 45 - The LST docked at about noon. I went ashore in the afternoon, cashed a $50 money order and bought $40.58 worth of stamps and envelopes. Returned to our area. They unloaded LST and were done about midnight. Didn't get to bed until 2 a.m.

Aug. 17, 45 - Sold the stamps. Some mail came in from one of our squadron planes coming up from Clark Field. More mail than we ever got at one time. Handed it out at night and sorted newspapers also. Am in tent with orderly room. I got six letters, two 'Times' and over a dozen newspapers. They were supposed to have come over to Ie Shima[2] today, Jap officials, to sign the peace but they didn't show up.

Aug. 18, 45 - Sold the rest of stamps. Went to P.O. (post office) twice and rode around in jeep most of the day. Had to go six miles to get a shower. No laundry set up as yet. Moved over to another tent, the mail room, in with the medics and orderly room. We do have a floor in now. Am squadron mail clerk up here. Pretty good job. Have it pretty easy so far.

1 - The Indianapolis was sunk on 7/30/45, on the return leg of a secret mission to deliver .....the first atomic bomb to be dropped on Hiroshima. Approximately 300 men went down with the ship. More than 900 others spent four days and five nights in the ocean. By the time they were rescued only 316 crewman survived.... many were lost to sharks. Netwide Development, *USS Indianapolis - Still at Sea*, 2005, www.ussindianapolis.org.

2 - "Small island three miles to the west of Okinawa. During the 2nd week of April, 1945 US forces occupied the island...Site of a Japanese airfield that was converted into a major base by American forces after its occupation. Japanese ambassadors and Army representatives flew here aboard a G4M1 Betty in surrender markings. They were then flown to Manila aboard a C-54.", Justin Taylan, *Pacific Wrecks*, 2005, www.pacificwrecks.com.

Group area at Okinawa

Aug. 19, 45 - Two new crews came in yesterday and that makes thirty crews in all. Still they haven't started to send any more crews home. The rumor now is that we go to Japan in five more weeks, that Gen. Whitehead gave 5th Air Force the honor of going first as it's the oldest Air Force overseas. The Jap plane showed up today on Ie Shima. Some fellows saw it but I only saw the P-38 escort. It was painted white with green crosses, about 1 p.m. it showed up. Drove a jeep today to P.O. Which was closed. Went six miles for shower. Got mail out in morning. Wrote letter at night and saw "Tarzan in the Desert" at the show. Went to bed early.

Japanese surrender plane at Ie Shima

Aug. 20, 45 - The mail room is still a part of the orderly room. Sent mail out in the morning. Took orderly jeep to post office which is five miles about. Got almost $40 worth of stamps and envelopes again. Sold them all at night. Was going to move to another tent but they changed it. Went about five miles for a shower tonight. It is a creek and very cold water.

Aug. 21, 45 - Got mail out in the morning. We have to have it at group by 10 a.m. Combs[1] my helper came yesterday from Clark along with quite a few other fellows. Got a little mail in. Bought $40 more of stamps and sold them. I buy them out of my money. Took a shower tonight. It rained towards night. Quite cold too. Moved to the back of the supply tent which is now the mail room and had a detail assigned to me. I had them build up the mail room with tin around all the sides, a counter and I am sleeping in here to(o). Also Combs. Very good place to(o) and good lights. A floor and got a good table. Made shelf to put our things on.

Aug. 22, 45 - Rained all last night and part of the day. Mud is pretty bad here. Got $49 worth of stamps. Wrote two letters. Had a little mail come in and got three letters myself. Rained again at night. Schoen came up from Clark and a lot of others. Six of our planes came up. In a couple of days our planes are taking paratroopers up to Japan. They're starting to take out some of the turrets out (of the planes) now. The rumor is we'll be a cargo outfit. Got word that my orders are going in. Bridge they said would leave Clark in a couple of days.

Aug. 23, 45 - Got mail out in the morning. There is a fellow, Stevens in one squadron that has over 1000 combat hours and 100 missions. Supposed to be the most of anyone in the Pacific. He came in a while ago. I think they are sending my orders in to go home, twenty (orders) in all. That is a good rumor now. Went to take shower at night. Wrote a letter. Leo (Brundshuk) gave me a pie at night.

Aug. 24, 45 - Had one letter today. Sorted mail, had mail call at 5 p.m. Wrote 2 letters. Had another pie Leo gave me tonight. Got laundry back and had to dry it. Put up a mosquito net as they are pretty bad here. Lt. Williams said my orders were typed up ready to send in. They are sending in twenty orders so the rumor goes.

Aug. 25, 45 - Got mail out in the morning. Very hot today. Had a little shower in afternoon. Had one letter. At night they came out with orders for all men to go home, ground men with 85 points or over. Thirty-six were to go out by plane to Manila at 1 a.m. and they worked up to then getting their records checked. Then it was canceled that night but the men are on alert. They were really celebrating.

---

1 - Most probably Paul Combs deceased., 2nd Squadron Newsletter, December 2001.

Aug. 26, 45 - The men didn't go home today though they expected to. Yesterday the squadron pulled a mission to Japan. They had bombers, going up the middle of Kyushu and down southern Honshu just to see if the Japs had dismantled their guns. If they (were) fixed on (by radar) they were to drop their bombs but they weren't. The fellows flew over where we first dropped that atomic bomb (Hiroshima) and said it was really level. They landed with the bombs. A mission for today was canceled but one is up for tomorrow. Got mail in but (I) didn't get any. Wrote two letters. Saw the new two engine Navy fighter plane. Also a 33rd ship cracked up on landing.[1] It really is a mess. I saw (it) with a Catalina and C-46 wrecked right beside it, last night. There are more rumors about my orders going in. Joe Tosto wrote Faletti today and he was on train going to Jefferson Barracks (Missouri) and then home.

#44-41538, Round Trip Ticket

Aug. 27, 45 - Heard more rumors on my going home. Kaplin and Balmenti came up from Clark Field today. The mail records were sent up and we had a little mail. Wrote letters. Reading a book "Leave Her to Heaven". We have girls doing our laundry now. They don't speak English and are short.

Aug. 28, 45 - Heard they landed paratroops in Japan. Two days ago two P-38's from group next to us here landed in Japan as they were running low on gas. We sent a weather recon plane to Japan at 12:00 noon and it

1 - "B-24-l #44-41538, Round Trip Ticket….(was) on a ferry flight from Clark Field…(to) Motubu Strip, Okinawa,…during the landing the right tire blew out….(causing it to) careen off the runway, smashing the nose…One of the passengers….was thrown out of the plane through the broken fuselage and was found dead under the #3 engine." Lawrence Hickey, The 22nd Bombardment Group in World War II, Volume III, Photo Supplement, ed. Don Evans (Bonsall, California: Alliance Business Services, 2001), 230

Aug. 28, 45 (cont.) - got back at twelve midnight. Am definite that my orders are written up but not sent in yet. Got some bomb photos censored. (These are the photos that Mr. Bates brought back with him and are included in this work)

Aug. 29, 45 - Washed my B-4 bag in morning. Traced Red Raider on it in afternoon, got paint and Perry is going to paint it on.

Aug. 30 - Sept. 4, 45 - Got this far behind in my diary but nothing much happened. Rumor is we're moving pretty soon, very soon to Japan and I'm sweating it out whether my orders will come back. They are at group now. I have 74 discharge points and with eight more for recount. Got Parker pen and some other things at PX. Saw "Back to Bataan" at movie. Got Red Raider insignia painted on B-4 bag.

Sept. 5, 45 - Today they dropped censorship on letters and I wrote three. Had PX supplies. Packed my B-4 bag, the things I'm not using.

Sept. 6, 45 - Am starting to get every man in the outfits name in this book now (see List). Leo gave me a pie tonight. Not much doing. Those having 80 points or over are going home soon. They checked out of squadron today.

Sept. 7, 45 - Got a carton of Luckies (brand of cigarettes) from supply. Wrote two letters today. Got a lot of mail in about 4:30 p.m. and had a late mail call. Got more fellows to sign this book. Got four cloth maps at operations. They took me off the records over there. Schoens orders are going in. He had 98 combat points.

Sept. 8, 45 - Had a lot of mail come in early and called off mail early also (easy way to deliver mail - mail clerk would stand in a general area, soldiers would gather around and he would call the names off of those who received mail). I had three letters. Our squadron planes are taking our prisoners of war to Luzon from here tonight. Wrote letters.

Sept. 9, 45 - Went to chapel this morning, my first time here. It is just a wooded pine area, very pretty with low pine trees, very thick to hide the sun and at the alter there is a large clump of tall thick fern like bushes which really sets it off. Mail came in, got three letters. Wrote two letters.

Sept. 10, 45 - Not much doing today. Not much mail came in. I have a very bad right ear, being infected and went to dispensary. Packed part of my bag and got things ready. Have nine cartons of cigarettes to take home.

Sept. 11, 45 - Heard our orders might come back tomorrow. Signed payroll, supplementary for $25 yesterday. Hardly any mail came in. Wrote one letter.

Sept. 12, 45 - Had rest of my pictures and other things censored and sealed today. Packed just about everything in B-4 bag. Got $25 pay. Hardly any mail came in. Twelve officers are ready to go home, their orders are back. Perry is too, Coleman and Raymond. They are thinking about signing up for Army, again. I didn't find out about my orders. Went to dispensary about my ear again. Lt. Lawrence[1] who is from Elmira came back from B-32 outfit they were transferred to that broke up. Faletti and Crocketts orders are in and Schoens are already in.

Sept. 13, 45 - Got Joe Zieglers[2] address and tried to get jeep at night to go early in morning to see him but Capt. O'Connell was asleep. Barton came over from 408th and saw me today.

Sept. 14, 45 - Awoke early to get jeep and go to Yontan but didn't get started until 9:30. Took Capt. O'Connell's[3] jeep and Masciangelo[4] and myself went past Yontan strip,[5] about 60 miles altogether and saw Joe Zeigler. Didn't have a hard time finding him and he's just the same as ever. Then we went to the 6th Marine Cemetery (see photo next page) a beautiful place and saw where Bryce Hardiman was buried. It's up on a large hill almost overlooking a cliff and - from there you can see a full view of the ocean, an island, airstrip and everything. A wonderful view. It has a chain fence around it and place to park in front. Has a carved bible with 23rd Psalm on it at entrance and chapel at other end. Row upon row of white crosses, Bryce was in the 19th row number 451 white cross. I got a small splinter of wood from his cross. Got back about 4:30 p.m. and had to go to medics with my ear.

---

1 - Lt. Edward Lawrence - last known address listed in diary as Gaines St., Elmira, NY.

2 - Joe Ziegler lived on Franklin Street in Horseheads, NY prior to the war. He served in the Navy. Al Frost (see research resources) married Joe's Zieglers' sister Carolyn.., Frost, Al in personal conversation with author, 2003.

3 - H.J. O'Connell Jr. - see "List" - page 181.

4 - Remo Masciangelo - see "List" - page 180.

5 - Located next to the village of Sobe, Okinawa. Major American airfield that based Army, Marine and Navy aircraft., Justin Taylan, *Pacific Wrecks*, 2005, www.pacificwrecks.com.

6th Marine Division Cemetery, Okinawa - BP

Sept. 15, 45 - Perry was called at group this morning for records. His orders are back. This squadron is flying thirteen planes back to states soon. All men over 80 points are moving to 380th Bomb Group down past Yontan tomorrow. I have 91 points and had my name on orders but had them cancel it. Am going to move down to 380 (Bomb Group) tomorrow with the rest, as another outfit with not enough points to go back, are moving in with our squadron tomorrow. Perry is staying here. Don't know what the score is here as yet. Got Form 5 for my flying record and took to orderly room along with all my other records. 1st Sgt. told me my orders and everything will follow me down in three days. Packed tonight. Saw baseball short (movie clip) tonight at the show tonight. Still am going home as combat orders they said.

Sept. 16, 45 - Got up early, packed bunk, blankets and miscellaneous bag. Fell out at 9:00 a.m. and got orders. Am going home on discharge points instead of combat. On (my) orders it says I'm transferred to 380th Bomb Group to go home with them. Before 9:30 when we were to leave, it started to rain and the wind blew. It ended up, we had a typhoon with the wind blowing over 100 mph at 9 p.m. and it lasted all night. Not two tents or buildings stayed up. (see photo next page) I had (a) little sleep from 11 to 2 in morning in the supply (room) and then that blew down and we were out in wind and rain. I had a blanket over me to ward off wind. All bags and everything I had was in truck with tarp over it. They said it was to end at 2 a.m. but at about 9 a.m. it started to slacken up and only rain.

Damage left by typhoon on 09/16/45

Sept. 17, 45 - They set up most of tents in afternoon but a lot were ripped. We really had a tough time last night. Got some mail and had to call it off in mess hall as there wasn't a mailroom. They called off us going down to Yontan as they too were hit hard. Slept in supply which they put up again and didn't get much sleep. Typed one letter at night. Didn't have any lights but a gas light. Rained a lot and everything was all mud. Faletti is flying a B-24 back to states. They will leave for Yontan with us. (They will) fly and will probably get to states before us.

Sept. 18, 45 - Mail came in, in the a.m. They told us we were leaving at 1 p.m. Those flying left in the morning. Another outfit, 417th Bombardment Group the "Sky Lancers" an A-20 outfit is moving in with group to make up full group today. Rumor is they change to A-26 now. Only one B-24 outfit is to stay here overseas. The B-32 (group) broke up over here. Went to 380th in afternoon, about 50 miles down south to Yontan strip. It is close to the strip. They say we will be here to Oct. 1 any way. Those flying will go sooner. Went to PX here and got box of candy. Ate and took shower. Would like to go back up to squadron and get combat orders as I'd go sooner then. They should be back today. Got some combat papers from medics before I left. It says I have combat fatigue only. Am only a mile or so now from Joe Ziegler.

Sept. 19, 45 - Up at 7 a.m. Ate and then read "The St. Louis Cards" in morning. Straightened up my things. Slept some and at 6 p.m. went to see a Major about not going home on combat orders and this way. Went with Stanco (Michael) but don't know if it did any good.

Sept. 20, 45 - Called everyone out at 7:30 a.m. and told us that those having over 80 points are on 36 hour alert. We are to be transferred again, to the 312th Bomb Group and go with them, supposedly this week end. All our men are working on 380th planes and they said that as soon as the planes were fixed, they were taking off. Had to sign our home address in orderly room. It looks pretty bright now.

Sept. 21, 45 - They called us all out and told us that instead of the three APA boats they have one liner for all V B.C. (Fifth Bomber Command) going home. That we would load from Saturday morning until Sunday morning. Put us on alert again.

Sept. 22, 45 - They called us together again and this time they told us we would go home on the liner and gave us our shipping number. Mine is 162. Separated us by our states. Told us we'd load Monday.

Sept. 23, 45 - It rained today so didn't go to church as I wanted to. Called us over to 312th Bomb Group and put us through processing, checking records. I have 87 points by my service record instead of 91. Will load the first part of the week.

Sept. 24, 45 - Called us to the medics in the morning. It rained and slept all noon. Am not sure what day we are going but they put us on 10 min. alert. Went to bed early and they called us about 11:30 at night for a meeting. They told us that everything we've been told up to now just forget. That we were now casuals, not in any outfit and that V B.C. were making our orders, starting at noon today, as fast as they could. We are to get up at 3 a.m. pack and go over to 312th Bomb Group at six. They are going to call off 2,000 names then to load on the boat and (then) the rest, other 2,000, the day after.

Sept. 25, 45 - Got up at 3 a.m., ate and then packed. Went to mess hall at 5:30 and it started to rain. We then went to 312th Bomb Group in rain and mud was terrible. They took us in corps. I'm in 2nd Corps area so about noon we were all called out, lined up and put on trucks. There was a lot of men in 2nd Corps. Went to Naha and after waiting around, got on landing barge, took us out to APA 122 (see photo next page) and after they hauled our bags up, we climbed up a rope ladder. It is very big ship and a lot of bunks with not much room. 6,000 men are coming aboard. We are shoving off in two days.

Sept. 26, 45 - Stayed on board all day, read and slept. The boat is really crowded and more came on all day today. It rained at night. They have us get up at 5 a.m. A very big mess hall we eat by compartments.

AP - 122 (Admiral R.E. Contz)

Carried a crew of 618 and had a maximum speed of 19 knots. It could carry approx. 5,200 troops. It's armament consisted of 4 single 5"/38 dual purpose gun mounts, 4 twin 40 mm gun mounts and 14 twin 20 mm gun mounts., Yarnell and 'Navsource' team, *Navsource Naval History, Photographic History of the U.S. Navy, 2003* www.navsource.org.

Sept. 27, 45 - There isn't anything to do on board here. All the men are loaded, 6,000 they say and at 4 p.m. they were to shove off. They changed it till 4:30 p.m. and finally took off at 6:15 p.m. There are four aircraft carriers around us in the harbor. We are going by way of Saipan[1] and have another APA boat following us with one boiler out and it can't go fast so that slows us up. They say now it's from 15-16 days. Rained at night. The chow has been very good.

USS Enterprise (Aircraft Carrier)

An example of a typical aircraft carrier it carried a compliment of 2,217 crewman (including the air wing), 90+ airplanes, had a maximum speed of 32.5 knots. It's armament consisted of 8 single 5"/38 mounts, 4 quad 1.1" 75 machine gun mounts and 24 - .50 cal. machine guns., Yarnell and 'Navsource' team, *Navsource Naval History, Photographic History of the U.S. Navy*, 2003, www.navsource.org.

1 - Part of the "Marianas Islands ....was garrisoned.....by....30,000 (Japanese) troops....US Marines landed on June 15, 1944.....July 9, 1944....the island was declared officially secured by the US forces. By the end of the battle, there were 3,500 US casualties. ...the civilian population of Saipan committed mass suicide by jumping off cliffs at Marpi Point or committing suicide with hand grenades in caves. An estimated 22,000 civilians died in the battle...", Justin Taylan, *Pacific Wrecks*, 2005, www.pacificwrecks.com.

Sept. 28, 45 - Called at 5 a.m. had inspection in morning. This Navy is very strict about some things. Sold cokes in morning but I didn't get any. Read most of morning. Not much room to move around or sit down even.

Sept. 29, 45 - Yesterday and today we moved our watches ahead for a half hour each time. Last night we had a small typhoon and the ship really tossed. A lot of the men got sick. I wasn't feeling too good but not sick. The other ship that was following us to Saipan we left this morning. It really slowed us up and about 7:30 a.m. we pulled away and are going pretty fast now. The weather is a lot better today but still quite rough. The compartments where we sleep are very hot though they have good ventilation. Saw a show which I stood up for about Bataan.

Sept. 30, 45 - Moved our watches ahead another half hour which makes two hours difference from Okinawa. We had a sermon at aft of ship in the morning. Had ice cream at night. Read a book. They say we should get there next Sunday. I see a lot of flying fish all over here. Yesterday made it one year I've been overseas.

Oct. 1, 45 - Around noon we had engine trouble and they stopped the ship for a while to fix it. Then just at dusk we came by a mine and after passing it we turned around and came back quite a ways from it and they fired a lot of rounds at it. It didn't go off but some say they hit and sank it. They had 20 mm and 40 mm firing. There were two good shows on but I didn't get a good enough place to see it. The meals are getting worse.

Oct. 2, 45 - This morning it was very cool out. We had a shower and at night about supper time it rained and got real cold. Don't know where we are as nobody has told us lately. Some say we dock Sunday. A fellow next to me is from Elmira. We go to Ft. Dix (New Jersey).

Oct. 3, 45 - Moved our watches a half hour ahead every day we've traveled so far. The World Series are on tomorrow as we haven't passed the International Date Line yet. Noon today we were at 169 degrees (this refers to the ships location - not the temperature) and in 24 hours had traveled 451 miles. 3,100+ miles to go yet at noon. The weather feels close to freezing outside and the ocean is very rough today. Slept and read all day.

Oct. 4, 45 - At 7:00 a.m. this morning the World Series started with Cubs winning 9-0. We will pass the International Date Line today some time and then it'll be Wednesday again. Very cold out again today.

Oct. 4, 45 - We passed the International Date Line sometime last night so today is again Thursday. It is cold and the wind blowing. The sea was a lot calmer though. Heard the World Series second game at 7:40 a.m. Won $5 on Detroit who won 4-1. Have a little sore throat and stayed below most of day. Read and slept. Have been lucky not to pull any details as yet. Most everyone has. We are over half way there now having gone over 3,000 miles and about 2,600 to go as of yesterday noon.

Oct. 5, 45 - It is still very cold out with the wind blowing. I stayed below all morning. The World Series started at 8 o'clock this morning which the Cubs won 3-0. It rained at noon. Have a sore throat and stayed in bunk most of morning. Had a pretty good supper. It rained again at night. Haven't been able to sleep hardly any the past few nights because we have set our watches ahead so far. Tonight we set it ahead one hour. Five and one-half hours difference so far. Went to sleep about 1 a.m.

Oct. 6, 45 - As usual, it rained and wind blowing. Not as cold as it has been though. The World Series started at 9 a.m. with the Tigers winning to even the series. This afternoon this ship got orders to dock at Seattle, Wash. instead of Frisco (San Francisco) because of the Third Fleet coming there. There is a lot of rumors as to when we get there but so far nothing is definite.

Oct. 7, 45 - Had a good breakfast this morning. Went to protestant services on the upper deck. Heard the series game at 9:30 a.m. as we set our watches another half hour last night. Detroit won 8-4. The weather is a lot better but cloudy and misty.

Oct. 8, 45 - Instead of Seattle we are now going to Tacoma, Washington and then to Ft. Lewis, Washington.[1] There was a very heavy fog all day and the water was calm. We went very slow as at noon we were only 200 miles off the coast. Turned our watches ahead a half-hour. Read "Canal Town".

Oct. 9, 45 - Today we came to the U.S.A. and it sure looked good. Went in Puget Sound and picked up a pilot to guide us. It is very foggy and about 10 a.m. we saw land through the fog. Then at about 3 p.m. we had it (land) on both sides and the fog cleared up a lot just misty. A flock of

---

1- "....Fort Lewis began as Camp Lewis in 1917....named after Meriwether Lewis of the Lewis and Clark expedition....At the conclusion of World War II, the northwest staging area of Fort Lewis became a separation center and discharged its first soldiers in November 1945.", John Pike, Military, *GlobalSecurity.org*, 2005, www.globalsecurity.org/military/facility/sheppard.htm.

Oct. 9, 45 (cont.) - birds followed us and we passed some small boats. We don't get off until tomorrow morning at 4:30 a.m. We aren't to Seattle as yet. We came in Tacoma just at dusk and small boats pulled us in to dock. A few people were there and they took a lot of pictures. We weren't expected until Friday. Stayed on board all night. Sent a telegram to Mary Alice. Went to bed at 2 a.m.

Two views of the "boat home"

Oct. 10, 45 - We unloaded in the morning and the Red Cross gave us milk and donuts. We unloaded fast off the ship and in to waiting trucks, all new ones and an awfully lot of them. Went to northeast Fort Lewis and they gave us barracks and told us the set up. We had tickets for a steak dinner but I went to the service club and ate. Had a wonderful dinner and bought everything there was. Went and filled out a clothing issue in afternoon and they give us only enough winter

Oct. 10, 45 (cont.) - clothing to get us to Ft. Dix, New Jersey,[1] one suit of o.d's.[2] Called up Mary Alice and also sent telegram home. She was waiting to go to the station when I called at 8 o'clock. She's coming here.

Oct. 11, 45 - I had it fixed up to see Mary in the service club. We weren't supposed to have any visitors here. Had our issue of clothing in the morning and went back to barracks, cleaned up and went to service club. Met Mary Alice. She'd had a hard time finding this place and had a girl, Virginia Russell with her. I went over to headquarters and tried to change my destination and get discharged here but they wouldn't let me. We were due to leave tomorrow morning at 9:30 but it is held over for 24 hours and I got a pass until tomorrow night. We went to Seattle where Virginia lives and Mary is staying. Went to the show and stayed at Virginia's house all night. She had a sailor with her who is stationed here.

Pass to Seattle, Washington

Oct. 12, 45 - Had a swell breakfast at Virginia's place and met her folks. Went down town in Seattle, looked around and went to a girl friend of Mary Alice. After staying there a while we went back in town and Virginia went to work. We ate supper and then saw "G.I. Joe" after

---

1 - "Construction began in June 1917, and on July 18 the War Department named the cantonment Camp Dix....(it) grew quickly and became the largest military reservation in the Northeast. On 8 March 1939, Camp Dix became Fort Dix as the installation became a permanent Army post. Fort Dix served as a reception and training center for men inducted under the draft of 1939. Ten divisions and many smaller units trained and staged here before entering the battlefields of World War II. At the end of the war, the reception center became the separation center, returning more than 1.2 million soldiers to civilian life." "Welcome to Fort Dix 'Home of the Ultimate Weapon", 2005, http://www.dix.army.mil/history/history.html

2 - an abbreviation for the common name used for the United States military uniform, which was an olive drab color - hence, o.d.'s

Oct. 12, 45 (cont.) - which we picked up Virginia again. Went sight seeing and then I had to come back so we went to the bus station. Mary is leaving tomorrow morning for home. Got back to camp about 1 a.m. and found out we were leaving at 9:30 a.m.

Oct. 13, 45 - After dickering around (slang for doing nothing but waiting around) all morning we finally left about 1 p.m. on the train which went very slow. Have a good Pullman car.

Oct. 14, 45 - As we woke up we were coming in (to) Spokane (Washington). We had just a short time here and I tried to get off to call Mary but they said there wasn't time, though we did finally stay there over a half hour but I couldn't get to call her. This almost brings this diary up to date and this is where I'm stopping as I only intended having it for over seas. Am glad I kept this to use in later years. Good bye diary.

Discharged October 23, 1945
Fort Dix Separation Center

SEPARATION QUALIFICATION RECORD

SAVE THIS FORM. IT WILL NOT BE REPLACED IF LOST sk 9

This record of job assignments and special training received in the Army is furnished to the soldier when he leaves the service. In its preparation, information is taken from available Army records and supplemented by personal interview. The information about civilian education and work experience is based on the individual's own statements. The veteran may present this document to former employers, prospective employers, representatives of schools or colleges, or use it in any other way that may prove beneficial to him.

1. LAST NAME—FIRST NAME—MIDDLE INITIAL: BATES JACK E.

2. ARMY SERIAL No.	3. GRADE	4. SOCIAL SECURITY No.
32 838 983	S Sgt	unknown

5. PERMANENT MAILING ADDRESS (Street, City, County, State): 303 Mill St Horse Heads NY Chemung County

6. DATE OF ENTRY INTO ACTIVE SERVICE	7. DATE OF SEPARATION	8. DATE OF BIRTH
27 Feb 43	23 Oct 45	11 May 23

9. PLACE OF SEPARATION: Fort Dix, New Jersey

MILITARY OCCUPATIONAL ASSIGNMENTS

10. MONTHS	11. GRADE	12. MILITARY OCCUPATIONAL SPECIALTY
3	Pvt	Basic Infantry (521)
4	Pfc	Rifleman (745)
9	Cpl	Student (629
16	S Sgt	Airplane Armorer and Gunner (612)

SUMMARY OF MILITARY OCCUPATIONS

13. TITLE—DESCRIPTION—RELATED CIVILIAN OCCUPATION

AIRPLANE ARMORER AND GUNNER

As armorer-gunner took care of all guns on the ship, and could handly any gun position, waist, turret, tail, belly, or nose guns. Flew 41 Combats missions on a B-24 with 5th Air Force in the Pacific. Awarded Air Medal with 3 Oak Leaf Clusters and 8 Battle Stars.

WD AGO FORM 100 JUL 1945
This form supersedes WD AGO Form 100, 15 July 1944, which will not be used.

Separation Papers

ENLISTED RECORD AND REPORT OF SEPARATION
HONORABLE DISCHARGE

1. LAST NAME - FIRST NAME - MIDDLE INITIAL	2. ARMY SERIAL NO.	3. GRADE	4. ARM OR SERVICE	5. COMPONENT
BATES JACK E	32 838 983	S-SGT	AAF	AUS

6. ORGANIZATION	7. DATE OF SEPARATION	8. PLACE OF SEPARATION
2ND BOMB SQ 22ND BOMB GP	23 OCT 45	SEP CTR FT DIX NJ

9. PERMANENT ADDRESS FOR MAILING PURPOSES	10. DATE OF BIRTH	11. PLACE OF BIRTH
303 MILL ST HORSEHEADS NY	11 MAY 23	HORSEHEADS NY

12. ADDRESS FROM WHICH EMPLOYMENT WILL BE SOUGHT	13. COLOR EYES	14. COLOR HAIR	15. HEIGHT	16. WEIGHT	17. NO. DEPEND.
SEE 9	BLACK	BROWN	5-4	120 Lbs.	0

18. RACE	19. MARITAL STATUS	20. U.S. CITIZEN	21. CIVILIAN OCCUPATION AND NO.
W	X SINGLE	YES	COST CLERK II 1-01.35

MILITARY HISTORY

22. DATE OF INDUCTION	23. DATE OF ENLISTMENT	24. DATE OF ENTRY INTO ACTIVE SERVICE	25. PLACE OF ENTRY INTO SERVICE
20 FEB 43		27 FEB 43	BINGHAMTON NY

26. REGISTERED	27. LOCAL S.S. BOARD NO.	28. COUNTY AND STATE	29. HOME ADDRESS AT TIME OF ENTRY INTO SERVICE
YES X	503	CHEMUNG CO NY	SEE 9

30. MILITARY OCCUPATIONAL SPECIALTY AND NO.	31. MILITARY QUALIFICATION AND DATE (marksmanship badges, etc.)
AIRPLANE ARMORER GUNNER 612	M1 CARBINE EXP 179 7-13-43 AAF TECH BADGE AR 600-80 1943

32. BATTLES AND CAMPAIGNS
AIR OFFENSIVE JAPAN BISMARCK ARCHIPELAGO CHINE LUZON NEW GUINEA RYUKYUS SOUTHERN PHILIPPINES WESTERN PACIFIC GO 33 WD 45 AS AMENDED

33. DECORATIONS AND CITATIONS
AIR MEDAL W/ 3 OAK LEAF CLUSTERS ASIATIC PACIFIC SERVICE MEDAL GOOD CONDUCT MEDAL PHILIPPINES LIBERATION RIBBON

34. WOUNDS RECEIVED IN ACTION NONE

35. LATEST IMMUNIZATION DATES				36. SERVICE OUTSIDE CONTINENTAL U.S. AND RETURN		
SMALLPOX	TYPHOID	TETANUS	OTHER	DATE OF DEPARTURE	DESTINATION	DATE OF ARRIVAL
30MAR44	23MAR44	30MAR44	NONE	29 SEP 44	WPTO	7 OCT 44
				27 SEP 45	US	10 OCT 45

37. TOTAL LENGTH OF SERVICE				38. HIGHEST GRADE HELD
CONTINENTAL SERVICE		FOREIGN SERVICE		
YEARS	MONTHS DAYS	YEARS	MONTHS DAYS	
1	7 15	1	0 12	S-SGT

39. PRIOR SERVICE NONE

40. REASON AND AUTHORITY FOR SEPARATION CONVENIENCE OF GOVERNMENT AR 615-365 15 DEC 44 AND RR 1-1 DEMOBILIZATION

41. SERVICE SCHOOLS ATTENDED	42. EDUCATION (Years)		
BUCKLEY FIELD, COLO. ACFT ARMAMENT 20 MAR 44 HARLINGEN, TEXAS AERIAL GUNNERY 27 MAY 44	Grammar 8	High School 4	College 0

PAY DATA

43. LONGEVITY FOR PAY PURPOSES	44. MUSTERING OUT PAY			45. SOLDIER DEPOSITS	46. TRAVEL PAY	47. TOTAL AMOUNT	NAME OF DISBURSING OFFICER
YEARS MONTHS DAYS	TOTAL	THIS PAYMENT					
2 8 4	$300	$100	NONE		$13.55	417.25	J HARRIS COL FD

INSURANCE NOTICE
IMPORTANT IF PREMIUM IS NOT PAID WHEN DUE OR WITHIN THIRTY-ONE DAYS THEREAFTER, INSURANCE WILL LAPSE...

48. KIND OF INSURANCE	49. HOW PAID	50. Effective Date of Allot.	51. Date of Next Premium Due	52. PREMIUM DUE	53. INTENTION OF VETERAN TO
Nat. Serv. U.S. Govt. None	Allotment Direct to Treasurer		EACH MONTH	Continue Discontinue	
X	X V.A.	31 OCT 45	30 NOV 45	6.50	X

54. REMARKS
LAPEL BUTTON ISSUED
ASR SCORE (2 SEP 45) 87
INACTIVE ERC FROM 20 FEB 43 TO 26 FEB 43

56. SIGNATURE OF PERSON BEING SEPARATED	57. PERSONNEL OFFICER (Type name, grade and organization - signature)
Jack E. Bates	J E WHITE JR CAPT A C

WD AGO FORM 53-55
1 November 1944

Separation/Discharge Papers

Discharge Papers

Honorable Discharge Certificate

THE LIST

Under the heading of "My Buddies in the Service", is a list of individually signed names replicated as best as possible. Included is a notation: "After I was through my missions at Clark Field I helped out at the mail tent while waiting to go home and these people I had sign my book from the mail tent." The blanks across from each name are due to either illegible handwriting or no entry. This list has been alphabetized.

NAME	CITY	STATE
Frank M. Adam	Winchester	Virginia
Bruce Ahrens		New York
Joe F. Allen	Albany	New York
Don Angle	Carrollton	Illinois
Robert Arand[1]	Cincinnati	Ohio
George T. Astereades	Phoenix	New York
Jack Baarstad	Valley City	North Dakota
Joseph P. Balmenti	Youngstown	Ohio (diary entry 08/27/45)
George Barnes Jr.	(Knoxville, Tennesee - NL - 04)	
Leonard Battaglia	Brooklyn	New York
Russel Batten	Ladd	Illinois
Karl Bednarik	Barberton	Ohio
(Genoa, OH - NL - 04)		
Charles Bell	Chicago	Illinois
R.F. Bennett	Oblong	Illinois
R. Bensall		Pennsylvania
Ralph Bergman	Boulder	Colorado
Stanley F. Bialecki Jr.	Racine	Wisconsin
Naldel O. Bier		New York
Lawrence Blais		New Hampshire
P.E. Boitano	San Francisco	California
James A. Borg	St. LaPorte	Indiana
R. L. Bork	Della	Wisconsin
C.R. Bowen	San Francisco	California
Royal Brantle	San Marcos	Texas
Gerald O. Brooks	Madero	California
Robert Brown		
Leo R. Brundshuk	Fremont	Oregon
(diary entry dated July 13, 45)		
J.H. Bushnel	Fort Lewis	Washington

1 - Paul Davies in letter to the author dated October 14, 2004 writes: "I did know Dick (Richard) Faletti....In regards to (the mission on) June 18th (45) I flew that day with Bob Arand and what was my most regular crew."

NAME	CITY	STATE
James Carder	Detroit	Michigan
Howard B. Carlisle	Spartanburg	South Carolina
William Carlson	Grosse Pointe	Michigan
Robert J. Carmen	Orange	Texas
James Canepa	Vineland	New Jersey
(diary entry 11/14/44 - deceased - NL)		
Arthur T. Challis	Salt Lake City	Utah
Arlington Charter	Oakland	California
Paul H. Combs	New Brunswick	New Jersey
(diary entry 08/21/45 - deceased - NL)		
Andy E. Comerford	St. Louis	Missouri
William Colsten[1]		Washington, D.C.
(deceased - NL)		
Roger W. Cook	Lynn	Massachusetts
William Cook	Fredonia	New York
Fred T. Conner	New York City	New York
Elwood L. Corsa Jr.	Cold Spring Harbor	New York
Bill Cortes	Middletown	New York
Willis E. Crisley	Peoria	Illinois
Ervin L. Curtis	Phoenix	Arizona
Arthur Dahl	Staughton	Wisconsin
Paul Davies	Waukesha	Wisconsin
(see Research Resources)		
John Davis	Highland Park	Michigan
Joseph Dicaro	New Brunswick	New Jersey
Thomas C. Die		Massachusetts
David Drewy		Wisconsin
George Drury	Chicago	Illinois (deceased - NL)
Myron Eckstein	Cleveland	Ohio
(Shaker Heights, OH - NL - 04)		
H. L. Edwards	Blanco	Texas
Harold Ernst	Forrest Hills	Pennsylvania
Eugene Eshelman	Paradise	Pennsylvania
Wesley Faist	Sacramento	California
Harry J. Falvey	Detroit	Michigan
Bob Farst	W. Manchester	Ohio
(Hamilton, OH - NL - 04)		
Robert L. Ficek	Dickinson	North Dakota

1 - William Colsten was the bombardier on Charles Mason's original crew. Mason, Charles, personal correspondence with author, September 2004.

NAME	CITY	STATE
Gene R. Fields	Lancaster	Ohio
James Ford Jr.	Clovis	New Mexico
(deceased - NL)		
Robert Frantz	Ferguson	Missouri
(deceased - NL)		
Al Freidman	Bronx	New York
Kenny Frontwine	Kansas City	Kansas
Patrick Gaffney	Akron	Ohio
Thomas H. Gallivan	Columbia City	Indiana
Thomas Gannon	Detroit	Michigan
Maurice L. Gardner	Revere	Missouri
George W. Garrett	Adamsville	Alabama
Stanley Garrison	Brooklyn	New York
Clyde L. Garruch	Columbus	Ohio
Donald Gow	Staten Island	New York
H.F. Gray	Portland	Oregon
B.L. Groeppen Jr.		Missouri
R.A. Hague	Camden	New York
(Rome, NY - NL - 04)		
Edward L. Hambrick		Virginia
Robert J. Hanley	Jersey City	New Jersey
Joseph Hargrove	(Conroe, TX - NL - 04)	
L. Hasty	Gadsden	Alabama
Willard Head	Pontiac	Michigan
(deceased - NL)		
Robert E. Hemberger	Greenville	Indiana
Henry E. Henrich	Farrell	Pennsylvania
(deceased - NL)		
Archie Henson	San Antonio	Texas
Saul C. Herman	Baltimore	Maryland
Sheldon M. Hodes	Chicago	Illinois
Robert P. Hoffman		
Benjamin Holden	Louisburg	North Carolina
(deceased - NL)		
George Howell		Georgia
John Hrehov		Ohio
Robert Hublitz	Richmond Hill	New York
Lee Hunter	Denton	Texas
John Ide	New Brunswick	New Jersey
(Santa Cruz, CA - NL - 04)		
Arthur N. Iseh	McGehee	Arkansas

NAME	CITY	STATE
Leonard Jackson (deceased - NL)	Port Arthur	Texas
Lyle W. Jackson	Eugene	Oregon
Bill Johnson[1] (deceased - NL)	Springfield	Ohio
Everett A. Johnson	Sioux City	Iowa
Charles Jones Jr.		
George Jones	Petersburg	Virginia
F.J. Kacar	Cleveland	Ohio
Charles Kanady[2]	Fairfield	Illinois
Albert Kaplan[3]	Norfolk	Virginia
Stanley W. Kave	Omaha	Nebraska
Ronald E. Keeley	Farrell	Pennsylvania
Norman L. King	Georgetown	Delaware
W.N. Kirkendall	Burlington	Colorado
Leo Kluczynski	Chicago	Illinois
Arthur Knuesen	Chicago	Illinois
J.M. Krantz	Raceland	Kentucky
Glenn Krueger	Menasha	Wisconsin
Russ Kulm	Jerome	Idaho
S.O. Kyle	Greenfield	Missouri
Joe Lanser	Lakewood	Ohio
Armond Lavadaun	Adams	Oregon
Chuck Lavoy	Brooklyn	New York
Roy C. Lehman	Elkhart	Indiana
Armil Lervis	Enid	Oklahoma
Milton Levine	New York	New York
James T. Little (deceased - NL)	Taylorsville	North Carolina
Henry Loiselle	Chelmsford	Massachusetts
John A. Lockridge	Hamilton	Alabama
Herman Longshore	East Orange	Nevada

1 - Bill Johnson was a gunner with Charles Mason's original crew., Mason, Charles personal correspondence with author, September 2004.

2 - In a letter to the author in October of 2004 Charles Kanady writes: "I worked in the office and scheduled the missions, along with the crew, and posted it on the board. I had very little contact with the crews. I enlisted on 8 Oct. 1942 and was discharged 5 Jan. 1946 at Jefferson Barracks, Mo. as a Sgt in the U.S. Air Force. I was a member of the 5th Air Force, 22nd Bomb Group, 2nd Bomb Squadron."

3 - Most probably the same person noted in diary on July 4, 1945 - as Caplin and Aug. 27, 1945 entry as Kaplin).

NAME	CITY	STATE
William P. Lopez	Arlington	Massachusetts
D.J. Lusignon	Port Arthur	Texas
W.C. Lynch	Detroit	Michigan
Joseph E. Marecha	Brooklyn	New York
J.R. Martin	W. Frankfort	Illinois
Remo Masciangelo (diary entry 09/14/45)	Detroit	Michigan
J.E. Mash	Chicago	Illinois
Charles Mason (see research resources)	Augusta	Maine
Jack Matthews	Kansas City	Missouri
Charles S. McCelland	Detroit	Michigan
Allen McCombs	Sumas	Washington
Harry M. McCully (deceased - NL)	Allison Park	Pennsylvania
William McKay	Danville	Virginia
N.C. McKensie	Fresno	California
Preston McReynolds	New Orleans	Louisiana
Edward Melle	Pittsfield	Massachusetts
Ernest V. Miller	Asheville	North Carolina
Floyd C. Miller	Candler	North Carolina
Lester E. Miller	Brooklyn	New York
Ferdinand Monus	Trenton	New Jersey
Wilson J. Moore		
Carl Morgan[1] (Cicero, NY - NL - 04)	Watertown	New York
Frank N. Morgan	Greensburg	Indiana
Robert C. Morrison (deceased - NL)	Lincoln	Nebraska
C.W. Morse	Waltham	Massachusetts
Jay L. Moss	Wichita Falls	Texas
Samuel Moss	Brooklyn	New York
Ralph Muchison		
Aaron Nail	McKinny	Texas
L. Napier	Memphis	Tennessee
W.L. Neely	Pittsburgh	Pennsylvania
C.C. Nicoloff	New Bedford	Massachusetts
John A. Norris		Tennessee

1 - Carl Morgan - passed away June 2, 2004. He was a Captain in the 22nd B.G., 2nd B.S. inducted into the service May 8, 1942 and discharged October 29, 1946., O'Brien, Yvonne personal correspondence with author, October 2004.

NAME	CITY	STATE
John Novicky	Red Bank	New Jersey
H.J. O'Connell, Jr.	Staten Island	New York
(see diary entry 09/14/45)		
Edward E. Offner	Erie	Pennsylvania
Walter Olsen	Hempstead	New York
William Parfitt	Shenandoah	Pennsylvania
(Longhorne, PA - NL - 04)		
Edward Peck		
W.B. Peterson	San Diego	California
(Martinez, CA - NL - 04)		
Lyle K. Plantin	Minneapolis	Minnesota
Robert Porter		Massachusetts
Ted A. Pozysk	Houston	Texas
(deceased - NL)		
Robert Read	San Jose	California
James Reiten	Toledo	Ohio
Glenn Remmer	Denver	Colorado
H.D. Richardson	Dallas	Texas
Ervin T. Riesz	Cincinnati	Ohio
Robert N. Roller	Cincinnati	Ohio
Alfons Rosenstrauss	Sydney	Australia
(North Bondi, Aust. - NL - 04)		
Edward Rosette	Denver	Colorado
Oscar Russell	Grand Prairie	Texas
Merle J. Sayer	Eldora	Iowa
H.W. Saunders		Oklahoma
F.C. Sepp	Elmhurst	New York
Sylvester M. Schreifels	St. Cloud	Minnesota
(Minn., MN - NL - 04)		
L. Schwartz	Elizabeth	New Jersey
Paul Shapiro[1]	Baltimore	Maryland
(diary entry 11/ 08/45)		
Ralph W. Shapman	Dallas	Texas
Clem Silvestro	New Haven	Connecticut
Alexander Sirkin	Miami Beach	Florida
Jack Slasson	Van Nuys	California
Carlton A. Smith		Wisconsin
James W. Smith	Oakboro	North Carolina
Harry Smith	St. Paul	Minnesota
Eugene P. Snook	Lewiston	Pennsylvania

1 - Mr. Bates notes: "met him at Owi – radio operator in my tent – nice fellow"

NAME	CITY	STATE
William P. Soeder	Cleveland	Ohio
(diary entry 07/19/45)	(Glendale, AZ - NL - 04)	
Lennart A. Soderling	Chicago	Illinois
Vincent Somma	Brooklyn	New York
Albert E. Songer [1]	Wichita	Kansas
(deceased - NL)		
Douglas Stallings	West Annapolis	Maryland
Michael Stanco	Oakville	Connecticut
(deceased - NL)		
Gilbert E. Stevens	Portland	Oregon
Wanetta Stevens		
Jess Steward	Valdosta	Georgia
Harold G. Stonick	Chicago	Illinois
Arnold Stoutland	Fargo	North Dakota
Stuart E. Strickler [2]	York	Pennsylvania
(deceased - NL)		
B.L. Stutler	Green City	Missouri
Dan Swierenga	Seattle	Washington
(deceased - NL - 04)		
Edwin L. Talashe	Detroit	Michigan
Harold Talley	Wilmington	Delaware
George J. Tasca	Dearborn	Michigan
Hal Taylor	Sacramento	California
William A. Walker	Purcell	Oklahoma
(deceased - NL)		
Thomas L. Warren	Pacoma	California
Irvin Weiss	Chicago	Illinois
Ed Wellman	Everett	Washington
F.P. White	Newark	Ohio
Jack B. Williams	El Paso	Texas
James Williams	Saginaw	Michigan
Robert Whitlaw	Richmond	Virginia
C.F. Woodard	Denver	Colorado
R. L. Von Petnold	Brooklyn	New York
Mario J. Zito	Detroit	Michigan
(Dresden, TN - NL - 04)		

1 - Albert Songer the radioman on Charles Mason's original crew. Mason, Charles personal correspondence with author, September 2004.

2 - Stuart Strickler was a gunner with Charles Mason's original crew. Mason, Charles personal correspondence with author, September 2004.

ODDS & ENDS

In the back of the diary are many interesting items and rather than "edit" these I include the following notations:

Won divisional championship while in infantry. (probably softball)

Only one in company to get expert on M-1 rifle, machine gun and carbine.

Places I Have Been:

San Antonio, Texas, The Alamo and some old places there.
San Francisco from the air. Saw a submarine, battleship, blimp and an aircraft carrier.
Saw the Sierra Nevadas and the Rocky Mountains. Saw Boulder Dam and Mt. Shasta from the air.
Went to Honolulu, Waikiki, Oahu, John Rodgers Field and saw Pearl Harbor from the air.
Went to Canton Island in the Phoenix Islands as stop over to Pacific.
Townsville, Australia, Garbutt Field.
New Guinea - Nadzab.
Netherlands East Indies, Owi.
Palau Islands - Anguar.
Philippines - Leyte, Tacloban.
Samar - Guiuan.
Manila - Clark Field - Bataan.
Morotai - down near Celebes.
Okinawa - up west coast.

Some places I have flown over:

Reno (NV), San Francisco (CA), Los Angeles (CA), Phoenix (AZ), Sacramento (CA), Las Vegas (NV), Eugene (OR). Flew over Loyalty Island and stopped at Nandi. Flew over New Caledonia and on to Townsville, Australia, then on to Nadzab, New Guinea. Went to Owi in Netherlands, East Indies. Went to Wewak on first mission in New Guinea. Palmyra in Hawaii, Phoenix Islands, Figi Islands, New Caledonia. In New Guinea - Port Moseby, Leahe (Lae), Finschafen. Netherlands, East Indies - Biak, Jaepon (Yapen), Morotai. Palau Island - Peleliu. Philippines - Davao, Mindanao, Manila, Corregidor, Bataan. Clark Field, Nichols Field, Nicholson, Neilson-Cebu, Negros and almost every island in Philippines. Formosa - all over it, China, Hong Kong - Canton. Morotai - Moluccas, Celebes, Borneo.

Overseas places I've been:

Oahu, Hawaiian Islands - Sept. 29 - Oct. 1, 1944
Canton, Phoenix Islands - Oct. 1-2, 1944
Nandi, Figi Islands - Oct. 3-5, 1944
Townsville, Australia - Oct. 5-9, 1944
Nadzab, New Guinea - Oct. 9-23, 1944
Owi, Netherlands East Indies - Oct. 23 - Dec. 3, 1944
Anguar, Palau Islands - Dec. 3 - Jan. 15, 1945
Tacloban, Leyte - Dec. 26 - 28, Feb. 12 - 14, 1945
Guiuan, Samar - Jan. 15 - April 7, 1945
Clark Field, Luzon - April 13 - Aug. 2, 1945
Morotai, Moluccas - June 23 - 30, 1945
Okinawa, Ryukus - Aug. 14 - Sept. 25 back to the states.

Service Record:

From Home to Fort Niagara, NY reception center on Feb. 27, 1943
From Fort Niagara, N.Y. to Camp Swift Texas, Infantry, 97th Division
Mar. 7 transferred from infantry to cadets
Went from Camp Swift, Texas to Sheppard Field, Texas on Oct. 18, 1943 was eliminated from cadets
From Sheppard Field to Buckley Field, (Denver) Colo., Dec. 3, 1943
From Buckley Field to Harlingen, Texas, March 27, (44)
From Harlingen to Lemoore Field, Calif., June 26, (44)
From Lemoore Field to Tonopah, Nev., June 14, (44)
From Tonopah to Hamilton Field, Calif., Sept. 15, (44)
From Hamilton to Fairfield-Suisun Field, Sept. 26, (44)
From Fairfield to Hawaii, John Rodgers Field, Sept. 29, (44)
Oct. 1st (44) went to Canton in Phoenix Islands.
Oct. 2nd (44) went to Nandi in the Figi Islands and passed the international date line so landed Oct. 3rd
Went to Townsville, Australia at Garbutt Field, Oct. 5, (44)
Went to Nadzab in New Guinea, Oct. 9, (44)
Went to Owi in 5th Air Force, Oct. 23, (44)
To Anguar in Palau Island, Dec. 3, (44)
To Samar, Guam, Jan. 15, (45)
To Clark, April 12, (45) Luzon
To Morotai June 23 - 30, (45)
To Okinawa Aug. 14, 1945
To States Sept. 27, 1945

Changes in Rank:

From Private, to Private First Class, Infantry - July 30, 43
From P.F.C. to Corporal - May 25, 44
started overseas flight pay in July 44
started overseas pay Sept. 29, 44
Got Sergeant rating Feb. 20, 1945, Samar
Staff Sergeant April 1st at Samar

Citations, Awards, Decorations:

Received wings at gunnery school on May 25, 1944
May 17, 1945 Air Medal by Brig. General Crabb
From May to July got 3 oak leaf clusters to air medal

Have campaign stars for:

New Guinea
Anguar, Western Pacific
Southern Philippines
Northern Philippines
China
Ryukyus

Buddies List:

The following were written in by Mr. Bates, in a section, under the heading of "My Buddies"

Staff Sergeant Walter Jascott - infantry - platoon Sergeant
Sergeant Clarence Arnold - infantry - section Sergeant roomed with him and his runner
1st Sergeant Copeland - infantry - 1st Sergeant of our company
Victor Barghi - in my machine gun squad
John Pashko - in my machine gun squad
Leonard Eggleston - in my machine gun squad
Staff Sergeant Deichberg - platoon Sergeant of no. 3 platoon
Sergeant Young - mortar section Sergeant
Warren Lannigan - in machine gun squad and was wounded in Italy and slept next to me
Larry Taylor - a Fin who was naturalized after entering the service - changed name (from) Lauri Tae Janla
Staff Sergeant Rhinehart - platoon Sergeant of 2nd

Buddies List: (cont.)

Cpl. Moralis - he's from New York City and a swell friend
Robert Berter - played on softball team. Went on three day pass with him
Arthur Deter - engineer in my crew
Joe Tosto - radio operator in crew
William Bridge - nose gunner and assistant radio operator
Richard Schoen - martin upper and assistant engineer
James Perry - tail gunner and my assistant
Robert Brodsky
Tallison
Summers
Dean

The following are written under the title "Fellow armour gunners"

Robert Davis - went around with him for over six months and a swell friend
Wallace Bragley - both (Robert Davis and Bragley) are from Utah
Pete Brenna - Arizona
Beverly Barton - Nevada and Ohio
Pete Antinello - Pennsylvania
Sgt. Bacon - Syracuse, N.Y.
Sgt. Barker
Kenneth Black
Donald Black
Delsburg - killed in action

These are written in at the bottom with a different pen

Capt. William R. Lee – commanding officer while in infantry
2nd Lt. Robert Greenlee - platoon leader
1st Lt. William Mc Andrews - company adjutant

Article(s) and letters, clipped from paper, sent home and pasted in diary (origin unknown but probably the local paper known as the Star-Gazette).

Newspaper article:

"BOMBERS SCORE BIG HITS ON MANILA'S CLARK FIELD

MacArthur's Headquarters, Philippines - (AP) - A smashing New Year's Day bombing of Manila's Clark Field by Leyte-based Liberators was reported from a Fifth Air Force advance base as Gen. MacArthur's stepped up air assaults brought Formosa into his communiqué today for the first time.

Fighter escorted Liberators of the veteran Red Raiders flew through intense anti-aircraft fire to spill bombs on the busiest airdrome in the Philippines. Many bombers were pierced by flak, but all returned.

The fighters tangled with Japanese interceptors in numerous dog-fights and at least two enemy aircraft were seen to go down."

Newspaper article:

"U.S. DAYLIGHT RAID SURPRISES JAP FIELD; 100 PLANES SMASHED

MacArthur's Headquarters, Philippines, Sunday - (AP) - Headquarters today reported a smashing daylight air raid on Clark Field, near Manila, in which the majority of 100 grounded Japanese planes were destroyed, and said also that U.S. Troops had completed the destruction of Nipponese in the bloody Ormoc Corridor of Leyte Island.

Liberator bombers operating from Leyte, made the Clark Field raid Friday, Philippine time.

It was the first daylight Liberator operation against that main Japanese air center in the Philippines and an Army spokesman said it was a first class surprise to the Nipponese, who got only nine of their fighters in the air to meet the assault.

Eight of the nine interceptors were shot down by the U.S. Thunderbolts. The dispersal and taxi areas between the two of the airstrips were left enveloped in fire and smoke. Liberator crews reported one tremendous explosion from which a smoke column rose 5,000 feet.

"U.S. DAYLIGHT RAID" (cont.)

General MacArthur announced the knocking out of another 20 Japanese planes and another probable in an attack on Clark Field near Manila on Tuesday, bringing the total in three days of raiding to 144. Where MacArthur will strike next in the Philippines naturally remained a closely-guarded military secret. However, the Japanese have been predicting that he will send invasion forces ashore on Luzon, site of the capital city of Manila.

Escorted American Liberators continued their almost daily raids on the network of airfields around Manila with two attacks Saturday and Sunday on Clark Field. Forty tons of bombs were dropped. Sunday when escorting fighters shot down 18 to 20 of 50 to 60 intercepting Japanese planes. One American plane was lost.

MacArthur's troops brought the Leyte campaign to a close Christmas Day with amphibious landing at Palompon, 15 miles northwest of Ormoc and the last port on the island still in Japanese hands, and at Puerto Bello, due west across Ormoc Bay from Ormoc."

Article from "Eclipse" newsletter:

"Cpl. Jack E. Bates, formerly of Dept. 273, was recently decorated with the Air Medal in recognition of courageous service to his combat organization. His mother, Mrs. Esther Bates, is in receipt of a letter signed by General George C. Kenney, Commander of the Far East Air Forces, which contained the following:

Your son was cited for meritorious achievement while participating in aerial flights in the Southwest Pacific Area from November 14, 1944 to December 26, 1944. He took part in sustained operational flight missions during which hostile contact was probable and expected. These flights included bombing missions against enemy installations, shipping and supply bases, and aided considerably in the recent successes in this theater.

You Mrs. Bates, have every reason to share our pride and gratification.

Also to share in General Kenney's pride are Mr. Bates brothers, Wellington Jr., (see photo next page) formerly of Dept. 273, and now in France, and another brother Robert, S 1/C, now serving with the Navy in the Philippines, and his father, Wellington, Sr. foreman of Dept. 17 (now Dept. 164)."

Wellington Bates, Jr. - Mr. Bates brother

Excerpt from letter (date unknown), published in the Star-Gazette, sent to his Mother while stationed in Texas in the Infantry.

"Dear Mom:

I hope you have a nice Mother's Day. I have it easy so far today. I got up at eight and went to chow and at nine went to chapel. It is a little after eleven now and almost dinner time. I have finally finished up on the range. We finished our machine gun marksmanship yesterday afternoon and I think next week we go on the combat range. I don't know exactly what that is but I think it's moving targets.

I have been pretty good in my shooting. There were only three of us who got expert on the machine gun and I was the only one who had expert on the machine gun and rifle both and that's something. It is a lot harder to shoot the machine gun. It really sounds off when you fire it, too. To qualify, one has to get 180 points, a first class gunner 200 points, and an expert is 218 points out of a possible 256. I got 226 which wasn't bad. That makes two medals I can wear now.

In Co. A there was a fellow who had just come off the rifle range last night and was cleaning his gun when it went off.

Letter home to Mother (cont.)

The bullet went through two barracks and hit a soldier who was walking in the street in the head. It killed him and I pity the officer who was supposed to inspect the rifles to see that they were empty. He'll probably become a private.

I got my cookies o.k. and also my cake which was really swell. It wasn't broken up at all either. Our Lieutenant came up in my room last night and had a piece of it and thought it was really good. He's a very nice officer.

I'm feeling fine here and if I have off next weekend, I think I'll go into town. That's about all for now. I suppose Pop (Wellington Sr.) is going to all the 'Pioneer' (a local semi-pro baseball team) games. Tell Robert if he gets a chance to send me the 'Sporting News' because I don't get a chance to see how the games are coming out.

I suppose school is almost over or getting close. I sure wish I was back in school and so will Robert, too. He had better finish it. If he doesn't like school, I don't know what he'll do here. We have to learn three times as much here as we did in school and in just a short time. School is easy to learn compared to learning here. No one comes around and sees that you learn it. Either you learn it or else you don't, and I pity someone who doesn't when he goes across. If you don't learn it here, it might cost you your life, so you learn it......."

Newspaper article - letter excerpted from Star-Gazette:

"Interesting reactions to the news of the surrender of Japan and the end of the war are contained in these letters from S/Sgt. Jack E. Bates son of Mr. and Mrs. W. E. Bates of Mill Street............"

The letter from Sgt. Bates, written on August 15, 1945 follows: (handwritten in) "I was at Motabu, Okinawa"

"I suppose you, along with everyone else, are enjoying this day which is supposed to be the day of peace. I'd give just about everything to be there with you.

Through you all probably celebrated a lot more than we did here, we did not do anything different from any other day. The fellows here had more to be thankful for that there is peace because they or most of them had more at stake and it meant a safe way home again. There were doubts in

Newspaper article – letter excerpted from Star-Gazette: (cont.)

the fellows minds whether everything was entirely through and a lot, including myself, expected to still see it go on in some places. I only wish I could write further on this but maybe you will read something in the papers.

This peace, though I'm very happy over it, has done a lot to prolong my stay over here. In fact, I don't know how long it will be before I can go home, but I figure it'll be at least another two months. At present I'm just about ready to sweat out being home around Christmas. That is kind of hard to take when if everything had gone right in the first place, I could have and should have been enjoying the peace back there in America.

Maybe you notice my new APO number on the address. As you know that means I've moved again and this time it's out of the Philippines. Until a few more days this is all I can say, but will let you know more about it later."

POEMS

The following poems were written down in the back of the diary. I felt it important to include these, as I believe they reflect not only the thoughts and feelings of Mr. Bates but possibly all those who served.

Untitled

Ye heroes of the sky behold
Your irresistible so I'm told.
Each one is worthy his weight in gold
Fiddlesticks!

Ye combat men your furlough get
You'll get your time and go home yet.
You think so huh? You wanta bet.
We'll see.

A quart of whiskey'll do the trick
They'll give you points and make them stick
But once you stop. Alas a lack
No kidding.

Just cast your troubles to the wind
And sweat this blasted war to end
You may go home but not till then.
I'm thinking.

I'm disillusioned, empty breasted
For what I think, I'd be arrested.
I'm "P.O. ed" morbid and disgusted
Yeah, damn it.

Even the lowly vulture fly
So can new men, so let them try.
And send us home or tell us why.
How about it?"

(author unknown)

A note attached reads: "Note Remember after we were in the 2nd Bomb Squadron for a couple of months or so and the squadron was short of crews because so many went home after finishing their missions that the commander put out an order that the system in force to finish their missions was canceled and you had to fly until further notice. Someone put this poem on the bulletin board and I copied it. Jack"

Don't Quit

"When things go wrong as they sometimes will;
When the road you're trudging seems all up hill;
When the funds are low and the debts are high,
And you want to smile, but you have to sigh;
When care is pressing you down a bit,
Rest, if you must, but don't quit.

Life is queer with its twists and turns,
As every one of us some time learns,
And many a failure turn about
When he might have won had he stuck it out.
Don't give up, though the pace seems slow -
You may succeed with another blow.

Success is failure turned inside out -
The silver tint of the clouds of doubt -
And you never can tell how close you are -
It may be near when it seems so far.
So stick to the fight when you're hardest hit;
It's when things seem worse that you must not quit!"

(author unknown)

The 2nd Squadron Sad Sack

"Two zekes came in at ten o'clock
He flipped the switches and grabbed the stock
The nips came on at terrific speed
So he tried them out with a one rod lead.

Closer and closer these zeros came.
Oh!! Here was a chance to earn his fame.
He squeezed the triggers and heard the roar.
But the light was bad and his aim was poor.

He could tell at a glance they had called his bet.
For they still came on and he started to sweat.
He cut his lead in half again
With a ten round burst he poured em in.

The 2nd Squadron Sad Sack (cont.)

The sky was filled with a big loud boom.
And another nip had met his doom.
He watched it spiral into the sea.
It made quite a splash an occasion to see.

The bomber turned homeward as it swept along.
His heart was filled with a joyous song.
For he'd made a name for himself today.
He was feeling high and was pretty gay.

The bomber got home and though it was late
They called the crew to interrogate
He told his story and he told it straight
He couldn't help feeling his life was great.

Then the captain with a hot retort
Calmly handed him the flight report
He read it through with an awful shock.
Twenty claims for a zeke at ten o'clock

He left the room with his spirit low
For he'd just received an awful blow.
This was the end of his four hour fame
Twenty men got credit for one damn plane."

(author unknown)

A note is attached to the diary which reads: "<u>Note</u> Remember the raids at Clark Field we made and Perry shot a Zero down after he shot out our #3 engine the day after Christmas 1944. When we got back to Anguar in the Palau Islands and about twenty people tried to get credit for the four Zeros we shot down that day. Well, I copied this poem from our squadron bulletin board a few days later. Jack"

Soldier Longing

"When he comes home, and soon I pray.
Will come to all that happy day,
I'm sure he'll want to see.
The old home as it used to be.
His room, his pictures on the wall.
And Ma and me not changed at all.

When all the battle flags are furled.
He'll want the same old little world
That once he knew. He'll look to find
The things he long has kept in mind.
The shops, the church, the people good.
That long made up his neighborhood.

Tis not some visionary scheme.
However noble it may seem.
He longs for now, so far away,
But for those joys of yesterday:
The home he had and wants to see.
Just as it was Mom and Me."

(author unknown)

The Humble Prayer

"What does a soldier pray for
As he lowers his head in his pew?
He prays for simple, earthly things
Taken for granted by many like you

He prays for his dearly beloved ones,
Mom and Dad, sweet Sis and Drake,
Their faces appear before him -
He feels his heart will break.

He dare not look about him
As his eyes begin to burn,
For only a lonely soldier
Can know what it means to yearn.

The Humble Prayer (cont.)

He prays for the church in the valley,
With the wisteria over the gate;
He prays for the old-fashioned garden
Where loved ones silently wait.

He prays for the return of those Sundays
The Sundays now out of his span.
When life had a glorious meaning
And the future was his to plan.

He prays for friends across the sea,
For they too are so weary of strife,
They have had enough of ships and planes
And long for a peaceful life.

He prays for an end to this conflict,
And the thought of a world rid of war
Gives new hope to the forlorn soldier,
And his spirits hasten to soar.

For although he cannot cease yearning,
And his heart is still filled with pain,
The thoughts of future of freedom
Will suffice, for him to sustain.

Oh, I know that the Lord in His heaven,
His heaven so wondrous up there,
Will look down on this humble soldier
And hear his humble prayer."

(author unknown)

Since Time Began

"Since time began -
One heart has shared
The troubles of the world;
Tho sword and shield they carry not
Nor battle flags unfurled.

Since Time Began (cont.)

Since time began -
They sent their sons
To lands across the sea.
They send a heart of courage
To console a heart that's free.

Since time began -
I wonder who's the greatest of them all;
The strong and gallant warrior
Who stands while others fall?

Somehow I think -
Since time began -
By the valiant, hopeful Mother
Ever longing for her son."

(author unknown)

Untitled

"In a moment of darkest peril,
In our land's most dire need,
Who answered the call of battle?
Who answered with valorous deed?

Who back at the very beginning
When the odds against us were great,
Who with the other guy winning
Fought back with his hands and his hate?

Who blazed a glorious trail,
In those first dark days of war,
Who first trod the road to victory
And started to even the score?

Who fought from the very beginning
Till the day of victory is reckoned?
These questions are needlessly asked;
the FIGHTING 22nd!"

George L. Virgin

THE 22nd BOMB GROUP & 2nd BOMB SQUADRON

This work would not be complete without some information concerning the unit that Mr. Bates was assigned to - The 22nd Bomb Group and 2nd Bomb Squadron.[1]

"April 12, 1945 - Cincinnati Enquirer - Japs Know the Red Raiders! - Bombardment Group Makes History in Pacific With Long String of Firsts.

Washington, April......Maybe you haven't heard of the Red Raiders. But thousands of them looked up too late to see the bombs falling.

Formally, the Red Raiders are the 22nd Bombardment Group of the U.S. Fifth Air Force. The long story of their operations in the Southwest Pacific just released contains a string of "firsts" as long as a Liberator's fuselage.

Latest of the list, the Raiders were the first land-based Army bombers to hit Formosa from the Pacific side. They left Heito Air Base in flames. That was the day after their leader, Col. Richard W. Robinson of Wilkinsburgh, Pa., was killed in a take-off crash at a Philippines base.

It was from Robinson, a full colonel at 26, that the Raiders took their name, a tribute to his flaming red hair. Their insignia is a red-maned Viking warrior.

In 1940 the new 22nd took B-26's directly from the assembly lines and were the first unit equipped with them. On the day after Pearl Harbor they were on their way to Australia--which they reached in January 1942.

They were the first medium bomber unit to hit Rabual, New Britain, where they braved swarms of Jap interceptors and the fire of 100 flak ships. They got a presidential citation about this time.

The first fully armed bombardment unit to span the Pacific, the 22nd sent some planes into the battle of Midway. Four of their bombers were the first Army mediums to be used for torpedo bombing.

---

1 - "The 22nd Bomb Group was based at Mitchell Field, Long Island, New York in 1940 prior to movement to its permanent stateside base at Langley Field, Virginia in November, 1940. The 22nd Bomb Group consisted of the 2nd, 19th, 33rd and 408th Bomb Squadrons. The 2nd Bomb Squadron was activated at Bolling Field, Washington, D.C. until it was moved to Langley Field on November 13, 1940. The 22nd's first overseas base was at Townsville, Australia". Lawrence Hickey, The 22nd Bombardment Group in World War II, Volume III, Photo Supplement, ed. Don Evans (Bonsall, California: Alliance Business Services, 2001), 3 & 23

They helped to knock out that big Japanese convoy of 22 ships in the Bismarck Sea and worked their way up New Guinea coast over such historic targets as Buna, Lae, Salamua, Finschafen, Wewak and Wakde.

These were replaced by the long-range Mitchell B-25's, and the Raiders were the first group to fly that type of bomber in combat. They didn't lose a plane. Jumps between targets became even longer and the Raiders switched to Liberators (B-24's) and thus became the first to have flown three types of bombers in combat.

They were the first to hit Palau in daylight hours, first to hit the Philippines, and the first B-24's in action against Clark Field, Manila and Corregidor in the Philippines.

Meantime they took part in a two-day strike which knocked out oil refineries at the "Ploesti of the Pacific" at Balikpapan on Borneo.

Operating now from the Philippines, the Red Raiders are commanded by Lt. Col. Leonard T. Nicholson, an original member of the squadron, from Prescott, Ariz.

The ambition of the Red Raiders now, naturally, is to be the first Pacific-based Liberator unit to hit Tokyo." - contributed by Richard Faletti - January, 2001

The 15th annual reunion, 22nd Bomb Group, Park Sheraton Hotel, New York City; July 25, 1964....Mr. Bates is seated third from the right, front row

The 22nd Bomb Squadron "Red Raiders" adopted an emblem "The Viking" that was used to identify the squadron. This insignia was often used as patches on their flight jackets, attached to equipment bags (see diary entry dated Aug. 29, 1945) and more popularly painted on many of the squadron's planes.

An example of the Red Raider shield
painted on a squadron B-24

22nd B.G. patch worn by Mr. Bates

The 2nd Bomb Group adopted an emblem to signify their squadron, as well - the Peyote Bird. This emblem was most commonly employed as a patch on the individuals' flight jackets.

2nd Bomb Squadron insignia - CK

Unidentified crewman next to a signpost showing
the insignias of the 22nd Bombardment Group
Top left - 408th Bomb Squadron, Top right 19th Squadron
Bottom left – 2nd Bomb Squadron, Bottom right – 33rd Bomb Squadron

MEMORABILIA

Mr. Bates left a large collection of memorabilia concerning his service in WW II. All of the following memorabilia belong to his son Ken. I was assisted in the identification of some of the memorabilia as indicated.

Patches/Medals

Fourth Air Force - unit charged with defense of the West coast of the United States - TW

The Fifth Bomber Command - unit charged with combat in the South West and Western Pacific Theaters - TW

Army Air Corp - TW

China, Burma, India Patch - TW

Pacific Ocean Area patch of the Overall Coordination Command - TW

Army Air Corp Aviation Cadet Patch

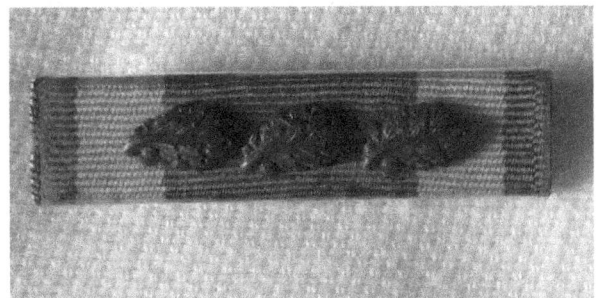
Air Medal Ribbon w/Three Oak Leaf Clusters signifying the awarding of four total medals - TW

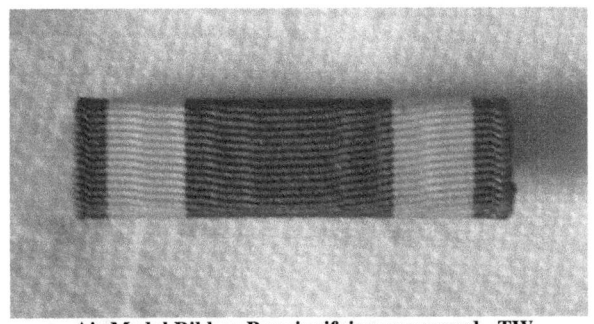
Air Medal Ribbon Bar signifying one award - TW

Good Conduct Ribbon awarded for, at least, three years of honorable service - TW

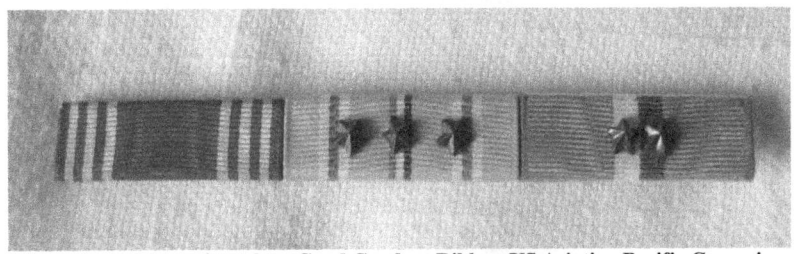
Ribbon Bar - shown in order - Good Conduct Ribbon US Asiatic - Pacific Campaign w/ 3 battle stars and the Philippines Liberation Medal with 2 battle stars - TW

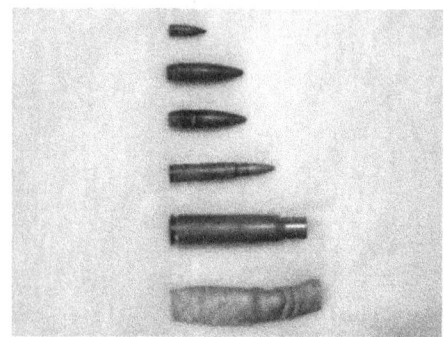
Shell casings and shells - origin unknown

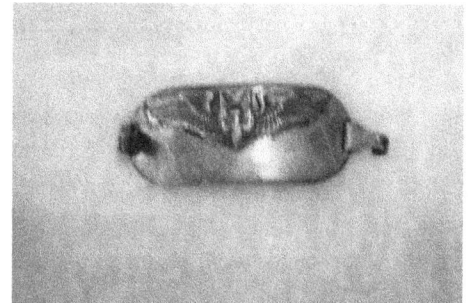
Bracelet with Aerial Gunner Wings insignia
Wore specifically by gunners to identify
them from other Air Corp personnel - TW

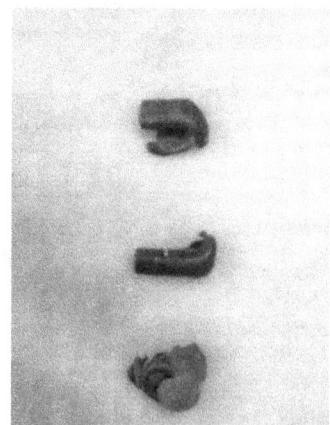
Shell fragments - origin unknown

Language guide for the Philippines

Hand sewn sash - origin unknown

GENERAL HEADQUARTERS
SOUTHWEST PACIFIC AREA
OFFICE OF THE COMMANDER-IN-CHIEF

PROCLAMATION

TO THE PEOPLE OF THE PHILIPPINES

Whereas, the military forces under my command have landed on Philippine soil as a prelude to the liberation of the entire territory of the Philippines; and

Whereas, the seat of the government of the Commonwealth of the Philippines has been re-established in the Philippines under President Sergio Osmena and the members of his cabinet; and

Whereas, under enemy duress a so-called government styled as the "Republic of the Philippines" was established on 14 October 1943 based upon neither the free expression of the peoples' will nor the sanction of the Government of the United States, and is purporting to exercise Executive, Judicial and Legislative powers of government over the people.

Now therefore, I, Douglas MacArthur, General, United States Army, as Commander in Chief of the military forces committed to the liberation of the Philippines, do hereby proclaim and declare:

1. That the government of the Commonwealth of the Philippines is, subject to the supreme authority of the Government of the United States, the sole and only government having legal and valid jurisdiction over the people in areas of the Philippines free of enemy occupation and control;

2. That the laws now existing on the statute books of the Commonwealth of the Philippines and the regulations promulgated pursuant thereto are in full force and effect and legally binding upon the people in areas of the Philippines free of enemy occupation and control; and

3. That all laws, regulations and processes of any other government in the Philippines than that of the said Commonwealth are null and void and without legal effect in areas of the Philippines free of enemy occupation and control; and

I do hereby announce my purpose progressively to restore and extend to the people of the Philippines the sacred right of government by constitutional process under the regularly constituted Commonwealth Government as rapidly as the several occupied areas are liberated and the military situation will otherwise permit; and

I do enjoin upon all loyal citizens of the Philippines full respect for and obedience to the constitution of the Commonwealth of the Philippines and the laws, regulations and other acts of their duly constituted government whose seat is now firmly re-established on Philippine soil.

DOUGLAS MacARTHUR,
General, U.S. Army,
Commander in Chief.

Proclamation issued to the Philippines people by General Douglas MacArthur, upon the liberation of the Philippines, by American forces.

MESSAGE TO THE PEOPLE OF THE PHILIPPINES FROM PRESIDENT OSMEÑA

MY BELOVED PEOPLE:

By the Grace of God, and by the honor of America, I am again with you. Happy as I am to be back on Philippine soil, I am sad that our late and beloved President Quezon is not here to witness the realization of the great cause to which he dedicated his life — the independence of the Philippines. I know, however, that you feel as I do, that he is here with us in spirit, to unite our people and to encourage us toward the achievement of the vital undertaking which lies ahead.

General MacArthur and I have returned together to accomplish a common objective: to restore to our people peace and prosperity, freedom and happiness. We were enjoying these blessings of democracy under the benevolent guidance of the United States when the enemy wantonly attacked us, interrupting our steady progress toward complete nationhood. This enemy is still on Philippine soil. It is thus our immediate purpose to destroy his power and to expel him from our country.

Primarily, this task belongs to the armies of freedom which are now, as during the fateful days of December, 1941, under the able leadership of General Douglas MacArthur, who is assisted by competent generals and admirals. With him are the brave soldiers, sailors, marines, and airmen of America and soldiers of our own race who have come to sacrifice their lives, if need be, so that Japan may be vanquished and the enslaved may be free again. No one, I believe, is better qualified than General MacArthur to accomplish this, for even during the dark period of the war, he had faith in the ability of the United States to obtain ultimate victory over the enemy in the Philippines. This view I shared with him. From what I have seen with my own eyes I can assure you that, as pledged by President Roosevelt, General MacArthur has at his disposal the men and resources needed to deal the enemy a mortal blow.

But it must be realized that the liberation of the Philippines is a joint enterprise which can only be speedily and thoroughly accomplished with the wholehearted support of our people. You in your homes, in the towns, in the barrios, in the mountains, whether or not you belong formally to the underground must do your part in accordance with the directives which the leaders of the underground and the guerrillas will receive from General MacArthur. You must do your utmost, as did your sons and brothers on Bataan and Corregidor, in Cebu and throughout our beloved land.

As the enemy is progressively driven out and order is restored in our country, so will the normal functions of civil government be resumed in the liberated areas. In my capacity as the head of the Philippine Commonwealth I will as promptly and effectively as possible direct the restoration of the democratic functions of government in the administration of the nation, the provinces and the municipalities. But I did not come back to the Philippines merely to see the reestablishment of the constitutional government which existed here before Pearl Harbor.

During the time that our government was compelled, by circumstances, to carry on in Washington, first under the leadership of President Quezon, and then under mine, it expanded the scope of its activities to include some of the prerogatives possessed only by independent nations. For the American Government did not only recognize the Commonwealth Government as the lawful government of the Filipino people, but also gave it the consideration accorded to governments of countries possessing the attributes of absolute sovereignty.

This more advanced government is the one which I have brought back to you. It is even more than that. We have the word of America that our country which has been ravaged by the war will be reconstructed and rehabilitated. Steps have already been taken to this end. With the return of normal conditions, law and order will be fully reestablished and democratic processes of constitutional government restored.

Letter to the people of the Philippines from their President

**HEADQUARTERS
ALLIED AIR FORCES
SOUTHWEST PACIFIC AREA**
OFFICE OF THE COMMANDER

March 10, 1945.

Dear Mrs. Bates:

Recently your son, Corporal Jack E. Bates, was decorated with the Air Medal. It was an award made in recognition of courageous service to his combat organization, his fellow American airmen, his country, his home and to you.

He was cited for meritorious achievement while participating in aerial flights in the Southwest Pacific Area from November 14, 1944 to December 26, 1944.

Your son took part in sustained operational flight missions during which hostile contact was probable and expected. These flights included bombing missions against enemy installations, shipping and supply bases, and aided considerably in the recent successes in this theatre.

Almost every hour of every day your son, and the sons of other American mothers, are doing just such things as that here in the Southwest Pacific Area.

Theirs is a very real and very tangible contribution to victory and to peace.

I would like to tell you how genuinely proud I am to have men such as your son in my command, and how gratified I am to know that young Americans with such courage and resourcefulness are fighting our country's battle against the aggressor nations.

You, Mrs. Bates, have every reason to share that pride and gratification.

Sincerely,

GEORGE C. KENNEY,
Lieutenant General, U. S. A.,
Commander.

Mrs. Esther Bates,
303 Mill Street,
Horseheads, New York.

Commendation letter

B-24 NOSE ART

These photo's of B-24 Nose Art are included in one of Mr. Bates scrapbooks with the notation "Pictures painted on our planes and planes based with us".

#44 - 40328, 8th A.F., 391st B.S.

#44 – 50768, 5th A.F., 43rd B.G., 403rd, B.S.

#44 - 40399, 5th A.F., 43rd B.G., 65th B.S.

#42 - 11019, 5th A.F., 22nd B.G., 33rd B.S.

#44 - 40402, 5th A.F., 22nd B.G., 33rd B.S.

#44 - 49827, 5th A.F., 43rd B.G., 65th B.S.

MEMORIAL

As I mentioned earlier and you have noted I attempted to find information concerning the people, places and events that Mr. Bates mentions in his diary. Little did I know that when I started researching the entry dated September 15, 1945 concerning Bryce Hardiman would I find such a treasure trove of information that I feel must be shared:

Bryce Edward Hardiman, was born April 6, 1924, son of Mr. & Mrs. Francis Hardiman. His family, before his entry in the service, lived on the corner of John's Street and Grand Central Avenue, in Horseheads, NY. Bryce and his family were known, not only by Mr. Bates, but many other people in the Horseheads area. He attended Horseheads High school and quit school to enlist in the Marines.[1] Bryce saw action with the Sixth Marine Division where he was a listed as a PFC in the 22nd Regiment, 1st Battalion, A company. He was KIA (killed in action) on May 30, 1945 when we was fighting on Okinawa.[2] Bryce was originally wounded by a grenade and as he was being carried to the rear on a stretcher; he and the stretcher bearers were hit by another grenade killing Bryce and one of the bearers.[1] Bill Pierce, a member of the 6th Marine Division, and who hosts a web site of the same name notes: "May 30th the regiments reached the outskirts of the capital city, Naha. I was WIA (wounded in action) on May 29th with a recon company who was up at the waters edge at night. Bryce had to be killed in the outskirts of Naha.....The division cemetery is gone since 1946 or so. Parents were given the choice of home internment or the Punch Bowl in Hawaii.[3] He was originally buried in the Sixth Marine Division Cemetery noted by Mr. Bates in his diary entry of September 9, 1945. Sometime later he was removed and brought home by his family where we was buried on April 22, 1949 in Woodlawn National Cemetery (veterans area - burial plot G O 4994) in Elmira, NY.

1 - Frost, Al in phone correspondence with author, 2003

2 - Hayes, Karen e -mail correspondence with author, September 2004

3 - Pierce, Bill e-mail correspondence with author, September 2004

A plaque, in tribute to Bryce, is located at the Horseheads Historical Society, Horseheads, NY.

The plaque has a picture of Bryce centered around the following (on the right hand side) it reads: "Presented to Horseheads American Legion Post 0442 April 22, 1999. Commemorating 50 years for 19 Horseheads Legion Members, who on the date each year place flowers on Bryce Hardiman's grave # 4994 U.S. War Veterans Cemetery, (Woodlawn National Cemetery), Elmira, NY. Also, sent corsage to (his) mother for Mother's Day, a gift to (his) Dad F. Raymond Hardiman for Father's Day until their death. (With) each gift a card from "Bryce's Buddies". On the left of the plaque (a list of Bryce's buddies): 50 Year Vow Donald Ball, Robert Comfort, Howard Colwell, Walter Cuyle, Carlton Edger Sr., Judson Eisenhart, Allen F. Frost, Stan Kowalski, James Lynch, Harold Messing, Grover Mott, John P. Murphy, Harry Noble, George Prindible, Frank Slavin, Fred Swartwood, Irving Treat, Charles Bater, Joseph Zeigler. Other donors: Donald Brown, William Jansen Sisters: Catherine Bush "Burt", Elizabeth Kocourek "Joe"

PFC. Bryce Edward Hardiman

(photo provided by Patty Bachman of the Horseheads Historical Society)

IN TRIBUTE

The poem "In Flanders Fields" is probably the most famous poem to come out of either WWI or WW II.

Flanders is the name of the whole western part of Belgium. This area saw bloody and continued fighting during WW I (1914-1918). Despite the fact this area saw four major battles neither army was able to advance. This area became a killing field scarred by trenches and dotted with thousands of bomb craters. Conditions among the trenches were unimaginable with the living laying amongst the dead. Statistics vary but for both sides of this conflict loses amounted close to 1 million casualties.

The poem, originally known as "We Shall Not Sleep" was written by Canadian Army physician John McCrae, as a result of his young friends and formers student death during the battle of Ypres, in the spring of 1915. Killed by a shell burst his remains were scattered all over the place. Soldiers gathered the remains and put them in sand bags which was laid on sand bags and closed with safety pins.

McCrae, greatly effected by this death, sat down the next evening and composed "In Flanders Field". Sitting on the rear step of an ambulance; it took him all of twenty minutes to scribble the fifteen lines in a notebook.

Surprisingly, the poem was very nearly not published. Not satisfied with the results he threw the poem away. A fellow officer retrieved the poem and sent it to newspapers in England. *The Spectator,* in London, rejected it and sent the poem back, but *Punch* published it on December 8, 1915.

I remember, as a young boy, listening to my father recite the poem word for word. I was greatly impressed with the words and meaning of the poem and determined to memorize the poem as well. It didn't take me long and I could recite the poem word for word.....the only poem I have ever memorized.

I believe this poem a fitting tribute to all of those who have given their lives for our county.

In Flanders Fields

By: Lieutenant Colonel John McCrae, MD (1872-1918)
Canadian Army

"IN FLANDERS FIELDS the poppies blow

Between the crosses row on row,

That mark our place; and in the sky

The larks, still bravely singing, fly

Scarce heard amid the guns below.

We are the Dead. Short days ago

We lived, felt dawn, saw sunset glow,

Loved and were loved, and now we lie

In Flanders fields.

Take up our quarrel with the foe:

To you from failing hands we throw

The torch; be yours to hold it high.

If ye break faith with us who die

We shall not sleep, though poppies grow

In Flanders fields."

LEST WE FORGET

Jack Bates gravesite
Woodlawn National cemetery
Elmira, NY

Bryce Hardiman gravesite
Woodlawn National cemetery
Elmira, NY

September 1, 2011 - 10th Year Remembrance of September 1, 2001 - Horseheads, NY

BIBLIOGRAPHY

Written Resources:

Ambrose, Stephen. The Wild Blue, The Men and Boys Who Flew the B-24's Over Germany. New York: Simon and Schuster, 2001.

Gunston, Bill. The Illustrated Directory of Fighting Aircraft of World War II. London: Salamander Books Ltd., 2002.

Hickey, Lawrence Edited by Col. Don L. Evans, USAF (Ret.). The 22nd Bombardment Group in World War II, Volume III, Photo Supplement - 1941-1945. © 22nd BG Association, Huntsville, Alabama, March 2001. For distribution to 22nd Bombardment Group veterans and their families

Mason, Charles, Secretary - Editor. 2nd Bomb Squadron Newsletter December 2001.

RESEARCH RESOURCES

References to written/oral correspondence, personal research noted as follows:

Bates, Ken son of Jack Bates, of Erin, NY. Personal correspondence with author.

Bates, Robert the brother of Jack Bates. He quit school in the eighth grade and worked at the Eclipse, Elmira Heights, NY with Jack, their brother Wellington Jr. and their father Wellington Sr. He was drafted in to the Navy in March of 1943. He served on APA # 44 (Attack Transport) USS Fremont. Among many of the engagements he served in was the invasion of Leyte/Luzon, Iwo Jima and Saipan. He was discharged in March of 1945.

Bates, Louise - wife of Jack Bates, personal interview with author in 2005.

Benesh, Joe via telephone, 2003. Joe Benesh now lives in Penn Yan, NY.

Cucurullo, Constantino "Cookie" via e-mail, December 2001. A gunner in the 22nd Bomb Group, 2nd Squadron. He flew four missions with Mr. Bates.

Dilworth, Bonnie and Jason - 90th Bomb Group historical information via e-mail, May 15, 2005

Davies, Paul, via letters to the author, October 2004. Davies of New Port Richey, Florida entered the Aviation Cadet Program on February 22, 1943 and was commissioned a 2nd Lt. on February 8, 1944. Flew twin engine Beechcraft bombardier training planes at Roswell, New Mexico until December 1944 when he was sent over seas and assigned to the 22nd Bomb Group, 2nd Bomb Squadron. He did not have a regular crew and flew as co-pilot on an as needed basis. Records show he flew with Mr. Bates on the June 20, 1945 mission to Shinchiku, Formosa.

Evans, Don, Col. USAF (deceased), via e-mail, February 2003. Don graduated from Hollywood High School, California in January of 1941. Directly afterwards he entered UCLA. While attending college he joined ROTC and worked at Lockheed building P-38's. Don joined the Army Air Corps on September 10, 1942 as an aviation cadet. He was called up in March of 1943. In January of 1944, he graduated from Ellington Field, Texas and was commissioned a 2nd Lieutenant. He flew fifty-two

Evans, Don (cont.) - missions, as a navigator, with the 408th Squadron of the 22nd Bomb Group. He returned home, as a Captain, October of 1945. He left the service in January of 1946 but remained on call in the Air Corp Reserves. He resumed his education at Caltech in Pasadena, Cal. In 1949, he volunteered for active service during the Korean War. He saw extensive service first as a squadron navigator and then as a navigator in B-26's; where he flew a 50 mission combat tour. After the war he continued to serve in the Air Force in many interesting capacities (missile development, space technology, research/development and teaching) retiring as a Colonel in September 1, 1975. He was a co-author of the 22nd Bomb Group and it's history "Revenge of the Red Raiders". Don passed away on September 10, 2005.

PS

Capt. Don Evans, on the left taken, just after the war ended.

Faletti, Richard via e-mail and mail, January 2001. He was a member of Mr. Bates original crew and was the co-pilot and/or pilot on many of the missions that Mr. Bates flew on. After the war Mr. Faletti graduated from the University of Illinois Law School. He joined the practice of Winston and Strawn and remained there until his retirement in 1989. He was widely known for his collection of African art. Dick passed away December 25, 2005.

Frost, Al in telephone conversation with author, 2003. He lives in Miller Street, Horseheads, NY and attended Horseheads High School with Jack Bates, Joe Benesh and Bryce Hardiman. He was drafted in to the US Navy on July 6, 1943 and served on LSI (Landing Ship Infantry) # 543 and discharged on December 3, 1945. He noted every year after Bryce's death some of his friends would gather together as a commemoration. After 50 years this tradition was ended (see memorial). Al remembers the Hardiman and Bates families well and states, "We had a great deal of respect for both families."

Hayes, Karen, via e-mail, September 2004. Has a web site dedicated to the Sixth Marine Division, in which her father was a member.

Horseheads Historical Society - Information on public display at the societies museum.

Kanady, Charles, via letter to author, October 25, 2004. He lives in Fairfield, IL - a member of 22nd Bomb Group, 2nd Bomb Squadron.

Klimesh, Cyril, www.redraidersbg.com and via e-mail, April 2005. Cy was a bombardier with the 22nd Bomb Group, 19th Bomb Squadron.

Mason, Charles, via e-mail, September 2, 2004. Charles enlisted in late 1942 and after pilot school was assigned to 22nd Squadron, 2nd Bomb Group and served with the group until the end of the war. He was the secretary/editor of the squadron newsletter and lives in El Dorado, AR

O'Brien, Yvonne of Coventry, CT, via letter to author, October 5, 2004. Daughter of Carl W. Morgan, who signed Mr. Bates diary (see The List).

Pierce, Bill, www.sixthmarinedivision.com, June 2002

Tosto, Joseph, via mail June 23, 2005, 2nd Bomb Squadron, 22nd Bomb Group, radio operator, original member of Jack Bates crew. Born 11/19/1919, in Cleveland, Ohio to Thomas and Mary Tosto. Graduated from East Technical High School in 1938. Graduated from John Carroll University 1960 with certificate in Business Management. Entered the Army Air Corp in June 13, 1942 at Camp Perry, Ohio. Joseph flew in a total of 25 missions with Mr. Bates. Discharged October 9, 1945 at Santa Ana, Calif. Married Betty Gall, November 24, 1945. Children - Joseph Jr, Joan (Gercely). Contact was made with Mr. Tosto through his son Joseph Tosto Jr. via e-mail, Oct. 2004.

Williams, Ted (TD), via e-mail May 19, 2006. A member of the "B-24 Best Web" research team and a combat veteran of WW II. He was navigator on the crew of 1/Lt Carl D. Magee (Crew 91) of the 531st Bomb Squadron (H), 380th Bomb Group (H), 5th Air Force, Southwest Pacific. His aircraft was SAD SACK, a B-24J and they flew 36 missions over the East Indies and New Guinea.

Yarnell, Paul, R., - 'Navsource' created and maintained by Paul R. Yarnell and the 'Navsource' team, copyright 1996-2003, www.navsource.org, June 2003

PHOTO CREDITS

All photographs, documents and other memorabilia contained in this work, unless otherwise noted as follows, are a part of the Jack Bates collection provided by his son Ken Bates.

AF - Air Force Historical Research Agency, http://www.afhra.af.mil/shared/media/photodb/photos/080128-f-3927s-038.jpgpage, Page 156

BJ - Dilworth, Bonnie and Jason, page 98

BP - Pierce, Bill http://www.sixthmarinedivision.com, © Sixth Marine Division Association Inc. – all right reserved, a non-profit 501 (C) organization. Web design and maintenance by Texasnova, hosting donated by 3dxhosting.com, Page 163

BW - Stockton, Dan, http://www.b24bestweb.com, © 1997 B-24 Best Web, Pages 86, 112, 115

CK - Klimesh, Cyril, www.redraiders22bg.com, "The Red Raiders ", Pages 56, 68, 70, 79, 84, 86, 98, 110, 111, 119, 132, 202, 203

CS - Snyder, Charles E. Jr., Major USAF (Retired), Snyder's Treasures, www.snyderstreasures.com, Page 60

DH - Hanson, Dave, www.daveswarbirds.com, Pages 17, 52, 54, 61, 82, 88, 102, 106, 110, 114, 134, 160

FG - Fiddlersgreen.net © 1994 – 2009, http://www.fiddlersgreen.net, Page 26

TK - Taki, Imperial Japanese Army, http://www3.plala.or.jp/takihome/88.aahtm, Page 39

JT - Teeuwen, Jaap "British Aircraft of WW II", http://www.jaapteeuwen.com/ww2aircraft, Page 142, 143

JW - Warakomski, Joe and Judy, Page 220

KK - Katoh , "Internet - Museum of Imperial Japanese Aircraft", http://home.interlink.or.jp/~katoh00, Pages 42, 43, 44

PHOTO CREDITS

ME - US Army Patches, www.usarmypatches.com,
Copyright 2004 - 2011 - All Rights Reserved. Courtesy of Michael Everson, Pages 206, 207

MF - Military Factory, http://www.militaryfactory.com, Photo Public Domain, courtesy of United States Department of Defense. Page 57

NS - Navsource Naval History, http://www.navsource.org, Created and maintained by Paul R. Yarnall and the Navsource Team. All pages copyright © 1996–2009 Paul R. Yarnall & NavSource Naval History All Rights Reserved. Pages 63, 108, 153, 154, 157, 166

PC - Hyperwar US Navy in World War II, http://www.ibiblio.org/hyperwar/USN/index.html, compiled and formatted by Patrick Clancey, Page 109

PS - The 22nd Bombardment Group in World War II, Volume III, Photo Supplement - 1941-1945 © 22nd BG Association, Huntsville, Alabama, March 2001, Pages 72, 75, 119, 134, 144, 225

RF - Falletti, Richard, Page 36, 128

TX - The University of Texas at Austin, Perry-Castaneda Library Map Collection, http://www.lib.utexas.edu/maps, Page 37

WP - Wikipedia, http://www.en.wikipedia.org/wiki/Mitsubishi_J2M, Page 42

INDEX

A-20 'Havoc', 87, 164
A-26 'Invader', 165
Adam, Frank M., 176
Ahrens, Bruce, 176
Air Corp (Army) 6, 25, 50, 99, 162, 188, 200
Air Force, 41, 66, 70, 156, 158, 189
Alamo, The, 184
Alcatraz, 46
Allen, Joe F., 176
America(n), vii, ix, 2, 3, 41, 42, 71, 93, 122, 129, 131, 152, 154, 189, 192
American Legion Post 0442, 217
Amoy (Xiamen), China, 34, 132
Angeles, 123, 149, 150, 152
Angle, Don, 176
Anguar, 32, 33, 67, 71, 77, 78, 81, 89, 184, 185, 186, 196
Antinello, Pete, 187
APA, 109, 165, 166
Arand, Robert A, 176
Armor Gunner, 6
Army (Canadian)), 218, 219
Army (US), 1, 5, 8, 97, 139
Army (New Zealand), 48
Arnold, Sgt. Clarence, 186
Arnold, Major General Henry H., 140
Astereades, George T., 176
AT-6, 17
Australia(n)/Aussie, 2, 22, 46, 48, 49, 50, 51, 87, 93, 109, 116, 140, 142, 146, 184, 185, 200
B-17 'Flying Fortress', 25, 110, 111, 113

B-24, 'Liberator', vii, ix, 18, 21, 22, 25, 26, 27, 28, 32, 33, 34, 35, 39, 41, 46, 51, 56, 57, 67, 68, 74, 85, 87, 98, 101, 106, 110, 111, 154, 155, 164, 201, 214
B-25 'Mitchell', 21, 87, 154, 201
B-26, 'Marauders', 200
B-29, 'Super Fortress', 106, 154
B-32, 'Dominator', 141, 154, 162, 164
Baarstad, Jack, 176
Bacon Sgt., 187
Baggio (Baguio), 87
Baker, 149
Balacap (Macbalacat), 79
Balikpapan, 57, 140, 201
Ball, Donald, 217
Balmenti, Joseph P., 160, 176
Bamban/Bambam, 83,84
Barghi, Victor, 186
Barker Sgt., 187
Barnes, George Jr., 176
Barrett, William, 139
Barton, Beverly, 71, 73, 127, 141, 162, 187
Bater, Charles, 217
Bates, Clark, 5
Bates, (Austin) Esther, 5, 189
Bates, Gene, 5
Bates, Gloria, 5
Bates, Helen, 5
Bates, Ken, vii, ix, 6, 124, 204
Bates, Jack, vii, ix, 2, 3, 5, 6, 21, 22, 25, 28, 31, 39, 41, 93, 107, 124, 137, 144, 149, 161, 186, 189, 191, 194, 196, 200, 204, 214, 216
Bates, John E., 6

Bates, (Bednarchik) Louise, 6
Bates, Robert, 5, 64, 78, 95, 96, 128, 149, 189, 191
Bates, Wellington, 5, 189, 191
Bates, Wellington Jr., 5, 107, 189
Bataan, 81, 91, 161, 167, 184
Battaglia, Leonard, 176
Batten, Russell, 176
Bax (Bax, Elmer), 144
Beaufighter, 142
Bednarik, Karl, 176
Bell, Charles, 176
Benesh, Joe, 64, 65, 96, 97, 98
Bennett, R.F., 176
Bensall, R., 176
Bergman, Ralph, 176
Bergstrom Field, Texas, 9
Berry, 2/Lt. Lawrence R., 35, 139
Berter, Robert, 187
Biak, 57, 61, 184
Bialecki, Stanley F. Jr., 176
Bier, Naldemar O., 176
Binghamton, NY, 5, 8
Black, Donald, 187
Black, Kenneth, 187
Blais, Lawrence, 176
Bismarck Sea, 201
Bogo, 33, 92
Boitano, P. E., 176
Borg, James A., 176
Bork, R. L., 176
Borneo, 35, 51, 57, 140, 144, 145, 146, 184, 201
Boulder Dam, 184
Bowen, C.R., 176
Bragley, Wallace, 187
Brantle, Royal, 176
Brenna, Pete, 187
Bridge, William F., 21, 22, 61, 62, 63, 66, 67, 76, 111, 140, 146, 149, 150, 152, 159, 187

British Navy, 112
Brock, 106
Brodsky, Robert, 187
Brooklyn, 96
Brooks, Gerald O., 176
Brown, Donald, 217
Brown, Robert, 176
Brundshuk, Leo R., 149, 159, 161, 176
Buckley Field, 13, 185
Buna, 201
Bush, Catherine, 217
Bushnel, J.H., 176

C-46, 101, 102, 160
C-47, 52, 61, 80, 85, 96, 101
C-54, 140
Caballo Island, 91, 109
Camp Swift, 5, 8, 9, 185
Canada, 8
Canepa, James, 32, 63, 77, 177
Canton (Guangzhu), China, 132, 184
Canton Island, 47, 49, 184, 185
Carder, James, 177
Carlisle, Howard B., 177
Carlson, William, 177
Carmen, Robert J., 177
Casa Loma, 135
C.B. (Construction Battalion/Seabees), 68, 107, 107
Cebu, 32, 33, 69, 71, 72, 92, 96, 184
Celebes, 35, 144, 184
Challis, Arthur T., 177
Charter, Arlington, 177
'Chemung Valley Reporter', 106
China, 34, 112, 127, 128, 129, 130, 131, 132, 138, 184, 186
Cincinnati 'Enquirer", 200

Clark Field, 32, 33, 34, 35, 73, 74, 76, 77, 78, 79, 80, 81, 82, 83, 84, 88, 100, 101, 102, 103, 104, 106, 107, 109, 115, 118, 123, 146, 157, 159, 160, 176, 184, 185, 188, 189, 196, 201
Cohen, Lt., 105
Combs, Paul H., 159, 177
Comerford, Andy E., 177
Company L, 9
Coleman, William D., 21, 60, 61, 62, 65, 68, 69, 70, 74, 78, 79, 80, 87, 101, 103, 117, 118, 123, 125, 137, 139, 141, 146, 153, 162
Colsten, William, 177
Colwell, Howard, 217
Comfort, Robert, 217
Conner, Fred T., 177
Conrad, 151
Consolidated Book Publishers, 1
Consolidated Aircraft, 25
Cook, Roger W., 177
Cook, William, 177
Copeland 1st Sgt., 186
Corregidor, 81, 87, 89, 91, 109, 184, 201
Corsa, Elwood L. Jr., 177
Cortes, Bill, 177
C.Q., 105, 106, 107
Crabb, Jimmy, Brigader General, 125, 186
Crisley, Willis E., 177
Crockett, Wilford, W., 21, 22 52, 65, 68, 69, 71, 112, 162
Cunningham, Horice, Lt. 34, 126, 128
Curtis, Ervin L., 177
Cuyle, Walter, 217

Dahl, Arthur, 177
Davao, 32, 66, 92, 96, 184

Davies, Paul, 35, 177
Davis, John, 177
Davis, Robert, 51, 187
Dawson, Edward, 111
Deichberg, S/Sgt., 186
Deis, 74
Delsburg, 187
Denver, Colorado, 13, 16, 185
Dean, Jack, 127, 187
Dembs, Henry, 149
Deter, Arthur, 21, 22, 49, 65, 68, 69, 70, 76, 83, 100, 102, 104, 110, 111, 135, 137, 138, 139, 141, 146, 147, 148, 187
Dicaro, Joseph, 177
Die, Thomas C., 177
Dovey, Aunt, 123
Drewy, David, 177
Drury, George, 177

Eckstein, Myron, 177
Eclipse, 5, 6, 8
'Eclipse News', 78, 95, 100, 189
Edger, Carlton Sr., 217
Edwards, H. L., 177
Eggleston, Leonard, 186
Eisenhart, Judson, 217
Elmira Free Academy, 6
Elmira Heights, NY, 5
Elmira, NY, 6, 162, 167, 216, 217
Elmira/Corning Regional Airport, 28
English, 49, 81, 155, 160
Ernst, Harold, 177
Eshelman, Eugene, 177
Eugene (OR), 184

F4U 'Corsair', 41, 82, 85, 86, 87
Fabrica, 32
Faist, Wesley, 177

Fairfield-Suisun Field, California, 20, 46, 185
Faletti, Richard, 21, 22, 32, 33, 34, 35, 49, 54, 63, 71, 78, 80, 83, 112, 116, 118, 123, 124, 126, 138, 140, 153, 160, 162, 164, 201
Falvey, Harry J., 177
Farst, Bob, 177
Ficek, Robert L., 177
Fields, Gene R., 178
Figi, 47, 48, 184, 185
Filipino(s), 76, 81, 82, 83, 87, 89, 95, 96, 97, 100, 102, 103, 104, 107, 111, 118, 127, 150, 151
Finschafen, 55, 184, 201
Flanders, Belgium, 218, 219
Flora, 152
Florida Blanca, 147
Ford, James Jr., 178
Fort Dix, New Jersey, 167, 170, 171
Fort Drum (Philippines), 91, 109
Fort Lewis, Washington, 168, 169
Fort Niagara (New York), 5, 8, 185
Fort Stotsenburg (Strotsburg), 81, 88, 149, 150
Formosa, ix, 31, 33, 34, 35, 38, 82, 84, 85, 88, 97, 98, 100, 103, 105, 111, 112, 113, 115, 116, 117, 118, 124, 125, 127, 128, 132, 133, 138, 139, 146, 150, 184, 188, 200
Formosa Straits, 112
France, 48, 189
Frantz, Robert, 178
Freidman, Al. 178
Fresno (California), 46
Frontwine, Kenny, 178

Frost, Allen F., 217
Gaffney, Patrick, 178
Gallivan, Thomas H., 178
Gamble, John, 102
Gannon, Thomas, 178
Garbutt Field, 51, 52, 184, 185
Gardner, Maurice L., 178
Garrett, George W., 178
Garrison, Stanley, 178
Garruch, Clyde L., 178
Garside, Mary Alice, 52, 53, 86, 100, 126, 147, 169, 170
Garzinski, Gary, 124
Geltz, Wayne, J., 143
Golden Gate, 46
Gow, Donald, 178
Grace Park, 134
Grande Island, 87, 89, 91, 153
Gray, H.F., 178
Greenlee, 2nd Lt. Robert, 187
Groeppen, B.L. Jr., 178
Grumman 'Avenger' TBF, 61
Guadalcanal, 49
Guam, 185
Guiuan, 87, 184, 185

H2X (Mickey), 35, 115, 116, 124, 133, 140
Hague, R.A., 178
Hainan, 127
Hambrick, Edward L., 178
Hamilton Field, California, 20, 21, 45, 46, 185
Hanley, Robert J., 178
Hardiman, Bryce, 162, 216, 217
Hardiman, F. Raymond, 217
Hardiman, Mr. & Mrs. Francis, 216
Hargrove, Joseph, 178
Harlingen, Texas, 16, 185
Hasty, L., 178
Hawaii, 2, 46, 55, 184, 185, 216,

Head, Willard, 178
Hedge, Tellie, J., 141
Heito, 97, 141, 200
Hemberger, Robert E., 178
Henrich, Henry E., 178
Henson, Archie, 178
Herman, Saul C., 178
Hickham Field, 46
Hiroshima, 160
Hodes, Sheldon M., 178
Hoffman, Robert P., 178
Holden, Benjamin, 178
Hong Kong, 107, 137, 184
Honolulu, 46, 47, 50, 184
Honshu, 151, 160
Horseheads American Legion, 217
Horseheads Central School, 5, 216
Horseheads Historical Society, 217
Horseheads, NY, 5, 216
Howell, George, 178
Hrehoy, John, 178
Hublitz, Robert, 178
Hunter, Lee, 178

Ide, John, 178
Ie Shima, 157, 158
IFF (Identification Friend or Foe), 154
International Date Line, 47, 167, 168, 185
'International' Night Club, 135
Iseh, Arthur N., 178

Jackson, Leonard, 179
Jackson, Lyle W., 179
James, Sgt., 155
Jansen, William, 217
Japan, ix, 41, 118, 121, 122, 129, 154, 155, 156, 158, 159, 160, 161, 191

Jap(s), 55, 56, 57, 63, 66, 67, 68, 69, 70, 71, 74, 76, 77, 78, 80, 82, 87, 91, 92, 93, 96, 101, 102, 109, 110, 111, 116, 118, 119, 134, 137, 138, 140, 142, 143, 151, 154, 155, 156, 157, 158, 160, 188, 200
Japanese, 33, 39, 41, 93, 115, 132, 138, 188, 189, 201
Jascott, S/Sgt Walter, 186
Java, 140
Jefferson Barracks, 160
John Rodgers Field, 46, 184, 185
Johnson, Bill, 179
Johnson, Everett A., 179
Jones, Charles Jr., 179
Jones, George, 179

Kacar, F.J., 179
Kamikaze, 41
Kanady, Charles, 179
Kaplan, Albert (Caplin/Kaplin), 147, 160, 179
Karitsky, 68
Kave, Stanley W., 179
Kawanishi N1K1 Shiden "George", 110
Keeley, Ronald E., 179
Kenney, General George C., 189
Kiirun, 34, 35, 128, 133, 139, 140
King, Norman L., 179
Kirkendall, W.N., 179
Kluczynski, Leo, 179
Knuesen, Arthur, 179
Kocourek, Elizabeth, 217
Kowalski, Stan, 217
K.P. (Kitchen Patrol), 53, 66, 68, 97, 103, 104
Krantz, J.M., 179
Krgei/Kagi, 118

Krueger, Glenn, 179
Kulm, Russ, 179
Kyle, S.O., 179
Kyushu, 160

L-5, 155
Lae (Leahe), 54, 55, 184, 201
Lannigan, Warren, 186
Lanser, Joe, 179
Las Vegas, 184
Lavadaun, Armond, 179
Lavoy, Chuck, 179
Lawrence, Lt. Edward, 162
Lee, Captain William R., 187
Legaspy (Legaspi), 33
Lehman, Roy C., 179
Lemoore Field, California, 19, 185
Lervis, Armil, 179
Levine, Milton, 179
Leyte, 62, 63, 65, 66, 67, 68, 69, 70, 73, 75, 76, 77, 78, 83, 104, 108, 109, 184, 185, 188, 189, 224
Limboeng, 144
Lingayen, 140
Lingayen Gulf, 88, 137
Little, James T., 179
Loiselle Henry, 179
Lockridge, John A., 179
London, 218
Longshore, Herman, 179
Lopez, William P., 180
Los Angeles, 184
Loyalty Island, 49, 184
LST, 63, 64, 103, 105, 106, 108, 152, 154, 155, 156, 157
Lusignon, D.J., 180
Luzon, 32, 33, 80, 82, 83, 87, 91, 96, 102, 111, 115, 123, 132, 137, 153, 161, 185, 189, 224
Lynch, James, 217
Lynch, W.C., 180

MacArthur, General Douglas, 54, 188, 189
Mandai, 144
Manila, 33, 72, 73, 76, 80, 81, 87, 91, 93, 101, 102, 109, 118, 134, 135, 141, 148, 149, 150, 159, 184, 188, 189, 201
Manila Gulf/Bay/Harbor, 33, 83, 91, 101, 109
Mann, 95
Marauder, 89, 100
Marudes, 105
Marecha, Joseph E., 180
Mare Island, 49
Marine(s), 1, 69, 77, 155, 216
Martin, J.R., 180
Matsuyama, 34, 117
Masciangelo, Remo, 162, 180
Mash, J.E., 180
Mason, Charles, 180
Matthews, Jack, 180
Mc Andrews, 1st Lt. William, 187
McCrae, John, 218, 219
McCelland, Charles S., 180
McCombs, Allen, 180
McCully, Harry M., 180
McKay, William, 180
McKensie, N.C., 180
McReynolds, Preston, 180
Melle, Edward, 180
Melody Gardens, 8
Messing, Harold, 217
Midway, 200
Miller, Ernest V., 180
Miller, Floyd C., 180
Miller, Lester E., 180
Mindanao, 32, 64, 65, 66, 67, 92, 184
Mindoro, 77, 109
Mitsubishi A6M 'Zero', 41, 70, 73, 74, 76, 78, 118, 195, 196
Mitsubishi J2 "Raiden", 41

Mitsubishi J2 "Raiden", 41
Moluccas, 184, 185
Montepart, 149, 151, 152
Monus, Ferdinand, 180
Moore, Wilson J., 180
Moralis Cpl., 187
Morgan, Carl, 180
Morgan, Frank N., 180
Morrison, Robert C., 180
Morotai, 35, 140, 141, 142, 145, 184, 185
Morse, C.W., 180
Mosquito (bomber), 142
Mosquito (net, barrier), 47, 60, 96, 124, 159
Moss, Jay L., 180
Moss, Samuel, 180
Motabu, 155, 156, 191
Mott, Grover, 217
M. P. (Military Police), 96, 151
Mt. Shasta, 184
Muchison, Ralph, 180
Murphy, 107
Murphy, John P., 217

Nadzab, 22, 32, 52, 80, 112, 184, 185
Naha, 155, 165, 216
Nail, Aaron, 180
Nakajima Ki-43 'Oscar', 41
Nakajima, Ki-84 'Frank', 41
Nandi, 47, 48, 49, 184, 185
Napier, L., 180
Nati, 135
Navy (U.S.), 1, 2, 67, 71, 77, 91, 96, 97, 106, 107, 109, 110, 123, 139, 142, 154, 155, 160, 167, 189
Neely, W.L., 180
Neilson-Cebu, 184
Neilson Field, 148
Negros, 32, 33, 71, 84, 96, 184
New Caledonia, 49, 50, 184

New Guinea, 22, 32, 52, 56, 57, 112, 184, 185, 186, 201
Netherlands East Indies, 56, 184, 185
Niagara, NY, 5
Niagara Falls, 8
Nichols Field, 184
Nicholson, 184
Nicholson, Lt. Col. Leonard T., 201
Nicoloff, C.C., 180
Nipponese, 188
Nina, 135
Noble, Harry, 217
Norris, John A., 180
Novicky, John, 181

Oahu, 46, 184, 185
O'Connell, H.J., 162, 181
Offner, Edward E., 181
Olsen, Walter, 181
Okinawa, 138, 139, 147, 150, 151, 152, 154, 156, 167, 184, 185, 191, 216
Ormoc, 188, 189
Ormoc Bay, 189
Owen, Graham, 100
Owi, 32, 56, 57, 68, 83, 99, 184, 185

Pashko, John, 186
PBY 'Catalina', 111, 113, 160
PB4Y2 'Privateer', 110
P-38 'Lightning', 41, 54, 56, 69, 76, 140, 158, 160
P-47 'Thunderbolt', 41, 54, 55, 73, 74, 78, 188
P-51, 'Mustang', 41, 115, 133, 140
Palau Islands, 32, 66, 67, 68, 71, 184, 185, 196, 201
Palmyra, Hawaii, 184
Palompon, 189

Parfitt, William, 181
Pearl Harbor, 2, 46, 184, 200
Peck, Edward, 181
Peleliu, 184
Perry, James J., 21, 22, 61, 62, 67, 76, 79, 87, 107, 111, 118, 123, 125, 137, 140, 141, 146, 149, 150, 152, 161, 162, 163, 187, 196,
Peterson, Harold, 35, 140
Peterson, Mary, 8
Peterson, W.B., 181
Philippines, ix, 31, 57, 60, 61, 62, 64, 72, 78, 79, 93, 135, 148, 152, 184, 186, 188, 189, 192, 200, 201
Phoenix (Arizona), 22, 184
Phoenix Islands, 47, 184, 185
Pierce, Bill, 216
Pike, Clinton, 97, 100
'Pioneer', 191
Plantin, Lyle K., 181
Port Moseby, 184
Porter, Robert, 181
Pozysk, Ted A., 181
Pratt & Whitney, 26
Prescott, Arizona, 201
Prindible, George, 217
Puerto Bello, 189
Puget Sound, 168
'Punch', 218
Punch Bowl, Hawaii, 216
PX (Post Exchange), 53, 62, 63, 69, 86, 127, 161, 164

Rabual, New Britain, 200
Raymond, Camillus A., 21, 22, 50, 52, 60, 61, 69, 125, 139, 141, 145, 146, 153, 162
Read, Robert, 181
Redding (California), 46
Red Cross, 96, 142, 169
Reiten, James, 181

Remmer, Glenn, 181
Reno (Nevada), 184
Rhinehart S/Sgt., 186
Richardson, H.D., 181
Riddle, Raymond, 137
Ridenour, Gordon, 95, 96, 97
Riesz, Ervin T., 181
Robinson, (Richard W.) Colonel, 85, 200
Rocky Mountains, 184
Roller, Robert N., 181
Roosevelt, Franklin, 111
Rosenstrauss, Alfons, 181
Rosette, Edward, 181
Rosita/Rosie, 95, 150, 152
Russell, Oscar, 181
Russell, Virginia, 170
Ryukyus, 185, 186

Sacramento (California), 184
Salamua, 201
Saipan, 166, 167, 224
San Antonio, Texas, 184
Samar, 33, 78, 80, 81, 87, 96, 111, 184, 185, 186
San Francisco, California, 20, 46, 168, 184
Sayer, Merle J., 181
Saunders, Dick, 139, 147, 149
Saunders, H.W., 181
Seattle, Washington, 168, 169, 170
Sepp, F.C., 181
Schreifels, Sylvester M., 181
Schwartz, L., 181
Scudder, 105
Shanghai, 151
Shapiro, Paul, 62, 65, 99, 181
Shapman, Ralph W., 181
Sheppard Field, Texas, 6, 12, 185
Shinchiku, 33, 35, 113, 117, 140, 224

Schoen, Richard, E., 21, 22, 61, 68, 69, 70, 75, 78, 83, 86, 87, 104, 110, 113, 126, 135, 140, 141, 146, 149, 150, 151, 152, 159, 161, 162, 187
Sierra Nevadas, 184
Silvestro, Clem, 181
Sirkin, Alexander, 181
Slasson, Jack, 181
Slavin, Frank, 217
Smith, Carlton A., 181
Smith, James W., 181
Smith, Harry, 181
Snook, Eugene P., 181
Sydney (Australia), 80, 112, 116, 139
Soeder, William P., 134, 150, 182
Soderling, Lennart A., 182
Somma, Vincent, 182
Songer, Albert E., 182
'Spectator, The', 218
Spitfire, 110, 142
Spokane (Washington), 171
'Sporting News', 124, 191
Stallings, Douglas, 182
Stanco, Michael, 164, 182
'Star-Gazette', 188, 190, 191, 192
'Stars & Stripes', 100
Stevens, 159
Stevens, Gilbert E., 182
Stevens, Wanetta, 182
Steward, Jess, 182
Stonick, Harold G., 182
Stoutland, Arnold, 182
Strickland, 150
Strickler, Stuart E., 182
Stutler, B.L., 182
Subic Bay, 33, 89, 91, 152
Summers, 187
Swartwood, Fred, 217
Sweeney, (James E.) Major, 68, 83
Swierenga, Dan, 182
Tacloban, 73, 75, 76, 78, 79, 87, 95, 96, 100, 108, 184, 185
Tacoma, Washington, 168, 169
Taichu, 35, 139
Taihoku/Taipei, 33, 34, 116, 117, 132
Tainan, 33, 34, 115, 118, 125, 126, 128
Takao, 34, 128, 138
Talashe, Edwin L., 182
Talley, Harold, 182
Tallison, 187
Tanawan, 108
Tarawa, 49
Tasca, George J., 182
Taylor, Hal, 182
Taylor, Larry, 186
'Time', 149, 151, 157
Tokyo, 155, 201
Tonopah, Nevada, 19, 20, 21, 45, 141, 185
Toshien, 34, 35, 124, 128, 141
Tosto, Joseph N., 21, 22, 67, 76, 83, 86, 102, 104, 110, 111, 128, 133, 135, 141, 146, 148, 160, 187
Townsville Australia, 2, 22, 49, 50, 51, 184, 185
Toyohara, 35, 146
Treasure Island (California), 46
Treat, Irving, 217
'Tropic', 135
Truman, Harry S., 156, 157

U.S.(A.), 52, 168, 188, 189, 200, 217
U.S.O., 152
U.S.S. Indianapolis, 157
Virgin, George L., 199
Von Petnold, R. L., 182

WAC (Women's Army Corp), 46, 146, 150
Waikiki, 47, 184
Wakde, 201
Walker, William A., 182
Warren, Thomas L., 182
Weiss, Irvin, 182
Wellman, Ed, 182
Wewak, 22, 32, 56, 116, 118, 184, 201
White, F.P., 182
Whitehead, Lt. Gen., 156, 158
Williams, Jack B., 182
Williams, James, 182
Williams, Lt., 159
Whitlaw, Robert, 182
Woodard, C.F., 182
Woodlawn National Cemetery, 6, 216, 217
WW I, 218
WW II, vii, ix, 25, 204

Yamashita, General, 87
Yapen (Jaepon), 57, 184
Yontan, 162, 163, 164
Young, Sgt., 186
Ypres, 218

Ziegler, Joe, 162, 164
Zito, Mario J., 182

13th Air Force, 80, 142
13th Bomb Squadron, 101
13th Strategical Hospital, 96
15th Strategical Hospital, 96
19th Bomb Squadron, 61, 66, 85, 98, 99, 103, 111, 112, 124, 132, 139, 148
2nd Bomb Squadron, vii, 3, 57, 61, 194, 195, 196, 200, 203
2nd Corp, 165

22nd 'Red Raiders' Bomb Group, vii, 3, 22, 57, 199, 200, 202
22nd Regiment, 1st Battalion, A Company, 216
312th Bomb Group, 165
33rd Construction Battalion, 105
33rd Bomb Squadron, 61, 66, 97, 111, 124, 128, 140, 160
380th Bomb Group, 163, 164, 165
386th Infantry (Co. L), 5
403rd Bomb Squadron, 135
408th Bomb Squadron, 60, 61, 71, 73, 76, 77, 116, 118, 127, 141, 144, 145, 162
417th Bombardment Group (Sky Lancers), 164
43rd Bomb Group, 61, 63, 65, 67, 97, 98, 112, 126, 128, 141
5th Air Force, 66, 91, 156, 158, 185
5th Bomber Command (V B.C.), 125, 155, 165
5th Fighter Command, 139
59th Service Group, 96
6th Marine Cemetery, 162
6th Marine Division, 216
7th Air Force, 68, 78, 89
90th 'Jolly Rodgers' Bomb Group, 61, 65, 67, 81, 98
97th Division, 5, 9, 185